CHILD PROTECTION

CHILD PROTECTION

Using Research to Improve Policy and Practice

RON HASKINS
FRED WULCZYN
MARY BRUCE WEBB

Editors

BROOKINGS INSTITUTION PRESS
Washington, D.C.

Library of Congress Cataloging-in-Publication data

Child protection : using research to improve policy and practice / Ron Haskins, Fred
Wulczyn, Mary Bruce Webb, editors.
   p.   cm.
   Summary: "Reports the results of the National Survey of Child and Adolescent
Well-Being. Discusses implications and suggests alternatives for types of personal
and familial problems the programs are meant to address, the range of services and
interventions that the child protection system can make available, and an assessment
of these programs"—Provided by publisher.
   Includes bibliographical references and index.
   ISBN-13: 978-0-8157-3514-4 (cloth : alk. paper)
   ISBN-10: 0-8157-3514-6 (cloth : alk. paper)
   ISBN-13: 978-0-8157-3513-7 (pbk. : alk. paper)
   ISBN-10: 0-8157-3513-8 (pbk. : alk. paper)
   1. Child welfare—United States. 2. Abused children—Services for—United
States. 3. Foster children—Services for—United States. 4. Family services—United
States. 5. Problem families—Services for—United States. I. Haskins, Ron.
II. Wulczyn, Fred. III. Webb, Mary Bruce. IV. Title.

HV741.C4876 2007
362.7—dc22   2007015716

9 8 7 6 5 4 3 2 1

The paper used in this publication meets minimum requirements of the
American National Standard for Information Sciences—Permanence of Paper
for Printed Library Materials: ANSI Z39.48-1992.

Typeset in Adobe Garamond

Composition by Cynthia Stock
Silver Spring, Maryland

Printed by R. R. Donnelley
Harrisonburg, Virginia

Contents

Foreword

W e do not know enough about child abuse and neglect, and much of what we think we know is questionable. So when the Annie E. Casey Foundation was approached by Ron Haskins and Fred Wulczyn to cosponsor a forum on findings from the National Survey of Child and Adolescent Well-Being (NSCAW), we jumped at the chance. This landmark longitudinal study of children and families who come to the attention of the child protection system provides hard data and critical insights. Whether confirming or challenging strongly held beliefs and perceptions, this study contributes to our knowledge about what services and supports are most helpful.

Studies that examine the experiences of large groups of children and families touched by the child protection system are rare. In fact, NSCAW, mandated by Congress in 1996, provides the first and most comprehensive set of data on children and families who come to the attention of the child protection system. NSCAW focuses not only on those children who entered foster care as a result of being referred to child protection but also on those children who were referred but did not enter foster care. In addition, NSCAW involved a large, representative sample of children and families, offering a more comprehensive and long-term view of their strengths, problems, and experiences, not just a quick snapshot.

This kind of longitudinal survey and analysis is essential if we want to develop more effective programs and policies for the children and families served by child protection agencies and their community partners. These agencies must have current, high-quality data and research as well as the capacity to use them. Research must inform the education and training of frontline workers, supervisors, and managers. Policymakers, parents, community members, advocates, and researchers require accurate information about children and families and which approaches are most effective.

The Foundation is grateful for the expertise, leadership, and commitment of Ron Haskins, Fred Wulczyn, and Mary Bruce Webb, without whom this book would not have been possible. We thank the many researchers who have dedicated their careers to child welfare and countless hours to the research summarized in this book and the administrators at the Department of Health and Human Services, under the leadership of Mary Bruce Webb, who supervised the design and implementation of the study. Last and most important, we are indebted to the thousands of individuals, family members, and social workers alike who participated in NSCAW and shared their personal experiences in the child protection system with the investigators. We hope this book will inform the child protection field and that it will spark additional interest in child protection research.

Patrick McCarthy
Vice President for System and Service Reform
Annie E. Casey Foundation
Baltimore, Maryland

Acknowledgments

The Brookings Institution is grateful to the Annie E. Casey Foundation and other funders for their continuing support for the Center on Children and Families (CCF) and our work on poverty, family formation, children's development, child protection, and the looming problem of federal budget deficits. We especially thank Patrick McCarthy, Gretchen Test, and Wanda Mial at the Casey Foundation for their support of this project from its beginning as a small briefing for Casey staffers. We acknowledge that the findings and conclusions presented here are those of the editors and authors alone and do not necessarily reflect the opinions of the foundations or the Department of Health and Human Services.

We also thank the authors—Richard Barth, Rodney Baxter, Barbara Burns, Cynthia Connelly, Katherine Dowd, John Eckenrode, Pamela Frome, Rebecca Green, Shenyang Guo, Lauren Hafner, Brenda Jones Harden, Andrea Hazen, Michael Hurlburt, Charles Izzo, Kelly Kelleher, Patricia Kohl, John Landsverk, Arleen Leibowitz, Laurel Leslie, Arnold Levinson, Anne Libby, A. Russell Localio, Xianqun Luan, Julie McCrae, Amanda O'Reilly, Heather Orton, Ramesh Raghavan, Steven Rosenberg, David Rubin, Sunny Hyuckun Shin, Aron Shlonsky, Elliott Smith, Judith Wildfire, and Mary Bruce Webb—for working so hard on this project, despite their many other commitments. The discussions at the conference that preceded the volume, as well as ongoing feedback throughout the writing and editing process, helped create a thoughtful, coherent volume on a complex subject.

The team of senior officials at the Department of Health and Human Services, headed by Mary Bruce Webb (one of the editors of this volume), who planned the National Survey of Child and Adolescent Well-Being, deserve great recognition for the seminal contribution this study is making to the field of child protection and to our understanding of abused and neglected children and their families.

We recognize and acknowledge the exceptionally excellent help we received in planning and conducting the conference and editing this volume from Megan Yaple, Katie Lambert, and Henry Young of CCF at Brookings. We also thank Anthony Nathe for editing, Larry Converse for typesetting and printing, Susan Woollen for cover design coordination, and Julie Clover for managing the editing and production processes. The editors are especially grateful to Julie and Henry who guided the rather elaborate editing process that led to completion of the volume.

As always, the authors and editors are responsible for any errors of fact or judgment.

1

Using High-Quality Research to Improve Child Protection Practice: An Overview

RON HASKINS, FRED WULCZYN,
AND MARY BRUCE WEBB

Each year in the United States, nearly 900,000 children are physically harmed or neglected by their caretakers, and approximately 1,300 of them die.[1] In addition, a little more than a half million children live in foster care—a living arrangement that includes families previously unknown to the child, relatives, and various forms of group and residential care.[2] Given the well-known problems associated with foster care, in combination with the abuse or neglect itself, it is little wonder that these children have an elevated incidence of poor school achievement, school dropout, mental health problems, arrests, teen pregnancies, and other afflictions.[3] The number of child victims may vary from year to year, but it is a brute fact of the human condition that some adults caring for children harm them. The United States, responding to this grim reality, has evolved what on paper looks to be a reasonable federalist system for protecting children. The purpose of this volume is to use information from a landmark new study to describe how this system works and to suggest specific ways that those working in the system can use it to improve their practice and thereby improve the odds that these most unfortunate children will grow up to lead happy and productive lives.

The nation's child protection system has several major components and features. The first is mandatory reporting laws—written by and enforced in every state—that require various professionals who have contact with children, such as doctors, nurses, and teachers, to report incidents of suspected abuse or neglect.

Professionals who do not report their suspicions are generally subject to penalties. The second component is programs, which are operated by every state or are under the authorization of state government, that investigate these reports, determine whether children have actually been subjected to abuse or neglect, and make several determinations about what to do if abuse or neglect is confirmed. A third component of the system is a somewhat haphazard set of services that aims to help abusive families and their children. As established in federal and state statutes, the goals of the child protection system are to maximize child safety, keep children in permanent living arrangements, and promote the development of children in its care. In pursuing these goals, the public child welfare agency first must decide in confirmed cases of abuse or neglect whether it would be safe to leave the child with the child's family or whether the child should be removed and placed in a foster care home, often with a relative. If children stay at home, the agency has to determine whether to provide services. If children are placed outside their homes, the agency must make reasonable efforts to reunify them with their families, unless the situation is so dire that reunification would not be reasonable. If these efforts fail, the agency must make permanent arrangements in as timely a fashion as possible. In most cases of this type, adoption is the preferred option. These various and complex decisions about the child, which sometimes turn out to be life-and-death matters, are made by social workers, who often have caseloads of twenty or more children. The courts then review the decisions.[4] The entire child protection system—from reporting, to investigating reports, making placement decisions, obtaining services, and maintaining the court system—is paid for by a combination of federal, state, and local resources. Federal funds flow from Title IV of the Social Security Act, which establishes the outline of the federalist system and provides approximately $7 billion per year to states that agree to abide by the federal rules specified in Title IV and in the Child Abuse Prevention and Treatment Act, as well as in various regulations, administrative guidelines, and review systems.

If this system looks somewhat reasonable on paper, in practice it has flaws that are widely recognized. These include inadequate training of the professionals running the system, a shortage of high-quality foster homes, a shortage of effective intervention programs to provide needed services, a dearth of prevention services, an abundance of paperwork, and a somewhat ineffective, though improving, system of accountability.[5] Both the federal government and the states have attempted on many occasions to address these and similar issues, sometimes with modest success, sometimes with less.

Congressional Approval of a National Study of Child Protection

During the highly partisan debate on welfare reform in 1995–96 that led to sweeping reforms of many welfare programs, a bipartisan agreement, primarily between Republicans on the House Ways and Means Committee and then sena-tor Daniel Patrick Moynihan of the Senate Finance Committee, resulted in the appropriation of $6 million per year for seven years to mount a representative national survey of children in the child protection system. The text of the legis-lation, which passed as part of the 1996 welfare reform law, instructed the Department of Health and Human Services to conduct a study that followed children in the child protection system for several years to discover how their cases were handled by the system, whether they were removed from their homes, what types of services they and their parents received, what were their develop-mental outcomes, and whether measures of the way cases were handled and services obtained were related to developmental outcomes. Congress in general, and the House Ways and Means Committee in particular (where the original provision authorizing the study was written), was especially interested in two types of results from the survey. First, based in part on testimony received by the Human Resources Subcommittee of Ways and Means over several years, the view of Congress was that there were too few high-quality, large-scale studies of the nation's child protection system. Thus one goal of the study was to provide an overall picture of how the nation's child protection system works by studying a large representative sample of children and families exposed to the system. Such a study could provide reliable answers to fundamental questions about the nation's child protection programs:

—When a case of abuse or neglect is confirmed, what percentage of children remains at home?

—What percentage enters foster care?

—How often is foster care provided by kin?

—How long do children stay in foster care?

—How many different placements do children experience over time?

—Do children or families receive services, and, if so, what types of services?

—Do the services produce good outcomes?

These and other basic questions could be answered, at least in part, by a national survey that would supply abundant national information about child protection that had not been previously available.

A second goal of the study was to learn something about child outcomes. At the time of the 1996 legislation, federal statutes specified that the goals of the child protection system were to preserve child safety and to achieve permanent placements—whether with the family or through adoption—as quickly as possi-ble. But members of Congress and the Clinton administration were concerned about promoting child well-being as well as achieving safety and permanency. Reforms of the child protection system enacted in 1997, combined with the subsequent regulations and especially the new federal review system imple-mented after the 1997 reforms, established the promotion of child well-being as an important goal of the child protection system. Thus Congress approved funds for the national study for two major reasons: members wanted to know whether the placements of children and the services they received influenced their growth and development, and they wanted reliable data on this and related questions for the nation as a whole and for as many states as possible. Under the strict rules of social science, a survey cannot establish whether the placements or services received by children are causally related to child outcomes, but the correlations between placements and outcomes might be suggestive and might raise issues for further research that could establish causality. In Congress, research methodology and determinations of causality are not a major concern—in reality, for members of Congress and their staffs, correlation is often considered as causation, regardless of the obscure rules of social science.

As it often does, Congress gave the Department of Health and Human Services wide latitude in conducting the study. More specifically, the secretary was directed to conduct "a national study based on random samples of children who are at risk of child abuse or neglect."[6] The secretary was also required to ensure that the study was longitudinal (meaning that the same children and caretakers had to be followed over time) and that it yielded data that were reliable for as many states as possible. The secretary was also required to consider collecting data on the type of abuse or neglect involved; the frequency of contact of the child and family with state or local agencies; whether the child was separated from his or her family; the number, type, and characteristics of out-of-home placements; and the average duration of placements.[7]

The Department of Health and Human Services after extensive consultation with experts in child protection research, policy, and practice convened an internal work group to plan for the study. Decisions by this work group led to two of the more innovative features of the study. First, the group decided that rather than focusing only on children who were served in the child protection system the study should provide a broad overview of children's experiences both before entering the system and then once inside the system, so that pathways from an initial report of maltreatment to long-term outcomes could be explored. This decision meant that the study would include not only children who were placed in foster care or who received other child welfare services but also those who had been reported to child protective services (CPS) without the report of their maltreatment being substantiated, as well as children who remained at home even if their reports were substantiated.[8] Second, the work group decided that the study should emphasize a broad range of developmental outcomes and measures of how children were functioning in day-to-day living. In this respect, the study reflects what seems to be a growing emphasis among policymakers on the development of children in the child protection system.

Description of the National Survey of Child and Adolescent Well-Being

After the internal group studied the legislation and wrote a request for proposal (RFP) based on the statute, the Department of Health and Human Services sought bids to conduct a national survey that met the requirements set out by the RFP. The Research Triangle Institute won the competition for the contract and has been the primary agent responsible for collecting the complex and comprehensive data called for by the RFP (see the appendix for an overview of all the measures collected). The study was named the National Survey of Child and Adolescent Well-Being (NSCAW).

NSCAW includes two samples of children: the CPS sample of 5,501 children and the One Year in Foster Care sample of 727 children. The CPS sample is representative of all children in the United States who were the subjects of investigations or assessments of child abuse or neglect conducted by CPS agencies during the fifteen-month period that began in October 1999. Some of the children and families selected for the samples may have had prior experience with CPS or child welfare services.

Both samples were selected using a two-stage stratified sample design. At the first stage, primary sampling units were selected, which were defined as geographic areas encompassing a population served by a single CPS agency. In most cases, these sampling units represented single counties, although there were instances in which some large counties contained multiple sampling units and small, contiguous counties made up a single unit. The sample units were randomly selected using a procedure that gave a higher chance of selection to units having larger caseloads. A few counties that were anticipated to have caseloads too small to provide an adequate workload for a single field interviewer were excluded from the sample (these counties are estimated to contain less than 3 percent of the child welfare population).

The first-stage sample resulted in the selection of 100 sampling units. Seven of these were determined to be very small and were combined with adjacent counties for the study. Of the original 100 sampled units, only six refused to participate in the study and were replaced by randomly selected units of approximately the same size. Eight counties were dropped after the onset of data collection because their laws did not permit contact with study staff without explicit consent—a restriction that would result in an unacceptably low response rate. These counties were not replaced. Thus the final sample comprised 92 sampling units, representing 97 counties.

The second-stage sample was composed of children selected from the 92 sampling units. The frame for selecting children for the CPS sample within sampling units was constructed from lists of children who were investigated for child abuse or neglect during the months October 1999 through December 2000. Sampling domains were constructed that allowed for the inclusion of children in out-of-home care, children receiving child welfare services at home, and children not receiving child welfare services following the investigation. The sample was selected to provide an oversample of infants, sexually abused children, and children receiving child welfare services.

The sampling frame for the One Year in Foster Care sample was also constructed from lists obtained from the participating agencies located in the 92 primary sampling units. Children were eligible for this sample if they met the following criteria:

—they had been placed into out-of-home care approximately one year before the sample selection period,

—their placement into out-of-home care had been preceded by an investigation of child abuse or neglect or by a period of in-home services, and

—they were still in out-of-home care when the sample was selected.

The foster care sample selection period was December 1999 through February 2000. In many sampling units, the number of children available during the original time period was found to be too small to support the sample sizes required. As a result, the window of inclusion was extended in those sampling units to include children who were placed in out-of-home care between July 1998 and February 1999. As a result of this procedure, children in the foster care sample had spent between eight and twenty months in out-of-home care at the time of sampling.

Data were collected from four sources: the children themselves, their primary caregivers, their caseworkers, and, for school-aged children, their teachers. Extensive information was obtained from standardized assessments and interviews that covered children's health; children's social, emotional, behavioral, and cognitive functioning; caregiver characteristics and caregiving environment; and services needed and received (see the appendix). Data were collected at baseline (wave 1) and at twelve months (wave 2), eighteen months (wave 3), and thirty-six months (wave 4) after the baseline data collection.[9] All children with a completed interview at wave 1 were contacted for participation in subsequent waves. Agency-level contextual data were collected from state and county child welfare administrators at baseline. The complex design of NSCAW allows for more sophisticated statistical procedures than those that have traditionally been used in child welfare analyses. These statistical procedures include multilevel modeling, growth curve modeling, and various multivariate analyses. Some of these procedures are featured in this volume.

After Congress had appropriated funds for NSCAW, the National Institute of Mental Health decided to fund a companion study, Caring for Children in Child Welfare (CCCW), that obtained information on the characteristics, policies, and practices of the state and local institutions that deal with the physical and mental health needs of children involved with the child welfare system. This study was conducted in the same locations where the NSCAW sampling was done to permit the analysis of the relationship between services received by children and the characteristics, policies, and practices of the child welfare system and the institutions responsible for providing health services to the public. The contextual information was gathered primarily from written documents about local institutions and from interviews with 1,169 informants at the state and local levels who answered questions about relationships between agencies; the organization, financing, and policies regarding children in CPS; the policies of the child protection agency concerning screening, assessment, and monitoring; and CPS training and placement policies. Several of the chapters in this volume make use of the CCCW study.

This volume is the first collection of studies reporting on the nationally representative information available from NSCAW. The papers are divided into three sections representing three distinct types of information about the nation's child protection system. These include three chapters that describe problems of children and their families, four chapters that examine the services and intervention programs received by families, and six chapters that focus on outcomes for children. We turn now to a brief overview of each of these chapters.

Child and Family Problems

Research shows that children with disabilities do better when they receive treatment at an early age.[10] Steven Rosenberg and his colleagues aim to determine how many children under the age of three with a confirmed case of abuse or neglect are likely to be eligible for services through Part C of the Individuals with Disabilities Education Act. The authors used the NSCAW sample to estimate how many children have disabilities that qualify them for Part C services. In the first stage of the analysis, based on the nationally representative NSCAW sample of 1,138 cases of children under the age of three with substantiated cases of maltreatment, they estimated that there were about 156,000 children under the age of three in the nation with a substantiated abuse case. Next, using the measures of development from NSCAW, the authors estimated how many of these young children had a developmental delay that would qualify them for Part C services. NSCAW contains three measures of development that can be used to determine what share of abused and neglected children under the age of three qualify for Part C. These measures include a test of cognitive ability, a scale for preschool language ability, and a scale that measures how adequately children perform tasks of daily living. The authors followed the eligibility criteria for Part C services that are based on a child's performance that is 1 standard deviation below average on two of three tests or 1.5 standard deviations below average on one test. They found that a surprising 47 percent of the NSCAW sample of children younger than age three had a developmental delay that would qualify them for Part C services. They estimated that at least 58,000 children in the CPS system were likely to have been eligible for Part C services in 2000, but because few of these children were identified as having developmental problems by their caseworkers, it was unlikely that they were referred for Part C services.

If children with substantiated cases of abuse or neglect, all of whom are at high risk for long-term developmental problems, are going to receive timely services for developmental problems, a major national effort is needed to correctly identify these nearly 58,000 children and then to ensure that the child protection system works with the Part C system to obtain the required services. It is quite troubling that many of the children who likely would be entitled to developmental services under Part C were not receiving them. Rosenberg's results amount to a call for national action.[11]

In addition to developmental disabilities, another problem faced by children in the child protection system is that they often live in families in which intimate partner violence occurs. This violence between adults is correlated with the probability that children will also be the victims of maltreatment. Yet there is relatively little information about how many families involved with the child welfare system are also experiencing intimate partner violence. Using the nationally representative NSCAW data set, Andrea Hazen and her colleagues found that about 45 percent of the female caregivers in families involved with child welfare services have experienced intimate partner violence in their lifetime and nearly 30 percent in the past year, approximately twice the rate of violence for the general population. Victimization is correlated with major depression in the female caregiver and with a history of prior reports of child maltreatment. Adult violence is also correlated with both externalizing and internalizing behaviors by exposed children. The authors recommend training of child protection workers so that they can recognize family violence and recommend quality treatment programs to reduce the violence and deal with its aftermath in children.

Intimate partner violence is not the only indicator that children might be at risk for maltreatment. Aron Shlonsky uses NSCAW to perform the initial steps in trying to build an actuarial instrument, based on characteristics of the child or family, such as violence within the family, that will predict whether children will be reabused if left at home. An instrument that can predict reabuse would be of substantial value to child protection workers who decide on child placement. NSCAW presents the first opportunity to build an instrument that is based on a nationally representative sample of child protection cases. To perform the initial calculations, Shlonsky divided the sample of 5,501 NSCAW cases into two groups using one group to construct the risk assessment tool and the other to validate the tool. To be included in the initial sample, children had to have the NSCAW risk assessment instrument completed at baseline and had to have remained in the study for the twelve-, twenty-four-, and thirty-six-month follow-up assessments. From this group, he randomly selected 2,401 to use in developing the risk assessment tool.

The model building consisted of computing bivariate correlations between each of the predictor variables and instances of re-reports and correlations between each of the predictor variables and instances of resubstantiation. The thirty-four predictor variables from the NSCAW risk assessment instrument included case factors such as prior history of report, child characteristics such as age and race, and caregiver characteristics such as history of drug problems and domestic violence. Only eight predictors were significant at all three follow-up periods (twelve, twenty-four, and thirty-six months).

After further statistical analysis, the models that provided optimum prediction differed for prediction of re-report and prediction of resubstantiation. The former included child age, prior report of child welfare investigation of the family, history of domestic violence, a second supportive caregiver in the home, and high stress in the family. By contrast, the model for resubstantiation prediction included child age, poor parenting skills, and high stress in the family. Shlonsky then used a weighting scheme and computed scores for the families on each predictor in the models and summed these to reach a total risk index score. Finally, he found natural breaks in the distribution of scores to divide scores into risk categories that corresponded with low, medium, and high risk of reabuse.

As Shlonsky concludes, although more analysis remains, this initial attempt at building an actuarial model to predict reabuse is a promising beginning. In the long run, if Shlonsky or others can use NSCAW data to construct and validate a risk assessment instrument that improves caseworkers' ability to determine whether children are likely to be reabused if left at home, the child protection system would gain an important new tool that could improve its ability to protect children while keeping the number of children removed from their families to a minimum. Shlonsky makes the important point that, even when a risk assessment tool with good predictive powers has been developed, the assessment tool should not be used in a mechanical way as the sole determinant of placement decisions. Rather, its proper use is as a supplement to caseworker judgment.

Services and Interventions

In most child protection cases, even when maltreatment is substantiated, children remain at home with their parents. In a surprising share of these cases, as we will see, families receive no services other than, perhaps, visits from a caseworker. But when families do receive services, logic would suggest that parent training should be among the preferred offerings. After all, if parents are maltreating their children, they need a new set of parenting skills to replace those that brought them to the attention of the child protection agency in the first place. Michael Hurlburt and his colleagues use NSCAW and the CCCW study to examine several questions about the use of parent training by child protection agencies. The authors review studies in the field of child mental health that used random assignment and that showed parent training to be an effective intervention for changing parent behavior as a means to improve the behavior of their children. Indeed, Hurlburt and his colleagues review evidence regarding three specific programs that have been shown by random assignment studies to produce significant changes in parent behavior. The authors conclude that parent training in many counties could benefit from using these programs or from incorporating principles common to the programs into existing parent training services.

They also report that the CCCW study shows that 90 percent of counties say that parent training is part of the case plan for half or more of their families. Despite this encouraging finding, less than 2 percent of counties use the three curricula shown by random assignment studies to be effective. Only about 40 percent of the families actually receive parent training in the year following referral to child welfare services, and even then in most cases for only fifteen hours or less, not enough according to the authors to achieve desired outcomes. In addition, there was virtually no evidence that child protection agencies took steps to ensure that the parent training delivered in community settings maintained fidelity to whatever parent program the agencies were implementing. Given these unfortunate findings, the authors provide detailed recommendations for actions that local agencies could take to increase their use of effective parent training programs.

Underlining the need for more and better parent training, Anne Libby and her colleagues examine the relationship between mental health and substance abuse problems of the caregiver on the one hand and mental health problems of the child on the other. A major finding is that children with parents who have mental health or substance abuse problems are themselves at greatly elevated risk for mental health problems. This relationship held even when a variety of background factors were statistically controlled. Equally interesting, the study yielded evidence, based on observations by caseworkers, that these mothers provided substandard parenting for their children, thereby in all likelihood setting up their children for subsequent mental health problems. This finding shows how important it is for child welfare programs to provide effective parenting services if children with parents who are involved with drugs or have mental health issues themselves are to avoid serious mental health problems as they grow up. It could prove difficult, however, to provide effective parenting help to such parents. The parents' problems mean that they need at least two types of services: mental health or drug programs for themselves and parenting improvement programs so they can provide better care for their children. There is little evidence that such dual programs are available in most child protection programs.

One way to make these and other programs more widely available is to finance them through the Medicaid program. Ramesh Raghavan and Arleen Leibowitz investigate factors associated with coverage of mental health services for children in the child welfare system. Their research is timely because many states have adopted managed care plans as part of their Medicaid program and because nearly all children removed from their homes by child welfare agencies are covered by Medicaid. Thus changes in Medicaid have the potential to have important impacts on receipt of health services—including mental health services—by children in the nation's child protection programs. Because children in the child protection system use far more physical and mental health services than other children, provider networks could lose money on these children, since managed care caps their reimbursement rates. In addition to the states' adopting managed care plans, "carve-outs" for mental health services are another growing practice that have the potential to impact children in the child welfare system. Carve-outs refer to situations in which state agencies or their contractors sign subcontracts with providers that, in turn, assume responsibility for providing all mental health services. Whether these new health delivery structures will enable children in the child welfare system to receive the level of care they need is open to question.

The authors obtained data from three sources: from NSCAW, data on access to ambulatory and inpatient services by individual children in the child welfare system; from a telephone survey, conducted as part of the CCCW survey described above, of key NSCAW contacts from counties throughout the United States, descriptions of the type of Medicaid financing used by local child welfare agencies; and from the Area Resource File (ARF), a database of the number and type of health care and mental health providers in counties in the United States that is maintained by a private company under contract to the federal government. These three sources of data were merged into an integrated data set consisting of 3,460 children aged three and older. Children were judged to be in need of mental health services if they scored above sixty-three on the Child Behavior Checklist administered at baseline in NSCAW. Actual receipt of ambulatory and inpatient services was determined from the twelve-month follow-up interview.

Using multivariate methods, the authors found that, controlling for a wide variety of factors, children in managed care systems were not less likely than other children to receive ambulatory mental health services. However, children in counties using mental health carve-outs were only about half as likely to receive inpatient services controlling for need. Other factors related to receiving mental health care included the finding that children in out-of-home care were more likely to receive mental health services, that uninsured children were less likely to receive ambulatory care (though not inpatient care), that children with highly educated parents were more likely to receive ambulatory services rather than inpatient services, and that children in counties with a relatively high number of child psychiatrists were more likely to receive ambulatory mental health services. The authors conclude that there are four levers that can be pulled to increase the chances that children in the child protection system will receive needed mental health services: aggressive caregivers who fight for their children's medical care, caseworkers who fight for services, insurance coverage, and an abundance of medical providers in the county of residence. Medicaid is simply one of a number of factors—albeit an important one—that determines receipt of needed mental health services for children in the child welfare system.

John Landsverk and his colleagues analyze the mental health problems of children in the child protection system and the institutional arrangements designed to meet their mental health needs. The authors' review of NSCAW data, plus numerous other studies in the literature, leads them to conclude that as many as half the children involved with the child welfare system have mental health problems that require treatment. Because mental health problems are so prevalent among these children, the authors recommend that the routine admission procedures for children entering the CPS system should include a full assessment of mental health and not just a screening assessment for mental health. They also recommend that a national authority develop guidelines for how this full assessment should be conducted and that CPS agencies have close institutional ties with the agencies that provide mental health services because these services are so important for the well-being of children involved with CPS. Finally, they note that most of the mental health services for these children are financed by the Medicaid program. As Raghavan and Leibowitz show in their chapter, Medicaid programs in many states are undergoing a transition to managed care. Given how important Medicaid is to children involved in child protection, the CPS agency should ensure that the children are adequately covered by the new managed care plans now emerging across the country.

Outcomes of Child Protection

Under the federal child protection legislation enacted in 1997 and the subsequent regulations and federal review system, child well-being joined safety and permanency as major goals of the nation's child protection programs. Thus it is especially timely for NSCAW to yield nationally representative data on outcomes produced by child protection programs. Even though child well-being is a major goal of CPS, the long-standing goal of achieving permanency is still of major importance. For most children removed from their homes because of maltreatment, permanency is achieved when the child is returned home.

Because family reunification is the single most common method of achieving permanency following an out-of-home placement, and because reunification is the outcome that nearly all those involved with child protection would most like to achieve if possible, studies of reunification are of prime importance. In the chapter by Judith Wildfire and her colleagues, NSCAW data is used to examine factors that predict reunification. Unlike most previous studies, the richness of the NSCAW data set allows the authors to examine the relationship between reunification and child characteristics, family characteristics, and actions by both child protection agencies and the parents themselves in trying to promote reunification. The Wildfire study is based on multivariate analyses that permit the authors to examine the relationship between individual predictors while holding other predictors constant.

Of the original NSCAW sample of 5,501 children, 1,568 had entered out-of-home placement at some point after eighteen months (half in foster homes or therapeutic foster homes, one-quarter with a friend or relative and the rest in group homes or other settings). By the end of eighteen months after placement, about 30 percent of these children had been returned home. The authors' goal was to identify the factors that predicted a return home. Given the findings of substantial age differences in factors related to reunification in previous studies, the authors conducted their analyses separately within six age groupings.

As expected, both the overall probability of reunification and the specific factors related to the child, family, and agency that predicted reunification varied dramatically by age. Infants under the age of seven months were the least likely to reunify, while children older than ten were the most likely. None of the specific measures within the three classes of predictors (child factors such as race and delinquency, family factors such as family violence and history of involvement with child protection, agency actions such as the type of placement and use of various serves) yielded significant predictions at every age, but child characteristics and agency or parental actions had at least one predictor that was significantly correlated with reunification at every age. As the authors argue convincingly, this pattern of age-related differences strongly suggests that a one-size-fits-all approach to family reunification will not work. Rather it seems likely that child protection agencies must adopt strategies that are tailored to children's ages. By way of example, frequency of contact with the mother during the period of removal was an important predictor of reunification for children older than ten but not for children younger than ten.

Following on Wildfire's chapter examining factors related to permanency, the chapter by David Rubin and his colleagues is the first to report on the impact of placement stability on outcomes for a nationally representative sample of children entering out-of-home care. When children are placed in foster care, it is important to preserve the continuity of care they receive and to avoid, if at all possible, frequent moves to new foster care settings. The Rubin study, which examined stability in the placement of more than 1,000 children who entered out-of-home care, is important because it reports findings directly relevant to this issue. The authors found that 67 percent of children placed outside their homes were still in placement after eighteen months, but only 34 percent of them had achieved early stability under the study's definition of stability. In addition, 47 percent were still in placement after thirty-six months, of whom 20 percent had had additional placements between eighteen and thirty-six months after removal. Equally informative, for only 34 percent of the entire sample of out-of-home placements had reunification been attempted by thirty-six months—and a quarter of these attempts had failed. Clearly, the nation's child welfare programs have difficulty either reunifying children with their parents or achieving stable placements outside the home for most children taken into state custody.

Rubin and his colleagues then analyze children's scores on a test of adaptive behavior and find that children who scored in the normal range at baseline were more likely to achieve successful reunifications or to achieve early stability in placement than were children who scored poorly on adaptive behavior. Thus children exhibiting problem behaviors have more difficulty achieving stability in out-of-home placements, although whether the problem behaviors cause placement instability or vice versa is unclear. In analyzing adaptive behavior as an outcome at thirty-six months, the authors find that placement stability has an important impact on scores. For example, of the children scoring in the normal range for adaptive behavior at baseline, 85 percent were still within the normal range at thirty-six months if they had achieved early stability compared with only 70 percent of children within the normal range who were reunified and only 60 percent who never achieved a stable placement. These results underline the importance of achieving stability, as intended by the 1997 child protection reforms, because stability is associated with better child outcomes.

While Rubin and his fellow researchers aimed to study the importance of achieving stable placements, Barth and his colleagues examined placements in kin and nonkin foster homes to understand how each setting affects child well-being. Child welfare practice and federal statutes and the statutes of many states show a preference for placements with relatives since connections with the child's family are preserved. Their study deepens our understanding of kinship foster care and its strengths and weaknesses. Unlike other studies of kinship care, the Barth study is based on a representative national sample (NSCAW). A major problem with most research comparing kin and nonkin foster parents is selection bias; that is, children placed with kin and nonkin parents may be different in important respects at the time of placement. If these preexisting differences are also related to outcomes such as length of stay, permanency, or child well-being, then differences in the outcomes for children in the two settings cannot be attributed to the effects of kinship or nonkinship care themselves.

Using a specialized technique, the authors are able to at least partially control for selection bias by matching as closely as possible characteristics of children in foster care with those of children in kinship care. Following this procedure, the Barth study found that children in kinship care improved more on their scores of acting out (that is, externalizing behavior) on the Child Behavior Checklist than did children in nonkinship care. However, all the other differences seen between children in the two settings on the full sample disappeared in the matched sample, demonstrating clearly that selection effects are present. This result shows why studies that simply compare groups of children in regular foster care and kinship foster care, without adjusting for selection bias, are seriously flawed and their conclusions suspect.

One finding of the Barth study deserves special mention: about one-fifth of the foster parents in the two settings were rated low in responsiveness and high in punitiveness. Numerous studies have shown that this combination signals serious problems in parenting and a high risk that children's growth and development will be negatively affected.[12] As the authors point out, only a minority of children in either setting received services. Thus the major hope for helping foster children is that the foster parents themselves, whether kin or nonkin, provide good parenting for these unfortunate and often traumatized children. The finding that in both settings parenting was ineffective and potentially damaging suggests that a major goal of child protection programs should be to offer kin and nonkin foster parents training in improved styles of parenting. Unfortunately, as shown by the Hurlburt study summarized above, few biological parents or foster parents receive any type of parent training, and most of the parent training programs being used by child protection agencies lack any evidence of effectiveness. A clear implication of several of the papers in this volume is that child protection agencies need to invest in evidence-based parent education programs for biological and foster parents.

The study by Patricia Kohl and Richard Barth also contains important recommendations for the improvement of child welfare practice. Kohl and Barth examined the frequency of re-reports of child maltreatment and the factors associated with them. Studying the 3,143 children who remained at home following the index maltreatment investigation, the authors found that nearly a quarter of these children have re-reports within eighteen months. This seemingly high rate of re-reports involving children already known to child welfare agencies shows that children remain at risk even after their families have initially been reported to child welfare authorities. The authors found several factors that are associated with a greater likelihood of re-reports, including the child's age (younger children are more likely to be the subject of re-reports), prior involvement with the child welfare system by the family, receipt of parenting services (in part because CPS agencies may ration parenting services by serving only the most serious cases, among other reasons), the presence of family violence, and the presence of child behavior problems. As the authors note, and in line with Aron Shlonsky's attempt to develop a formal risk assessment instrument, these and other parent and child characteristics can be used by child protection workers to help predict which children are likely to be subject to further maltreatment after they have been reported to the child welfare system. Once cases with a high likelihood of reabuse are identified, families should be provided with services and should receive greater oversight by child protection workers. Kohl and Barth call attention to the system-wide financial constraints that limit oversight and services. Even so, they argue that the types of parenting services now provided by agencies are often not consistent with scientifically tested best practices. Better programs for parents could reduce the likelihood of reabuse and could improve children's prospects.

Kohl and Barth's finding that family violence predicts re-reports shows the importance of conducting more research on physical abuse. John Eckenrode and his colleagues examined the relationship between physical abuse and the occurrence of problem behaviors, psychosocial problems, and academic functioning in adolescents. The authors examined three sources of reports of abuse: caseworkers, caregivers, and the children themselves. Youths aged eleven and older at wave 1 ($N = 1,179$) were selected for the study. The importance of using multiple sources to detect abuse was demonstrated by the finding that about one-third of the cases (127 of 388) of physical abuse reported by one or more of the informants would have been missed if the measurement of abuse had been based only on case records. The reported incidence of abuse ranged from 9 to 27 percent among the three sources. A measure that combined the results from all sources suggested that as many as 40 percent of the youths were physically abused, a total that was nearly 50 percent higher than the highest rate (27 percent), which was reported by the youths themselves. Abuse was correlated with poor outcomes in all areas of youth behavior studied including problem behaviors, psychosocial functioning, and academic performance. Statistically significant correlations were found in all four waves, and the correlations were greatest at older ages. The reports by the youths were correlated with more outcomes than were those of caseworkers or parents. The Eckenrode study demonstrates the importance of caseworkers considering multiple sources for detecting physical abuse—especially the importance of interviewing the children themselves—and of improving treatment for the children and their families if long-term deleterious impacts on the children's development are to be avoided.

Perhaps even more important for avoiding negative impacts on the growth and development of children in the child welfare system is education in general and special education in particular. The chapter by Mary Bruce Webb and her colleagues explored the educational needs of these children and whether their educational needs are being met. The authors used two cognitive assessments and two tests of socioemotional behavior that were part of the standard

NSCAW child assessment battery to determine whether children were in need of special education. Caseworkers and caregivers provided information, again as part of the standard NSCAW assessment, on whether children had been referred for and had received special education services. The assessments showed that nearly 30 percent of the children met the study's criteria for needing special education services. Unfortunately, less than 60 percent of these children were actually receiving special education services. Thus around 40 percent of the children who were identified as needing special education were not receiving any services.

Like so many of the other findings produced by NSCAW, these results show that children in the child welfare system are being shortchanged. A major goal of the child welfare system is to promote child well-being. Although many social workers give their highest priority to ensuring safety—and with good reason—the federal statute and the statutes of nearly every state charge the child welfare system with taking the necessary steps to ensure children's adequate development. The federally mandated Child and Family Services Reviews, which have now incorporated the goal of meeting children's educational needs (along with the child's physical and mental health needs), are now being used to evaluate the child welfare program of every state. Statutes and a sense of equity for these children both dictate that the child welfare system improve its performance in making certain that children receive the educational services they need. The public schools must, of course, be part of this effort, especially because they too have legal mandates to serve children with special needs. But unless workers in the nation's child welfare programs take the lead, it seems likely that the educational needs of maltreated children will continue to go unmet.

The studies in this volume demonstrate that an important contribution of NSCAW has been to provide information that could enable researchers, policymakers, and practitioners to begin differentiating among the families and children who come into contact with the child welfare system. A more comprehensive understanding of children's developmental histories and trajectories, as well as of the links between the types of risks that are incurred by children and families in different circumstances and the subsequent outcomes for children, will enable providers to create or improve service systems that support the individual needs of the children they serve.

Lessons learned in this set of reports include the following:

—As many as 58,000 maltreated children qualify for federal Part C disability services. But only about 17,000 of these children are identified by child protection caseworkers as disabled. A national effort to connect all disabled children in contact with child welfare programs to appropriate early intervention services is needed. In mounting this effort, providers of early intervention services must understand that the special problems of parents in the child welfare system will require that parenting programs be tailored to the unique needs of parents.

—About 30 percent of the women involved with child welfare have been involved in intimate partner violence in the past year, and this violence is correlated with child abuse. Child protection workers should be trained to recognize intimate partner violence, and CPS programs should have programs for both the adults and children involved in family violence.

—About 90 percent of child welfare programs say their case plans for families include parent training. However, only about half the programs actually give parent training to even half their caseload. Moreover, the parent training that they offer could be improved substantially. In particular, counties should adopt or at least experiment with effective parent training curricula from children's mental health programs that have strong relevance to child welfare.

—Children whose parents have mental health or substance abuse problems are themselves likely to have mental health problems in part because their parents have poor parenting techniques. CPS programs should provide services to help parents with both their substance abuse and their poor parenting skills.

—Contrary to widespread concern, managed care does not seem to impede the ability of children in the child welfare system to obtain outpatient mental health services. Children in the child protection system are more likely to receive needed mental health services if they have parents or caseworkers who know how to insist that they get good care, if they have insurance coverage, and if they live in a jurisdiction with a large number of mental health providers.

—Nearly half the children in the child welfare system have mental health problems. Thus local programs should adopt the policy of conducting full mental health assessments of all children entering the child welfare system.

—Factors of the child, family, and agency that predict family reunification after the child has been removed vary greatly by age, suggesting that agencies must adopt reunification practices that are tailored to the age of the child.

—CPS is failing in most cases to achieve either family reunification or stable placements after children have been removed from their homes. Two-thirds of children removed from their homes are still in placement after a year and a half; half are still in placement after three years. Of the children removed from their families, only one-third are in stable placements by eighteen months. Policymakers and practitioners at the state and local levels should make every effort to promote placement stability.

—When preexisting differences between children placed with kin and children placed with strangers are controlled, differences between the two types of placements after thirty-six months are negligible.

—Most children remain at home following the investigation of a maltreatment report. Of those who remain at home, about one-quarter will be the subject of further maltreatment reports within eighteen months. Children most likely to be the subjects of repeated maltreatment reports include those children who are young, whose families have previously been involved with the child welfare system, who are in families in which violence between the adults is present, and who have behavior problems. Child protection agencies should target parents in families with these characteristics for services and should remain especially vigilant in taking steps to ensure that the families do not reabuse their children.

—In child maltreatment investigations, children, parents, and caseworkers are not equally likely to report physical abuse. Children are more likely to report physical abuse than parents or caseworkers, but the reported incidence of physical abuse rises by about 50 percent if positive reports of parents and caseworkers are added to those of children. CPS programs should evaluate all abuse cases reported by children, parents, or caseworkers to determine which ones should receive services.

—Physical abuse is correlated with poor outcomes in all areas of youth behavior including problem behaviors, psychosocial functioning, and academic performance. To uncover all cases of physical abuse, CPS workers must interview youths during their investigations.

Notes

1. Committee on Ways and Means, U.S. House of Representatives, *2004 Green Book: Background Material and Data on the Programs within the Jurisdiction of the Committee on Ways and Means,* 108th Cong., 2d. sess. (Washington: U.S. Government Printing Office, 2004), pp. 11–77.

2. Administration for Children and Families, U.S. Department of Health and Human Services, "The AFCARS Report, Preliminary FY 2005 Estimates as of September 2006 (13)" (www.acf.hhs.gov/programs/cb [December 15, 2006]).

3. Committee on Ways and Means, *2004 Green Book,* section 11.

4. Annie E. Casey Foundation, *The Unsolved Challenge of System Reform: The Condition of the Frontline Human Services Workforce* (Baltimore, Md., 2003), p. 36.

5. Ibid.

6. The authorizing language can be found in section 429A of the Social Security Act.

7. See the welfare reform law of 1996, "Personal Responsibility and Work Opportunity Reconciliation Act of 1996 (PRWORA)," Public Law (P.L.) 104-193, Section 503 National Random Sample Study of Child Welfare or Section 429A National Random Sample Study of Child Welfare of the Social Security Act.

8. The statute authorizing the study refers to including children "at risk of abuse or neglect," so this decision by the study group was consistent with the intent of the statute.

9. A fifth wave of data collection, which will assess the children's progress at five to six years after the baseline investigation, was begun in 2005 as new funding became available and is scheduled for completion in 2007. With the reauthorization of PRWORA (see note 7 above), funding was authorized through 2010.

10. Michael J. Guralnick, "Effectiveness of Early Intervention for Vulnerable Children: A Developmental Perspective," *American Journal on Mental Retardation* 102, no. 4 (January 1998): 319–45.

11. Congress apparently recognizes the importance of ensuring that maltreated children receive Part C services. In both the Child Abuse Prevention and Treatment Act (recently

amended and reauthorized by the Keeping Children and Families Safe Act of 2003, P.L. 108-36) of 2003 and the most recent reauthorization of Individuals with Disabilities Education Act (P.L. 108-446) in 2004, provisions were included that required child protection agencies to refer children under the age of 3 who have substantiated cases of maltreatment for early intervention services under Part C.

12. Gayla Margolin and Elana B. Gordis, "The Effects of Family and Community Violence on Children," *Annual Review of Psychology 51* (February 2000), 445–79; Alan J. Litrownik and others, "Long-Term Follow-Up of Young Children Placed in Foster Care: Subsequent Placements and Exposure to Family Violence," *Journal of Family Violence* 18, no. 1 (February 2003): 19–28.

Appendix

Overview of Information Gathered by Source and Wave

Construct	Measure	Author	Waves	Information gathered
Child module				
Child characteristics	Project-developed questions	. . .	1, 3, 4	Child's demographic information, height, weight, and head circumference for children less than four years of age[a]
Developmental and cognitive status	Kaufman Brief Intelligence Test (K-BIT)	Kaufman and Kaufman (1990)[1]	1, 3, 4	Standardized assessment tool composed of two subsets: vocabulary (expressive vocabulary and definitions) and matrices (ability to perceive relationships and complete analogies)
Developmental and cognitive status	Battelle Developmental Inventory (BDI) and screening test—cognitive skills section	Newborg and others (1984)[2]	1, 3, 4	Cognitive skills; administered to children aged four and older
Developmental and cognitive status	Bayley Infant Neurodevelopmental Screener (BINS)	Ayleward (1995)[3]	1, 3[b]	Basic brain function, ability to comprehend and express, and intellectual processes
Communication skills	Preschool Language Scales-3 (PLS-3)	Zimmerman, Steiner, and Pond (1992)[4]	1, 3, 4	Standardized assessment tool composed of three scales: expressive communication, auditory comprehension, and total language, which include prelinguistic and language skills
Academic achievement	Mini Battery of Achievement (MBA)	Woodcock, McGrew, and Werder (1994)[5]	1, 3, 4	Standardized test of academic achievement in reading and mathematics
Neighborhood factors	Abridged Community Environment Scale from National Evaluation of Family Support Programs	Furstenburg (1990)[6]	4	Behavior of emancipated youth in their community; items mirror community environment module in Current Caregiver Instrument

(continued)

Overview of *Information Gathered by Source and Wave (continued)*

Construct	Measure	Author	Waves	Information gathered
School engagement	Drug Free Schools (DFSCA) outcome study questions	Tashjian and others (1996)[7]	1, 3, 4	School achievement; student's disposition toward learning and school; administered only to children in school (excludes home-schooled children)
Peer relationships, including social rejection	Loneliness and Social Dissatisfaction Questionnaire for young children	Asher, Hymel, and Renshaw (1984)[8]; Asher and Wheeler (1985)[9]	1, 3, 4	Success in making and keeping friendships; school adjustment; administered only to children in school (excludes home-schooled children)
Protective factors	Resiliency Scale—LongSCAN	Runyan and others (1998)[10]	1, 3, 4	Resources that facilitate resiliency
Behavioral monitoring	Parental monitoring	NIMH (1995)[11]	1, 3, 4	Extent to which the caregiver monitors the child's activities
Independent living	Project-developed questions	. . .	4	Life skills that youth have developed and where they learned the skills
Child in out-of-home care; perceptions of permanency, disruptions, contact with family	University of California at Berkeley foster care study	Fox, Frasch, and Berrick (2000)[12]	1, 3, 4	Adjustment of child in out-of-home placement, including concerns about how well the child fits in with the foster family and how permanent the child views the placement
Youth in out-of-home care; perceptions of permanency, disruptions, contact with family	University of California at Berkeley foster care study	Fox, Frasch, and Berrick (2000)[12]	4	Adjustment of adopted and emancipated youth, including concerns about how well the youth fits in with the adoptive family (if applicable) and contact with biological family
Satisfaction with caseworker services	Project-developed questions	. . .	1, 3, 4	Degree of satisfaction with caseworker services

Domain	Instrument	Source		Description
Future expectations	Adolescent Health Survey—section on expectations about employment, education, and life span	Bearman, Jones, and Udry (1997)[13]	1, 3, 4	Expectations as related to children's life experiences
Social support and other family resources, including assistance with child rearing	Adapted from Duke Functional Social Support Scale and Sarason Social Support Questionnaire-3	Sarason and others (1983);[14] Sarason and others (1987)[15]	4	Perceived social support for emancipated youth; items mirror social support module in Current Caregiver Instrument
Physical health	Short-Form Health Survey (SF-12)	Ware, Kosinski, and Keller (1998)[16]	4	Physical health status of emancipated youth; items mirror physical health module in Current Caregiver Instrument
Mental health	Children's Depression Inventory	Kovacs (1992)[17]	1, 3, 4	All aspects of well-being, including behavior problems
Mental health	Trauma Symptom Checklist for Children—posttraumatic stress disorder section	Briere (1996)[18]	1, 3, 4	Indicators of posttraumatic stress disorder
Participation in activities	Social Competence Scale—youth self-report	Achenbach (1991)[19]	1, 3, 4	Involvement in activities that may promote social skills or cognitive development
Behavior problems	Syndrome and Total Problems Scale—youth self-report	Achenbach (1991)[19]	1, 3, 4	Magnitude of aggressive behavior and impulse control
Relationship with parents and other significant adults	Revised Adolescent Health Survey questions; Relatedness Scale from Research Assessment Package for Schools—self-report instrument for middle school students (RAPS-SM)	Connell (1990)[20]	1, 3, 4	Degree of supportive relationships between child and adult

(continued)

Overview of Information Gathered by Source and Wave (continued)

Construct	Measure	Author	Waves	Information gathered
Relationship with parents and other significant adults	Project-developed questions	. . .	1, 3, 4	Degree of supportive relationships between child and adult
Loss, violence, and other stressors in and out of the home	Violence Exposure Scale (VEX-R)—home set	Fox and Leavitt (1995)[21]	1, 3, 4	Violence observed and experienced in the home
Services received	Project-developed questions	. . .	1, 3, 4	Factors that affect the service provision process; includes items administered only at wave 4 for emancipated youth
Substance abuse	Drug Free School Community Act, outcome study questions	Tashjian and others (1996)[22]	1, 3, 4	Misuse of controlled substances as associated with depression and maltreatment
Sexual behavior	LongSCAN	Runyan and others (1998)[10]	1, 3, 4	Early sexual activity
Delinquency	Modified self-report of delinquency; revised Adolescent Health Survey questions	Achenbach (1991);[19] Elliott and Huizinga (1985)[23]	1, 3, 4	Participation in delinquent or criminal activities, includes items added at wave 4 on reasons for recent arrests
Maltreatment	Injury questions from Child Health and Illness Profile—adolescent edition	Starfield and others (1995)[24]	1, 3, 4	Nature and extent of injuries in the past twelve months
Victimization	Study of incidence and prevalence of drug abuse among runaway and homeless youth—shelter sample questionnaire	Green and others (1995)[25]	4	Emancipated youth's victimization, including things that may have happened to youth since he or she started living on own (for example, robbery, sexual assault, and so on)
Maltreatment	Adaptation of Parent-Child Conflict Tactics Scale (CTSPC)	Straus and others (1998)[26]	1, 3, 4	Additional maltreatment information to better understand the effects of the severity and specific type of abuse

Current caregiver instrument module

Module	Instrument/source	Citation	Modules	Description
...	Project-developed verification questions to drive instrument wording and flow	...	All	Verification of respondent contact information, relationship to child, out-of-home placement status, and legal guardianship
Family composition and demographics	Project-developed questions	...	All	Family composition and demographic information necessary for classification and description of subjects
Group home classification and composition	Project-developed questions	...	4	Composition of group home facility, including number of children in home and relationship to child, and demographics of group home caregiver
Disruption in living environment	Project-developed questions	...	1, 3, 4	Changes of household composition or placement situations
Neighborhood factors	Abridged Community Environment Scale from National Evaluation of Family Support Programs	Furstenburg (1990)[6]	1, 3, 4	Behavior of individuals and families in their community
Health and disabilities services received by child	Child and Adolescent Services Assessment (CASA); Child Health Questionnaire from National Evaluation of Family Support Programs; Brief Global Health Inventory; and project-developed questions on services	Burns and others (1996)[27]	All	History of health, injury, and disability status of child; services received by the child
Child's readiness to live on own	Project-developed questions	...	4	Most recent caregiver's perception of emancipated youth's readiness to live independently

(continued)

Overview of *Information Gathered by Source and Wave* (continued)

Construct	Measure	Author	Waves	Information gathered
Adaptive skills	Vineland Adaptive Behavior Scale (VABS) Screener—Daily Living Skills	Sparrow, Carter, and Cicchetti (1984)[28]	1, 3, 4	Regular behaviors the child exhibits
Global social competence	Social Skills Rating System (SRSS)—Social Skills Scale	Gresham and Elliot (1990)[29]	1, 3, 4	Level of development of social skills
Emotional regulation and temperament	How My Infant/Toddler/Child Usually Acts from National Longitudinal Survey of Youth	Baker and others (1993)[30]	All	Child's ability to express emotions and cope with highly charged emotional situations
Behavior problems	Behavior Problem Index, with addition of items from Social Skills Rating System—Social Skills Scale	Baker and others (1993)[30]	2	Added at wave 2 to collect child well-being measure from current caregiver
Behavior problems	Child Behavior Checklist	Achenbach (1991)[19]	1, 3, 4	Degree to which child exhibits different types of behaviors
Income	Project-developed questions	...	1, 3, 4	Financial resources available to the child's household
Services received by caregiver	Project-developed questions	...	All	Frequency and duration that services have been or are being received
Social support and other family resources, including assistance with child-rearing	Adapted from Duke Functional Social Support Scale and Sarason Social Support Questionnaire-3	Sarason and others (1983)[14]; Sarason and others (1987)[15]	1, 3, 4	Perceived social support for child and family
Physical health	Short-Form Health Survey (SF-12)	Ware, Kosinski, and Keller (1998)[16]	1, 3, 4	Caregiver's physical health status

Measure	Instrument	Reference	Cohort	Description
Services received by foster caregivers	Project-developed questions	...	All	Frequency and duration that services have been or are being received
Adoption possibilities for child	Project-developed questions	...	2, 3	Adoption possibilities for child, including factors that encouraged or discouraged adoption decision
Permanency planning possibilities for child	Project-developed questions	...	4	Permanency planning options for child, including adoption, legal guardianship, and long-term foster care
Mental health: depression	Composite International Diagnostic Interview, Short-Form (CIDI-SF)—module for depression	Kessler and others (1998)[31]	1, 3, 4	Caregiver experiences that indicate symptoms of depression
Mental health: substance abuse	Composite International Diagnostic Interview, Short-Form (CIDI-SF)—module for alcohol dependence	Kessler and others (1998)[31]	1, 3, 4	Caregiver experiences that indicate symptoms of alcohol dependence
Mental health: substance abuse	Composite International Diagnostic Interview, Short-Form (CIDI-SF)—module for drug dependence	Kessler and others (1998)[31]	1, 3, 4	Caregiver experiences that indicate symptoms of drug dependence
Criminal involvement of parents	Project-developed questions	...	1, 3, 4	Caregiver criminal history and involvement with the justice system
Behavioral monitoring and discipline	Parent-Child Conflict Tactics Scale (CTSPC) with neglect and substance abuse questions added	Straus and others (1998)[26]	1, 3, 4	Methods and frequency of discipline measures used by the caregiver during the last twelve months
Domestic violence in the home	Conflict Tactics Scale (CTS)	Straus, Gelles, and Smith (1990)[32]	1, 3, 4	Type and frequency of violence occurring in the home and directed toward female caregiver in the last twelve months and subsequent use of services
Satisfaction with caseworker	Project-developed questions	...	All	Satisfaction level with services received from caseworker

(continued)

Overview of Information Gathered by Source and Wave (continued)

Construct	Measure	Author	Waves	Information gathered
Emotional nurturing, cognitive and verbal responsiveness and stimulation	Home Observation for Measurement of the Environment—Short Form (HOME-SF)	Baker and others (1993)[30]	1, 3, 4	Scripted items about the child's home environment
Emotional nurturing, cognitive and verbal responsiveness and stimulation	Home Observation for Measurement of the Environment—Short Form (HOME-SF)	Baker and others (1993)[30]	1, 3, 4	Observations by field representative of the child's home environment
Teacher survey instrument				
Teacher-child relations	Project-developed questions	. . .	1, 3, 4	Subject area taught, average class size, knowledge of child
Peer relationships	Teacher Checklist of Reactive and Proactive Aggression	Dodge and Coie (1987)[33]	1, 3, 4	Student's relationship with peers in class
Social skills and school socialization	Social Skills Rating System (SRSS)	Gresham and Elliot (1990)[29]	1, 3, 4	Level of development of social skills possessed by the child
Student behavior	Teacher Report Form	Achenbach (1991)[19]	1, 3, 4	Behavior of student now and in the past two months
Academic performance, school absences	Project-developed questions	. . .	1, 3, 4	Grade progression, academic performance by subject, behavior and discipline problems, reading level
Special educational needs	Project-developed questions	. . .	1, 3, 4	Physical, emotional, or mental conditions that limit child; individual education plan (if applicable), classification of special needs

Investigative caseworker instrument module

	Source	Wave	Description
Case investigation	Project-developed questions	…	1	Circumstances surrounding the investigative report; background of the caseworker
Nature of abuse	Project-developed questions	…	1	Details about the specific nature of the alleged abuse or neglect
Risk assessment	Project-developed questions based on questions from Michigan, New York, Washington, Illinois, and Colorado risk assessment forms and checklists	…	1	Factors determining case decisions, including prior history of abuse or neglect, caregiver substance abuse, domestic violence in the home, caregiver mental health problems, poor parenting skills, excessive discipline, and so forth
Services to parents	Project-developed questions	…	All	Service needs, regardless of availability; asked only for long-term foster care cases at wave 1; asked for all cases at waves 2, 3, and 4
Services to child	Project-developed questions	…	All	Services the child may have received; asked only for long-term foster care cases at wave 1; asked for all cases at waves 2, 3, and 4

Services caseworker instrument

	Source	Wave	Description
Child welfare history	Project-developed questions	…	2, 3, 4	Child's history with the child welfare system since the case report that resulted in the child's selection for NSCAW
Services to parents	Project-developed questions	…	All	Service needs, regardless of availability; asked for long-term foster care cases only at wave 1
Services to child	Project-developed questions	…	All	Services the child may have received; asked for long-term foster care cases only at wave 1

(continued)

Overview of Information Gathered by Source and Wave (continued)

Construct	Measure	Author	Waves	Information gathered
Independent living skills	Project-developed questions	…	4	Independent living skills the child has developed and where each skill was learned
Adoption possibilities for child	Project-developed questions	…	2, 3	Adoption possibilities for children in out-of-home care; also factors that encouraged or discouraged the caregiver's decision about adoption
Permanency planning possibilities for child	Project-developed questions	…	4	Permanency planning possibilities for children in out-of-home care, including adoption, legal guardianship, and long-term foster care; also factors that encouraged or discouraged the caregiver's permanency planning decision; permanency planning module replaced the adoption planning module from prior waves
Prior reports of abuse or neglect	Project-developed questions	…	2	Child's history with the child welfare system before the case report that resulted in the child's selection for NSCAW; administered at wave 3 if the wave 2 caseworker interview could not be obtained
Involvement with juvenile justice and court system	Project-developed questions	…	2, 3, 4	History of court hearings related to the case, including type of hearing, recommendations made by the child welfare agency, and outcome of the hearing
Child's placement history and parental living situations	Project-developed questions	…	2, 3, 4	History of child's living situations since investigation, including type of living arrangement and child's contact with biological parents

Caseworker involvement with child and family	Project-developed questions	...	Caseworker's individual involvement with case, including referrals made for family members, caseworker contact with siblings, number of contacts with service providers and family, and attitudes about service to family
Family's compliance with case plan	Project-developed questions	...	Family's progress with and adherence to case plan
Caseworker demographic characteristics	Project-developed questions	...	Demographic information about the caseworker, including employment and educational history, and attitudinal questions about work as a caseworker; completed as a self-administered paper-and-pencil questionnaire or as a module of a computer-assisted interview; brief subset of items administered in subsequent waves
		2, 3, 4	
		2, 3, 4	
		2, 3, 4	

Source: Katherine Dowd and others, *NSCAW Data File Users Manual* (Washington: U.S. Department of Health and Human Services, Administration for Children and Families, 2006).

. . . = Not applicable.

a. Caregivers provided demographic information for very young children.

b. The BINS is not adminstered at wave 4 because sampled children have aged out.

1. Alan Kaufman and Nadeen Kaufman, *Kaufman Brief Intelligence Test (K-BIT): Expressive Vocabulary, Definitions, and Matrices* (Circle Pines, Minn.: American Guidance Service, 1990). Electronic version of K-BIT Individual Test Record items prepared by Research Triangle Institute with permission of publisher for research purposes only.

2. Jean Newborg and others, *Battelle Developmental Inventory, with Recalibrated Technical Data and Norms: Examiner's Manual* (Rolling Meadows, Ill.: Riverside Publishing, 1984).

3. Glen P. Aylward, *The Bayley Infant Neurodevelopmental Screener Manual* (San Antonio, Tex.: The Psychological Corporation, 1995), standardization manual published in 1992.

4. Irma L. Zimmerman, Violette G. Steiner, and Roberta P. Pond, *Preschool Language Scale-3* (San Antonio, Tex.: The Psychological Corporation, 1992).

5. Richard W. Woodcock, Kevin S. McGrew, and Judy K. Werder, *Woodcock-McGrew-Werder Mini-Battery of Achievement* (Itasca, Ill.: Riverside Publishing, 1994).

6. Frank Furstenburg, *Philadelphia Family Management Study, Parent Interview Schedule* (Philadelphia: University of Pennsylvania Population Studies Center, and Boulder: University of Colorado, Institute of Behavioral Science, 1990).

7. Christine A. Tashjian and others, *School-Based Drug Prevention Programs: A Longitudinal Study in Selected School Districts* (Washington: U.S. Department of Education, 1996).

8. Steven R. Asher, Shelley Hymel, and Peter D. Renshaw, "Loneliness in Children," *Child Development* 55, no. 4 (1984): 1456–464.

(continued)

Overview of Information Gathered by Source and Wave (continued)

9. Steven R. Asher and Valerie A. Wheeler, "Children's Loneliness: A Comparison of Rejected and Neglected Peer Status," Consulting Clinical Psychology 53, no. 4 (1985): 500–05.

10. Desmond K. Runyan and others, "LONGSCAN: A Consortium for Longitudinal Studies of Maltreatment and the Life Course of Children," Aggression and Violent Behavior 3, no. 3 (1998): 275–85.

11. National Institutes of Mental Health, Use, Need, Outcome, and Costs in Child and Adolescent Populations Steering Committee (Bethesda, Md., 1995).

12. Adair Fox, Karie Frasch, and Jill D. Berrick, Listening to Children in Foster Care: An Empirically Based Curriculum (Berkeley, Calif.: Child Welfare Research Center, 2000).

13. Peter S. Bearman, Jo Jones, and J. Richard Udry, "The National Longitudinal Study of Adolescent Health: Research Design, 1997" (Chapel Hill: University of North Carolina, Carolina Population Center) (www.cpc.unc.edu/addhealth [December 29, 2006]).

14. Irwin G. Sarason and others, "Assessing Social Support: The Social Support Questionnaire," Personality and Social Psychology 44, no. 1 (1983): 127–39.

15. Irwin G. Sarason and others, "A Brief Measure of Social Support: Practical and Theoretical Implications," Social and Personal Relationships 4 (1987): 497–510.

16. John Ware, Mark Kosinski, and Susan Keller, How to Score the SF-12 Physical and Mental Health Summary Scales, 3d ed. (Lincoln, R.I.: Quality Metric Incorporated, 1998).

17. Maria Kovacs, Children's Depression Inventory (North Tonawanda, N.Y.: Multi-Health, 1992).

18. John Briere, Trauma Symptom Checklist for Children: Professional Manual (Lutz, Fla.: Psychological Assessment Resources, Inc, 1996).

19. Thomas M. Achenbach, Manual for the Child Behavior Checklist/2-3 and 1992 Profile; Manual for the Child Behavior Checklist/4-18 and 1991 Profile; Manual for the Teacher's Report Form and 1991 Profile; Manual for the Youth Self-Report and 1991 Profile (Burlington: University of Vermont, Department of Psychiatry).

20. James P. Connell, "Context, Self, and Action: A Motivational Analysis of Self-System Processes across the Life Span," in The Self in Transition, edited by Dante Cicchetti and Marjorie Beeghly (University of Chicago Press, 1990), pp. 61–97.

21. Nathan A. Fox and Lewis A. Leavitt, The Violence Exposure Scale for Children (VEX) (College Park: University of Maryland, 1995).

22. Christine A. Tashjian, Silvia E. Suyapa, and Judy Thorne, School-Based Drug Prevention Programs: A Longitudinal Study in Selected School Districts (Washington: U.S. Department of Education, 1996).

23. Adapted from Delbert Elliott and David Huizinga, Self-Reported Delinquency Measure (Boulder: University of Colorado, Institute of Behavioral Science, 1985).

24. Barbara Starfield and others, "The Adolescent CHIP: A Population-Based Measure of Health," Medical Care 33, no. 5 (May 1995): 553–66.

25. Jody Green and others, Youth with Runaway, Throwaway, and Homeless Experiences: Prevalence, Drug Use, and Other At-Risk Behaviors (Washington: U.S. Department of Health and Human Services, Administration on Children, Youth and Families, 1995).

26. Murray Straus and others, "Identification of Child Maltreatment with the Parent-Child Conflict Tactics Scales: Development and Psychometric Data for a National Sample of American Parents," Child Abuse & Neglect 22, no. 4 (1998): 249–70.

27. Barbara J. Burns and others, "The Child and Adolescent Services Assessment (CASA)" (Duke University, School of Medicine, 1996).

28. Sara S. Sparrow, Allie S. Carter, and Domenic V. Cicchetti, Vineland Screener: Overview, Reliability, Validity, Administration, and Scoring (New Haven, Conn.: Yale University Child Study Center, 1993).

29. Frank M. Gresham and Stephen N. Elliot, Social Skills Rating System (Circle Pines, Minn.: American Guidance Service, 1990).

30. Paula P. Baker and others, *NLSY Child Handbook: A Guide to the 1986–1990 National Longitudinal Survey of Youth Child Data*, rev. ed. (Columbus, Ohio: Center for Human Resource Research, 1993).

31. Ronald Kessler and others, "The World Health Organization Composite International Diagnostic Interview Short-Form (CIDI-SF)," *International Journal of Methods in Psychiatric Research* 7 (1998): 171–85.

32. Murray Straus and Richard Gelles, with Christine Smith, *Physical Violence in American Families: Risk Factors and Adaptations to Violence in 8,145 Families* (New Brunswick, N.J.: Transaction Publishers, 1990).

33. Kenneth A. Dodge and John D. Coie, "Social-Information-Processing Factors in Reactive and Proactive Aggression in Children's Peer Groups," *Personality and Social Psychology* 53, no. 6 (1987): 1146–158.

2

Identifying Young Maltreated Children with Developmental Delays

STEVEN A. ROSENBERG, ELLIOTT G. SMITH,
AND ARNOLD LEVINSON

Part C of the Individuals with Disabilities Education Act (IDEA) was designed as an interagency program for the coordination of efforts within and across community and governmental agencies to address the needs of infants and toddlers with developmental delays and their families. Child welfare agencies are among the entities expected to be involved in these interagency efforts. Child welfare programs are responsible, under the Child Abuse Prevention and Treatment Act (CAPTA), for ensuring the safety and well-being of children who are maltreated by providing child protective services (CPS) and foster care services. Recent changes in federal legislation have mandated greater collaboration between Part C and child welfare services. CAPTA and IDEA now require states to ensure the referral of children who are younger than three-years-old with developmental delays and who are "involved in a substantiated case of child abuse or neglect to early intervention services funded under part C."[1]

Under the Part C program, each state is required to establish a definition of eligibility for services that addresses delays in five developmental domains: motor, communication, cognitive, daily living, and social-emotional. States' criteria for Part C must specify levels of developmental delay and diagnoses associated

Support for this research was provided by a grant from the U.S. Department of Education, OSEP Grant # H324T990026.

with developmental conditions that confer eligibility. States also have the option of creating eligibility criteria for children who are at risk of having a developmental delay. Children who are eligible for Part C services must receive an individualized family service plan (IFSP), which specifies services based on a multidisciplinary assessment that addresses the child's functioning in each of the five developmental domains. The IFSP is also expected to address those family concerns, priorities, and resources identified as important in assisting the family to support the child's development. Finally Part C requires that each child and family be provided a service coordinator to help the family obtain services by coordinating services across agencies and providers.

Maltreatment of children adversely affects their health and developmental status.[2] Evidence shows that maltreated children have high rates of illness, injuries, and developmental delays.[3] Chernoff and others examined the results of health examinations provided to children younger than five years of age at the time of entry into foster care and found 23 percent had abnormal or suspect results on developmental screening examinations.[4] Similarly, Halfon, Mendonca, and Berkowitz conducted a chart review of 213 young children in foster care and found that more than 80 percent had developmental, emotional, or behavioral problems.[5] Stahmer and others examined scores in the areas of cognitive, behavioral, and social skills of children younger than six years of age obtained from the National Survey of Child and Adolescent Well-Being (NSCAW).[6] They found 46 percent of these children had scores that would qualify them for early intervention services. This high rate of health and developmental problems among children in child welfare services is the result of the increased vulnerability to maltreatment that comes from having a disability and the fact that these problems can occur as a consequence of abuse and neglect.[7]

Of particular concern are very young maltreated children, whose developmental problems occur at a time when they are most vulnerable to lasting harm.[8] Children younger than three who have medical or developmental problems experience more removals from parental care, have longer stays in foster care, are placed in more settings, and are less likely to return to their parents at the end of foster care than peers who are unaffected by health and developmental conditions.[9] Although these children are candidates for early intervention under Part C, there is reason to believe that only a small number are actually enrolled in services.[10] Concerns about the high rates of developmental problems and under-enrollment in services have prompted federal requirements that maltreated children younger than three be referred for Part C early intervention services.

Evidence of high rates of developmental problems among young children who are maltreated and of low rates of their referral for early intervention, as well as the requirement that they be referred to the Part C program, highlight the need for studies that examine rates of Part C eligibility among young children who are victims of maltreatment. In this study, the nationally representative NSCAW sample was used to estimate rates of Part C eligibility for maltreated children and to examine the extent to which their developmental delays were recognized by intake caseworkers.

Methods

The NSCAW database has measures for three of the five developmental domains used to determine children's eligibility for Part C services from birth to three years of age. Children's skills in these three domains were assessed with three different instruments: cognitive skills using the cognitive subscale of the Battelle Developmental Inventory (BDI), communication skills using the total score of the Preschool Language Scale-3 (PLS-3), and daily living skills using the daily living skills domain of the Vineland Adaptive Behavior Scale (VABS) Screener.[11] Caseworker identification of children with developmental and behavioral problems was obtained from interviews of intake workers.

Victimization status of the children was obtained from the investigative caseworker's report of the outcome of the investigation. Children were classified as victims if the maltreatment under investigation was either substantiated or indicated. A similar definition for victimization is used in the *Child Maltreatment* report series, published by the U.S. Department of Health and Human Services.[12] For some children in the NSCAW database, the caseworker assigned a level of risk rather than a case disposition. These children were not considered to be victims and were not included in the analyses. The final sample consisted of 1,138 victims of maltreatment who were less than three years of age at the start of NSCAW. The characteristics of the sample are summarized in table 2-1.

Our estimate of the number of maltreated children having developmental delays relied on criteria commonly used to determine the eligibility of children for Part C services. In many states, children would be eligible for Part C services if they scored 1.0 standard deviation (SD) or more below the mean on developmental measures of two of Part C's five developmental domains, or 1.5 standard deviations below the mean on one measure of developmental functioning. These criteria were used to compute a composite that classified children into delayed and nondelayed groups.

Rates of Developmental Problems

A substantial proportion of maltreated children in NSCAW showed delays on one or more of the three measures of developmental functioning. Developmental scores were less than or equal to 1 standard deviation below the mean for 39 percent of the children on the BDI, 44 percent on the PLS-3, and 34 percent on the VABS (table 2-2).

Table 2-1. *Demographic Characteristics of Maltreated Children Younger than Age Three*[a]

Characteristic	Percent
Sex	
Male	51.3
Female	48.7
Race	
Non-Hispanic White	40.5
Non-Hispanic Black	30.3
Hispanic	21.7
Other	7.5
Child setting	
In-home, no services	32.3
In-home, services	35.8
Foster home	18.6
Kin care setting	12.5
Most serious alleged maltreatment	
Physical abuse	14.7
Sexual abuse	2.5
Emotional abuse	7.4
Neglect (failure to provide)	27.9
Neglect (lack of supervision)	33.2
Abandonment	3.5
Other maltreatment	9.2
Unknown	1.6

Source: Authors' calculations.

a. Table entries are percentages that are weighted to produce national estimates. Sample size is 1,138, representing 156,000 maltreated children younger than three years of age. Percentages may not add to 100 because of rounding.

Using the criteria of two or more scores less than or equal to 1.0 standard deviations below the mean or one score 1.5 SD below the mean, the study found that 46.5 percent of children were classified as having developmental delays that likely would make them eligible for Part C services. Generalizing from the NSCAW sample to the national population, we estimate that about 156,000 children younger than three-years-old were substantiated for maltreatment in the United States during the fifteen-month data collection period for wave 1. The estimated number of children in the nation classified as being eligible for Part C services would be 46.5 percent of 156,000 or about 72,660 for a fifteen-month period. On an annual basis, this result yields an estimate of 58,100 children eligible for the Part C program who were substantiated for abuse or neglect.

Table 2-2. *Child Performance on Developmental Assessments*[a]

Child Performance	Percent
Battelle Developmental Inventory (BDI)—cognitive scale	
No delay	60.9
1 to 1.5 SD below mean	12.5
More than 1.5 SD below mean	26.5
Preschool Language Scale (PLS-3)—total communication score	
No delay	55.9
1 to 1.5 SD below mean	21.3
More than 1.5 SD below mean	22.8
Vineland Adaptive Behavior Scales (VABS)—daily living skills	
No delay	66.3
1 to 1.5 SD below mean	16.0
More than 1.5 SD below mean	17.7

Source: Authors' calculations.
SD = standard deviation.
a. The number of valid cases for the BDI was 932; for the PLS-3, it was 958; and for the VABS, it was 1,138. Percentages may not add up to 100 because of rounding.

Recognition of Developmental Delays

Intake caseworkers were asked whether, at the time of the investigation, the child had major developmental or behavior problems. Their responses showed they were able to identify less than one-fourth (23 percent) of the children whose assessment scores indicated delayed development on the basis of the criteria used in this study.

Discussion

At the time of their entering into child welfare services, 47 percent of maltreated children younger than three years of age had developmental delays, making them likely to be eligible for Part C early intervention. This finding is consistent with reports of a high incidence of developmental problems among children in foster care.[13] However, these results are probably an underestimate of the true rate of delay in this sample because two of the five developmental domains, motor and social-emotional functioning, used to determine eligibility for Part C services could not be assessed for our sample using the data in NSCAW. Moreover this study did not attempt to identify children using diagnoses that determine Part C eligibility, which would also contribute to an undercount of eligible children.

As previously mentioned, caseworkers were able to identify only 23 percent of the children with developmental problems. This result suggests that the developmental needs of most of these children went unrecognized, and consequently it is unlikely that they were referred for early intervention by child welfare services. This evidence that developmental delays were underidentified and the consequent lack of referral for Part C services suggest that a concerted effort will be needed to overcome barriers to identifying and serving children who need Part C early intervention.

Increasing referrals for Part C services by child welfare agencies will not be easy. Problems of parental acceptance of Part C referrals and services will have to be dealt with if children are to be evaluated and served. Child welfare professionals need better information about Part C, particularly how to refer families for early intervention services. Differences between the organizational cultures of Part C and child welfare services will need to be addressed during any process that attempts to link these two systems. For example, voluntary family participation is a fundamental principle of Part C services. By contrast, coercion is a fact of life for many parents under supervision by child welfare services who must demonstrate their fitness to avoid losing custody of their children. The fact that some parents are ordered into Part C services will present a dilemma for many early intervention practitioners who have been taught that services are voluntary and that priorities for services should reflect parents' wishes. Ideally, child welfare and Part C agencies should have specialists who liaison between the two service programs, working with families that have children with developmental problems.

Other barriers can block the use of Part C services even when children are determined to be eligible and families have completed the individual family service plan (IFSP) process. Substantial numbers of high-risk families may drop out of Part C services after treatment has begun.[14] Families reported for abuse or neglect may not be highly motivated to participate in early intervention.[15] Parents who have maltreated their children are often dealing with multiple stressful events.[16] They may also be less effective in their day-to-day caretaking than other parents.[17] It is anticipated that they may have considerable difficulty learning to support their children's development.

Many Part C programs are not prepared to work with families that have a history of child abuse and neglect. Interventions needed by families in the CPS system, including parent education and training, may not be available through the Part C program. The most common services provided by the Part C program under IDEA are speech and language therapy, occupational therapy, physical therapy, and child educational interventions.[18] By contrast, such services as family training and counseling, psychological services, and social work are infrequently included in children's IFSPs. The emphasis of Part C on services that address child motor and communication skills means that families referred by child welfare services may not receive the services they most need. Moreover, these services are often delivered by a series of different professionals. It is likely that families with children who are maltreated will have difficulty making use of services that involve the provision of multiple therapies. Instead these families would benefit more if services were provided by a single, trusted professional. An additional concern regarding the appropriateness of typical Part C services for these families stems from the need of parents for direct teaching in home and group settings to achieve meaningful improvements in the care they provide their children.[19] In particular, the interaction between parents and their children should be a focus for early intervention.[20] However, parent-child interaction is an area with which Part C personnel typically have had little experience. Indeed Mahoney and others noted that in the Part C program there has been a tendency to reject the direct instruction of parents and other interventions that focus on parenting skills, because these services are seen as incompatible with the goal of developing a collaborative relationship with parents.[21] As a consequence, the interventions required to improve parents' caregiving skills are unfamiliar to many providers of Part C early intervention services. Therefore, Part C providers will need training so that they can work successfully with families referred by child welfare agencies.

Because many young children who have suffered from abuse or neglect are placed in foster care, their access to Part C services must also be addressed.[22] Biological parents whose rights have not been terminated and foster parents should be involved in Part C services to learn how to interact with these young children and to promote their development.

One complication of involving foster children in the Part C program has to do with obtaining parent consent for evaluation and services.[23] Parent consent is required for enrollment of the child in Part C services. Parents whose rights have not been terminated may consent to Part C evaluations and services for their child. However, problems enrolling children can arise when parents cannot be located. To ensure that children receive services in a timely fashion, educational surrogates are sometimes appointed to act on a child's behalf. Surrogates can be family members, such as grandparents, or others with whom the child has a relationship. State officials and county child welfare staff are typically not allowed to act in this role because of a potential conflict of interest. To ensure that foster children have access to Part C services, child welfare and Part C programs must work out procedures that provide children in out-of-home care with representation by their parents or by educational surrogates.

The Part C program served about 233,000 children in 2000.[24] This study found that at least 58,000 children in the CPS system were likely to have been eligible for Part C services in that year. Few of these children were identified as having developmental problems by their caseworkers, however. Thus it was unlikely that they were referred for Part C services. If most of these children had been properly identified and referred, the number of maltreated children needing developmental evaluations to determine their eligibility for Part C services would have increased drastically, as well as the number enrolling in Part C services. Such increases in assessments and enrollment can be expected to strain the capacity of many Part C programs. If state Part C systems are substantially overextended by increases in workload, it is possible that some will adopt restrictive eligibility criteria to reduce the total number of children who receive Part C services or will adopt ineffective strategies for enrolling families from the child welfare system into the Part C program. Consequently, planning must accompany any efforts to increase referrals from child welfare to Part C services to ensure that the Part C system has the capacity to adequately screen, conduct multidisciplinary assessments, and deliver early intervention services.[25] Advocates for children and families will need to monitor the responses of states to these new requirements to ensure that children who need Part C services receive them. Where capacity is inadequate, advocacy should make legislators aware of the need to expand programs so that these children can be appropriately served.

Staff of child welfare and Part C programs within states are now in the process of establishing procedures for providing developmental evaluations and Part C early intervention to young, maltreated children. A potentially useful partner in this process is the Interagency Coordinating Council (ICC) in each state. The ICC is the primary forum where Part C policy is debated and then recommended to the state's lead Part C agency. The ICC includes representatives from state agencies involved in providing or funding Part C services, as well as parent representatives. The goal of fostering collaboration between the child welfare and Part C systems would be advanced if the child welfare agency in each state had representation on the ICC. In addition, planning in each state should include providing Part C personnel with estimates of potential increases in referrals for eligibility determination and Part C enrollment. Projected referral data will help in determining the resources communities need to manage increases in referrals.

This study has shown that the child welfare population includes large numbers of children whose delays in development make them candidates for Part C services. However, the need for early intervention services will not be met unless action is taken by the child welfare system to identify these children and by the Part C system to serve them.

Notes

1. Keeping Children and Families Safe Act of 2003, Public Law 108-36, section 114(b)(1)(B)(xxi).

2. Neal Halfon and Linnea Klee, "Health Services for California's Foster Children: Current Practices and Policy Recommendations," *Pediatrics* 80, no. 2 (1987): 183–91; Jack P. Shonkoff and Deborah A. Phillips, "Executive Summary," in *From Neurons to Neighborhoods: The Science of Early Childhood Development,* edited by Jack P. Shonkoff and Deborah A. Phillips (Washington: National Academy Press, 2000).

3. Neil Hochstadt, Paula Jaudes, Deborah Zimo, and Jayne Schachter, "The Medical and Psychosocial Needs of Children Entering Foster Care," *Child Abuse & Neglect* 11, no. 1 (1987): 53–62; Robin Chernoff and others, "Assessing the Health Status of Children Entering Foster Care," *Pediatrics* 93, no. 4 (1994): 594–601; Neal Halfon, Ana Mendonca, and Gale Berkowitz, "Health Status of Children in Foster Care," *Archives of Pediatrics and Adolescent Medicine* 149, no. 4 (1995): 386–92; Jack P. Shonkoff and Deborah A. Phillips, *From Neurons to Neighborhoods: The Science of Early Childhood Development.*

4. Robin Chernoff and others, "Assessing the Health Status of Children Entering Foster Care."

5. Neal Halfon, Ana Mendonca, and Gale Berkowitz, "Health Status of Children in Foster Care."

6. Aubyn C. Stahmer and others, "Developmental and Behavioral Needs and Service Use for Young Children in Child Welfare," *Pediatrics* 116 , no. 4 (2005): 891–900.

7. Douglas Barnett, "The Effects of Early Intervention on Maltreating Parents and Their Children" in *The Effectiveness of Early Intervention,* edited by Michael Guralnick (Baltimore, Md.: Brookes, 1997), pp. 147–70; Paula K. Jaudes and Linda D. Shapiro, "Child Abuse and Developmental Disabilities" in *Young Children and Foster Care: A Guide for Professionals,* edited by Judith A. Silver, Barbara J. Amster, and Trude Haecker (Baltimore, Md.: Brookes, 1999): pp. 213–34; Patricia M. Sullivan and John F. Knutson, "The Association between Child Maltreatment and Disabilities in a Hospital-Based Epidemiological Study," *Child Abuse & Neglect* 22, no. 4 (1998): 271–88.

8. Jack P. Shonkoff and Deborah A. Phillips, *From Neurons to Neighborhoods: The Science of Early Childhood Development.*

9. Steven A. Rosenberg and Cordelia C. Robinson, "Out-of-Home Placement for Young Children with Developmental and Medical Conditions," *Children and Youth Services Review* 26, no. 8 (2004): 711–23.

10. Sarah M. Horwitz, Pamela Owens, and Mark D. Simms, "Specialized Assessments for Children in Foster Care," *Pediatrics* 106, no. 1 (2000): 59–66; Cordelia C. Robinson and Steven A. Rosenberg, "Child Welfare Referrals to Part C," *Journal of Early Intervention* 26, no. 4 (2000): 284–91.

11. Jean N. Newborg, John R. Stock, Linda Wnek, John Guidubaldi, and John Svinicki, *Battelle Developmental Inventory with Recalibrated Technical Data and Norms: Examiner's Manual* (Rolling Meadows, Ill.: Riverside Publishing, 1984); Irma L. Zimmerman, Violette G. Steiner, and Roberta E. Pond, *Preschool Language Scale-3: Examiner's Manual* (San Antonio, Tex.: Harcourt Brace Jovanovich, 1991); Sara S. Sparrow, Alice S. Carter, and Domenic V. Cicchetti, *Vineland Screener: Overview, Reliability, Validity, Administration, and Scoring* (New Haven, Conn.: Yale University Child Study Center, 1993).

12. U.S. Department of Health and Human Services, Administration for Children and Families, *Child Maltreatment 2003* (Washington: U.S. Government Printing Office, 2005).

13. Robin Chernoff and others, "Assessing the Health Status of Children Entering Foster Care"; Neal Halfon, Ana Mendonca, and Gale Berkowitz, "Health Status of Children in Foster Care"; John Takayama, Ellen Wolfe, and Kevin Coulter, "Relationship between Reason for Placement and Medical Findings among Children in Foster Care," *Pediatrics* 101, no. 2 (1998): 201–07.

14. Steven A. Rosenberg, Cordelia C. Robinson, and G. Edward Fryer, "Evaluation of Paraprofessional Home Visiting Services for Children with Special Needs and Their Families," *Topics in Early Childhood Special Education* 22, no. 3 (2002): 158–68.

15. Donna Spiker and Judith A. Silver, "Early Intervention Services for Infants and Preschoolers in Foster Care," in *Young Children and Foster Care,* pp. 347–71.

16. Susan P. Cadzow, Kenneth L. Armstrong, and Jennifer A. Fraser, "Stressed Parents with Infants: Reassessing Physical Abuse Risk Factors," *Child Abuse & Neglect* 23, no. 9 (1999): 845–53; Jonathan B. Kotch and others, "Stress, Social Support, and Substantiated Maltreatment in the Second and Third Years of Life," *Child Abuse & Neglect* 21, no. 11 (1997): 1025–037.

17. Douglas Barnett, "The Effects of Early Intervention on Maltreating Parents and Their Children."

18. U.S. Department of Education, Office of Special Education and Rehabilitative Services, Office of Special Education Programs, *25th Annual Report to Congress on the Implementation of the Individuals with Disabilities Education Act,* vol. 2, 2003 (Washington, 2005).

19. David Olds and Harriet Kitzman, "Can Home Visitation Improve the Health of Women and Children at Environmental Risk?" *Pediatrics* 86, no. 1 (1990): 108–16; Steven A. Rosenberg, Cordelia C. Robinson, and G. Edward Fryer, "Evaluation of Paraprofessional Home Visiting Services for Children with Special Needs and Their Families."

20. Mark Chaffin and others, "Parent-Child Interaction Therapy with Physically Abusive Parents: Efficacy for Reducing Future Abuse Reports," *Journal of Consulting and Clinical Psychology* 72, no. 3 (2004): 500–10.

21. Gerald Mahoney and others, "Parent Education in Early Intervention," *Topics in Early Childhood Special Education* 19, no. 3 (1999): 131–40.

22. U.S. Department of Health and Human Services, *Child Maltreatment 2003.*

23. Sheryl Dicker and Elysa Gordon, "Critical Connections for Children Who Are Abused and Neglected: Harnessing the New Federal Referral Provisions for Early Intervention," *Infants & Young Children* 19, no. 3 (2006): 170–78.

24. U.S. Department of Education, *25th Annual Report to Congress on the Implementation of the Individuals with Disabilities Education Act,* vol. 1, 2003 (Washington, 2005).

25. Cordelia Robinson and others, "Interagency Collaboration Guidebook: A Strategic Planning Tool for Child Welfare & Part C Agencies" (Denver, Colo.: JFK Partners and Department of Pediatrics and Psychiatry, University of Colorado at Denver, 2003).

3

Intimate Partner Violence in the Child Welfare System: Findings from the National Survey of Child and Adolescent Well-Being

ANDREA L. HAZEN, CYNTHIA D. CONNELLY,
KELLY J. KELLEHER, JOHN A. LANDSVERK,
AND RICHARD P. BARTH

More than twenty years of research has documented the fact that intimate partner violence (IPV) is a significant public health problem that affects the well-being of a large proportion of women and children in the United States. As recognition of its pervasiveness and harmful consequences has grown, so has interest in increasing our understanding of this problem in high-risk populations, such as families involved with the child welfare system. There has been relatively little research on this topic to date, and existing studies have generally been limited in scope. The purpose of this paper is to report findings from the National Survey of Child and Adolescent Well-Being (NSCAW) on rates and correlates of IPV and on the relationship between IPV and child behavior problems in a representative sample of families that came in contact with the child welfare system throughout the United States.

The information and opinions expressed herein solely reflect the position of the authors, and nothing should be construed to indicate the support or endorsement of its content by the Administration on Children, Youth and Families, U.S. Department of Health and Human Services. The NSCAW findings described here are reproduced with permission from *Child Abuse & Neglect* 28, no. 3 (2004): 301–19, and from *Pediatrics* 117, no. 1 (January 2006): 99–109. The work described in this chapter was supported, in part, by the National Institute of Mental Health grant MH59672 (to Dr. Landsverk), National Institute of Mental Health Mentored Research Scientist Development Award K01-MH65454 (to Dr. Hazen), National Institute on Drug Abuse Mentored Research Scientist Development Award K01-DA15145 (to Dr. Connelly), and National Institute of Justice grant 2002-WG-BX-0014 (to Dr. Kelleher). NSCAW was funded under a contract to Research Triangle Institute (RTI) from the Administration on Children, Youth and Families, U.S. Department of Health and Human Services.

National surveys conducted over the past two decades indicate that approximately 20 percent of women are physically assaulted by a current or former partner during their lifetime.[1] Women of child-bearing age are at highest risk of experiencing IPV.[2] Children, especially those younger than five, have been shown to be significantly overrepresented in households in which such violence occurs relative to the number of households with children in the general population.[3] Estimates have suggested that between 11 and 20 percent of youth have been exposed to incidents of IPV during their childhood.[4] There is also considerable evidence that children exposed to parental violence frequently have been the victims of other forms of child maltreatment.[5] IPV has been linked with verbal abuse of children, harsh physical discipline, physical abuse, and sexual abuse.[6] In a review of studies on the relationship between IPV and child maltreatment, Appel and Holden found a median co-occurrence rate of 40 percent using samples of abused women and child abuse victims.[7] In community samples, the co-occurrence rate ranged from 6 percent to 11 percent.[8]

There is a dearth of empirical information on the extent to which IPV is experienced by families that come in contact with the child welfare system. Prior research has been limited to a small number of single-county studies that used case record reviews. Findings from these studies suggested that IPV was a problem for approximately 30 to 40 percent of families involved with the child welfare system.[9] Clearly this research suggests that IPV is a common problem among families that come in contact with child welfare services, but the reliance on data that are based on an identification of IPV by a child welfare worker, the lack of standardized measurement, and the small sample sizes in prior studies limit the reliability and generalizability of the information that has been available to date for policymakers, administrators, and other stakeholders.

Numerous studies have found that children involved with the child welfare system are at risk for behavioral and emotional problems.[10] Research has similarly documented high rates of a variety of adverse psychosocial outcomes among children exposed to IPV.[11] Two recent meta-analyses concluded that children's exposure to IPV is associated with significant emotional and behavioral problems.[12] Compared with children from nonviolent homes, children exposed to parental violence are more likely to exhibit internalizing problems such as anxiety and depression as well as externalizing problems such as aggression, oppositional behaviors, and conduct problems.[13] The average effect size across studies examined in one meta-analysis suggested that 63 percent of children exposed to IPV were functioning more poorly than children who were not exposed.[14]

One longitudinal study of families referred to child protective services in Washington state did not find a direct relationship between IPV and child behavior but did find that the violence had indirect effects through associations with caregiver well-being, family functioning, and caregiver-child interactions.[15]

Given the growing evidence of the links between IPV and child functioning in other populations and of the prevalence of this type of violence in families involved with the child welfare system, there is a need for additional research on this topic. When analyzing these relationships, studies must control for other risk factors for child psychopathology; otherwise the influence of IPV on child outcomes is unclear.[16] In the literature on children's exposure to IPV, the extent to which adverse behavioral and emotional outcomes are associated with factors such as socioeconomic status, family structure, other maltreatment experiences, parental substance use, and community environment is not well understood.[17] There is some evidence, though, that smaller effect sizes are obtained when such variables are taken into consideration.[18] The fact that a large proportion of families in the child welfare system experience many psychosocial and environmental risk factors underscores the importance of taking such variables into account when investigating the impact of exposure to IPV in this population.[19]

This paper examines NSCAW findings on the lifetime and past-year prevalence of IPV in a nationally representative sample of families referred to child welfare services. Correlates of IPV in this population, which include sociodemographic characteristics, mental health and substance use problems, and history of contact with the child welfare system, are also described.[20] The relationship between reports of IPV by a female caregiver and child behavior problems and the moderating effects of caregiver parenting behaviors on this relationship are also discussed.[21] Most important, the implications of the paper's findings for providing services to families that come in contact with the child welfare system are discussed.

Study Design

The NSCAW child protective services (CPS) sample ($N = 5,501$) consists of children who were subjects of investigations of child abuse and neglect conducted by child protective services agencies during the sampling period (see chapter 2 by Rosenberg, Smith, and Levinson in this volume). The relevant NSCAW measures are listed in table 3-1.

Procedure

Current caregivers of children selected for the NSCAW CPS sample were interviewed about demographic characteristics, community environment, child functioning, caregiver mental health, substance use, criminal involvement, and experiences with IPV. Interviews were conducted in the caregivers' homes using computer-assisted interviewing. For the portions of the interview inquiring about IPV, mental health functioning, substance use, and criminal involvement, participants answered questions confidentially by entering responses directly into a laptop computer after listening to audio prompts heard on earphones.

Table 3-1. *Study Measures of the National Survey of Child and Adolescent Well-Being*

Domain	Measure	Informant
Caregiver history of arrest	Questions developed for the NSCAW study on caregiver's lifetime history of being arrested	Caregiver
Caregiver major depression and substance dependence	World Health Organization Composite International Diagnostic Interview, Short Form: Major Depression and Substance Dependence Modules (that is, alcohol and drug dependence) (CIDI-SF)[a]	Caregiver
Caregiver physical health	Short-Form Health Survey (SF-12)[b]	Caregiver
Child behavioral problems	Child Behavior Checklist: Internalizing and Externalizing Broad Band Scales (CBCL)[c]	Caregiver
Child health	Child Health Questionnaire, Overall Rating of Child Health (CHQ)[d]	Caregiver
Child maltreatment and history of involvement with child welfare	Interview modules developed for the NSCAW study	Child welfare worker
Community environment	Abridged community environment scale developed for the Philadelphia Family Management Study[e]	Caregiver
Demographic information	Questions developed for the NSCAW study concerning the caregiver and household: caregiver age, gender, race and ethnicity, marital status, education, income, number of household members, relationship of caregiver to index child, poverty status of household, urbanicity of residence; concerning the child reported for maltreatment: child age, gender, race and ethnicity	Caregiver
Intimate partner violence (IPV)[f]	Conflict Tactics Scale Physical Assault Scale (CTS1)[g]	Caregiver
Caregiver parenting	Parent-Child Conflict Tactics Scales (CTSPC)[h]	Caregiver

Source: National Survey of Child and Adolescent Well-Being.

a. Ronald Kessler and others, "The World Health Organization Composite International Diagnostic Interview Short-Form (CIDI-SF)," *International Journal of Methods in Psychiatric Research* 7, no. 4 (1998): 171–85.

b. John E. Ware Jr. and others, "Assessment Tools: Functional Health Status and Patient Satisfaction," *American Journal of Medical Quality* 11, no. 1 (1996): S50–S53.

c. Thomas M. Achenbach, *Manual for the Child Behavior Checklist/4-18 and 1991 Profile* (Burlington: University of Vermont, Department of Psychiatry, 1991).

d. Jeanne Landgraf, Linda Abetz, and John Ware, *The CHQ User's Manual* (Boston: Tufts–New England Medical Center, The Health Institute, 1996).

e. Frank Furstenburg, *Philadelphia Family Management Study: Parent Interview Schedule* (Philadelphia: University of Pennsylvania, Population Studies Center, and Boulder: University of Colorado, Institute of Behavioral Science, 1990).

f. IPV was assessed with the physical assault scale of the Conflict Tactics Scale (CTS1). This measure has "minor" and "severe" subscales. The minor (less severe) items include having something thrown at the person; being pushed, grabbed, or shoved; and being slapped. The severe items include being kicked, bitten, or hit with a fist; being hit or one's partner trying to hit with something; being beat up; being choked; being threatened with a knife or gun; and having a knife or gun used. Respective prevalence scores reflect one or more acts occurring in the overall scale or subscales.

g. Murray Straus, "Measuring Intrafamily Conflict and Violence: The Conflict Tactics (CT) Scales," *Journal of Marriage and the Family* 41, no. 1 (1979): 75–88.

h. Murray A. Straus and others, "Identification of Child Maltreatment with the Parent-Child Conflict Tactics Scales: Development and Psychometric Data for a National Sample of American Parents," *Child Abuse & Neglect* 22, no. 11 (1998): 249–70.

Results

In the following sections, findings are reported on the lifetime and past-year prevalence and correlates of IPV experienced by female caregivers of children in the NSCAW CPS sample. Results concerning the relationship between caregiver reports of IPV and child behavior problems and the moderating effects of caregiver parenting behaviors on this relationship are also described.

Prevalence of Intimate Partner Violence

Lifetime and past-year prevalence of IPV were determined for a subsample of the NSCAW core sample.[22] Because information on IPV was not obtained from nonpermanent caregivers of children placed in out-of-home care, results were only available for the portion of the sample that included children who were not in out-of-home placement at the time of the baseline interview. Among these 4,037 cases, 3,612 (89.5 percent) had baseline interviews with a female caregiver for whom data on IPV were obtained (364 cases had interviews with a male caregiver; 61 interviews with a female caregiver were missing IPV data). The age, gender, and types of maltreatment of children who were placed in out-of-home care were similar to those in the subsample who remained at home.[23] However, it could not be concluded that the families of children who were in out-of-home care had a similar prevalence or intensity of IPV as those families of the children who remained at home.

The mean age of the 3,612 female caregivers was 31.9 years (ranging from fifteen to seventy-seven years of age), and the racial and ethnic distribution was 50.8 percent non-Hispanic White, 25.5 percent Black, 16.7 percent Hispanic, and 7.1 percent were from other racial and ethnic backgrounds.[24] Approximately one-third (32.0 percent) had never married, 29.8 percent were currently married, and 38.3 percent were separated, divorced, or widowed. Median family income was $17,500, and 75.3 percent had a high school education or less. Some 54.0 percent of the households were at or below the poverty level.

Nearly all (93.9 percent) of the caregivers were biological mothers of the index child investigated as a possible victim of child maltreatment. The mean and median age of the index children was approximately seven years; 50.9 percent were males. With regard to racial and ethnic background, 46.1 percent of the children were non-Hispanic White, 28.6 percent were Black, 18.2 percent were Hispanic, and 7.1 percent were of other racial and ethnic backgrounds.

Nearly 45 percent of the female caregivers reported that they were subjected to physical violence perpetrated by a spouse or partner at some time in their adult lives (table 3-2). Some 42.4 percent reported at least one incident of less severe physical violence (such as being pushed, grabbed, shoved, or slapped), and 32.6 percent reported at least one incident of severe violence (such as being beaten up, choked, or threatened with a weapon).

Table 3-2. *Lifetime and Past-Year Prevalence of Intimate Partner Violence*[a]

Type	Lifetime		Past year	
	Percent	95 percent CI	Percent	95 percent CI
Less severe physical violence				
Had something thrown	26.6	(23.1, 30.4)	15.5	(13.3, 18.1)
Pushed, grabbed, shoved	36.4	(32.9, 40.2)	23.6	(21.1, 26.3)
Slapped	26.5	(23.4, 29.9)	14.3	(12.2, 16.8)
Any less severe physical violence	42.4	(38.3, 46.5)	27.7	(24.8, 30.7)
Less severe physical violence only	12.1	(10.4, 14.1)	11.9	(10.3, 13.7)
Severe physical violence				
Kicked, bitten, or hit with fist	21.5	(19.3, 23.7)	9.5	(7.9, 11.5)
Hit or tried to hit with something	25.3	(22.3, 28.6)	13.0	(11.2, 15.2)
Beat up	18.1	(15.8, 20.6)	7.9	(6.3, 9.9)
Choked	17.1	(14.5, 20.2)	8.2	(6.6, 10.2)
Threatened with knife or gun	9.5	(7.7, 11.7)	4.6	(3.5, 6.2)
Knife or gun used	3.0	(2.1, 4.1)	1.1	(0.71, 1.8)
Any severe physical violence	32.6	(29.4, 36.0)	17.0	(14.8, 19.5)
Any physical violence	44.8	(40.7, 48.9)	29.0	(26.2, 31.9)

Source: Andrea L. Hazen and others, "Intimate Partner Violence among Female Caregivers of Children Reported for Child Maltreatment," *Child Abuse & Neglect* 28, no. 3 (2004): 301–19.

CI: confidence interval.

a. Table entries are the percentages of the sample of 3,612 female caregivers who experienced each type of violence.

Twenty-nine percent of caregivers indicated that they experienced physical violence in the past year, with 27.7 percent reporting less severe violence and 17.0 percent reporting severe violence. The women reported an average of 15.4 incidents of physical violence overall, 9.0 acts of less severe violence and 11.7 acts of severe violence during the preceding year.

Correlates of Intimate Partner Violence

The relationships between severe and less severe IPV experienced in the past year and sociodemographic characteristics, caregiver functioning, and previous contact with the child welfare system were examined using odds ratios (OR) obtained with polychotomous logistic regression (table 3-3).[25]

Caregiver major depressive disorder (OR = 2.63), caregiver drug dependence (OR = 2.42), and history of prior reports of child maltreatment (OR = 1.83) were all associated with increased odds for the caregiver being the victim of severe physical violence (relative to no violence). Caregiver age was also associated with severe violence, with increasing age of the caregiver related to decreasing odds of violence (OR = 0.96).

Few variables were significantly related to less severe violence. Only the presence of a male partner in the female caregiver's household (OR = 2.02) and

Table 3-3. *Odds Ratios for Relationship between Caregiver and Household Characteristics and Caregiver and Severe and Less Severe Intimate Partner Violence during the Past Year*[a]

	Odds ratios	
Characteristic	*Severe physical violence*	*Less severe physical violence*
Caregiver		
Age[b]	0.96***	0.99
Race and ethnicity		
Non-Hispanic White	Reference	Reference
Non-Hispanic Black	0.97	0.94
Hispanic	0.67	1.22
Other	1.25	1.13
Marital status		
Married	Reference	Reference
Never married	1.27	0.85
Separated; divorced; widowed	1.20	1.16
Education		
Less than high school diploma or equivalent	Reference	Reference
High school diploma or equivalent	1.00	1.02
Postsecondary	0.98	1.33
Major depressive disorder	2.63***	1.88**
Alcohol dependence	1.33	0.27*
Drug dependence	2.42*	1.76
Household		
Male intimate partner in household		
No	Reference	Reference
Yes	1.03	2.02**
Poverty status[c]		
Less than 50 percent	Reference	Reference
50–99 percent	1.21	0.93
100–149 percent	1.06	0.57
150–199 percent	0.97	0.68
Greater than or equal to 200 percent	1.61	0.50
Number of children in household		
One	Reference	Reference
Two	1.19	1.54
Three	1.04	0.96
Four	0.85	0.79
Five or more	1.41	0.55
Any prior reports of maltreatment	1.83**	1.49

Source: Andrea L. Hazen and others, "Intimate Partner Violence among Female Caregivers of Children Reported for Child Maltreatment" (see table 3-2).

*$p < 0.05$, **$p < 0.01$, ***$p < 0.001$.

a. Reference group for the polychotomous logistic regression was no physical violence (see Statistical Note in the text).

b. Age was taken as a continuous variable.

c. Poverty status is measured relative to the federal poverty threshold.

caregiver major depressive disorder (OR = 1.88) were associated with increased odds for the caregiver experiencing less severe violence (relative to no violence). Caregiver alcohol dependence was associated with lower risk for less severe violence (OR = 0.27).

Intimate Partner Violence and Child Behavior Problems

The association between IPV and child behavior problems was examined in families with female caregivers who had children who were between four- and fourteen-years-old and who were not in out-of-home care.[26] Among 2,491 such cases, 2,020 had interviews with female caregivers in which data on IPV and child behavior problems were obtained. The remaining 471 cases could not be included because data on IPV or on child behavior problems were missing or because interviews were conducted with a male caregiver.

The mean age of the caregivers was 33.8 years, and 50.7 percent were non-Hispanic White, 25.6 percent were Black, 17.8 percent were Hispanic, and 5.9 percent were of other racial and ethnic backgrounds. Thirty-one percent were currently married; 43.7 percent were separated, divorced, or widowed; and 24.9 percent had never been married. Some 30.1 percent had less than a high school education, 41.8 percent had a high school diploma or equivalent, and 28.1 percent had at least some postsecondary education or training. Slightly more than half (52.9 percent) of the families were living at or below the federal poverty threshold.

Nearly all (94.5 percent) of the female caregivers were the biological mothers of the index children. The mean age of the children was 8.6 years, and 50.5 percent were males. On racial and ethnic background, 46.6 percent were non-Hispanic White, 27.8 percent were Black, 18.2 percent were Hispanic, and 7.4 percent were of other racial and ethnic backgrounds.

Multiple regression was used to examine the associations of caregiver victimization with child externalizing and internalizing problems, while controlling for other risk factors. Caregivers' experiences with severe IPV ($B = 2.17$, $p < 0.05$) were significantly associated with child externalizing behavior problems but not caregivers' experiences with less severe IPV ($B = 1.44$, $p > 0.05$). Other significant predictors of externalizing problems were the older age of the child ($B = 0.34$, $p < 0.01$), male gender of the child ($B = 3.09$, $p < 0.001$), poor child health ($B = 5.43$, $p < 0.01$), caregiver history of arrest ($B = 2.36$, $p < 0.01$), caregiver substance dependence ($B = 4.58$, $p < 0.05$), and prior reports of child maltreatment ($B = 2.32$, $p < 0.01$). In addition, Hispanic children were less likely to have externalizing problems than were non-Hispanic White children ($B = -2.67$, $p < 0.05$). The following were not significantly related to child externalizing problems: caregiver education, poverty level of household, family size, urbanicity of county of residence, child physical maltreatment, child sexual maltreatment, and community environment.

Caregiver victimization by severe IPV was significantly associated with greater internalizing problems of the child ($B = 2.37$, $p < 0.01$), but victimization by less severe violence was not ($B = 1.27$, $p > 0.05$). Older age of the child ($B = 0.60$, $p < 0.001$) and poor child health ($B = 8.26$, $p < 0.001$) were also significant predictors of children's having internalizing problems. The following were not significantly related to child internalizing problems: child gender, child race and ethnicity, caregiver education, poverty level of household, family size, urbanicity of county of residence, caregiver history of arrest, caregiver substance dependence, child physical maltreatment, child sexual maltreatment, history of prior reports of child maltreatment, and community environment.

Moderating Effects of Caregiver Depression and Negative Parenting Practices

Multiple regression was used to investigate the potential moderating effects of caregiver depression and negative parenting practices (that is, caregiver use of psychological aggression and corporal punishment) on the relation between IPV and child externalizing and internalizing problems. These analyses examined whether each of the potential moderators had an effect on the relationship between IPV and children's behavior problems. For instance, caregiver use of corporal punishment might moderate the relationship between IPV and externalizing problems such that as corporal punishment increased, the association between violence and externalizing problems increased or decreased. In each regression model, child, family, and community environment used in the analyses described above were entered, along with the moderator of interest and the interaction term for IPV and the moderator. Moderation was indicated if the interaction term was significant.

Caregiver depression was not a significant moderator of the relationship between child externalizing problems and either severe IPV ($B = -1.31$, $p > 0.05$) or less severe IPV ($B = -0.25$, $p > 0.05$). Caregivers' psychological aggression directed toward their children was a moderator of the relationship between severe IPV and externalizing problems ($B = -0.10$, $p < 0.05$), with the association between severe violence and externalizing problems diminishing as use of psychological aggression increased. However, caregivers' use of psychological aggression was not a moderator of the relationship between less severe violence and externalizing problems ($B = -0.10$, $p > 0.05$).

Caregivers' use of corporal punishment was a significant moderator of the relationship between severe IPV and externalizing problems ($B = -0.21$, $p < 0.05$) and of the relationship between less severe violence and externalizing problems ($B = -0.22$, $p < 0.05$). The association of IPV and externalizing behaviors decreased as corporal punishment increased.

Similar to the results for externalizing problems, caregiver depression was not a significant moderator of the relation between internalizing problems and severe IPV ($B = -3.14$, $p > 0.05$) or less severe violence ($B = -1.45$, $p > 0.05$).

Caregiver use of psychological aggression moderated the relationship between less severe violence ($B = -0.09$, $p < 0.05$) and internalizing problems but did not moderate the relationship with severe violence ($B = -0.04$, $p > 0.05$).

Use of corporal punishment was found to moderate the relation between internalizing problems and both severe violence ($B = -0.16$, $p < 0.05$) and less severe violence ($B = -0.16$, $p < 0.05$). As use of corporal punishment increased, the relation between IPV and internalizing problems diminished.

Discussion

Female caregivers of children investigated as victims of maltreatment in the NSCAW CPS sample experienced high rates of IPV, with nearly 45 percent reporting physical violence at some time during their lives and 29 percent reporting such violence in the preceding year. Our findings are consistent with the limited previous research on families involved with the child welfare system, which has reported rates of IPV ranging from 30 to 40 percent.[27] Moreover, these lifetime and past-year rates of violence are approximately twice as high as community prevalence estimates obtained by the National Family Violence Surveys, the National Violence against Women Survey, and the National Comorbidity Survey.[28]

The rates of both severe and less severe IPV tended to not vary with most of the sociodemographic characteristics examined, including caregiver race and ethnicity, education, urbanicity of county of residence, poverty status of household, and number of children in household. Consistent with other research, younger women were found to be at greater risk of experiencing violence.[29]

The context in which these high rates of IPV were obtained bears consideration. As of August 2003, one state defined "exposure to IPV" as child maltreatment in its juvenile code, and a few other states included language in their child abuse definitions and reporting statutes that referred to "emotional harm" or "mental injury," which could be interpreted as including exposure to IPV.[30] In addition, cases involving exposure to IPV have been considered instances of neglect due to a caregiver's failure to protect her children from potential harm.[31] Overall, at the time the NSCAW data were collected, most states did not specifically address exposure to IPV in their child abuse statutes and did not explicitly mandate reporting of child abuse under such circumstances. It is noteworthy that there appears to be a growing trend in the United States to define exposure to IPV as a form of child maltreatment, and it is logical to predict that IPV will be a concern for caseworkers in an increasing number of families that have contact with child welfare systems in the future.[32]

Our findings also demonstrated that female caregivers' experiences with severe IPV, such as being kicked, bitten, beat up, choked, and threatened with a weapon, were associated with children's externalizing and internalizing problems when other potent risk factors including socioeconomic status, caregiver antisocial behavior, child maltreatment, and community environment were taken into account. No relationship was found, however, with victimization by less severe forms of violence, such as being pushed, grabbed, shoved, or slapped. In addition to IPV, children's externalizing problems were related to female caregivers' substance use and history of arrests, which is consistent with prior research on parental antisocial problems.[33] Prior maltreatment reports were also associated with externalizing problems, which suggests that children from families with chronic violence and abuse are at risk for behavior disorders.

Several limitations associated with the findings should be noted. First, the assessment of IPV was limited to physical violence and did not include other forms of victimization, including psychological or sexual abuse. As a result, it is likely that the rates of victimization are conservative estimates of experiences with IPV as it is more broadly defined. Second, the results described here are based on cross-sectional data, which limits conclusions about the direction of the observed associations. Third, this research would have been strengthened if information had been available on the attributes of the perpetrator of IPV. Such data would have permitted a more comprehensive analysis of the correlates of violence and of the relationship between perpetrator characteristics and child adjustment. Future studies should go beyond the assessment of maternal and child attributes and pay greater attention to variables associated with the IPV perpetrator.

The need for effective screening and identification of IPV in families referred to child welfare agencies is underscored by our findings on the high prevalence of this problem. Other recent findings from NSCAW suggest that IPV frequently goes undetected by child welfare workers. Kohl and others found that 31 percent of female caregivers reported that they experienced IPV in the preceding year, but child welfare workers identified violence in only 12 percent of all families.[34] Reports by the caregiver and child welfare worker overlapped in 8 percent of the cases, and workers did not identify IPV when the caregiver reported it in 22 percent of the cases. Underidentification by child welfare workers was associated with the female caregiver's drug or alcohol abuse, with a family having had prior contact with the child welfare system, and with the female caregiver having a history of childhood abuse or neglect. The association between prior involvement with the child welfare system and the low likelihood of a caseworker identifying IPV is a particular concern. Our findings and those of English and others suggest that families who have been involved with child welfare services and who are affected by IPV are likely to have had prior reports of maltreatment.[35] Thus the failure to identify and address IPV may contribute to a continuation of family problems and to repeated contacts with the child welfare system.[36]

Steps have been taken to address this issue of underidentification of IPV. Recently, the National Council of Juvenile and Family Court Judges and the

National Association of Public Child Welfare Administrators recommended that screening for IPV should be standard practice during all stages of a child protection case, from intake to case closure.[37] However, there has been little examination of screening and assessment procedures to identify IPV in families coming to the attention of the child welfare system. In small pilot studies conducted in New York City, the implementation of an IPV questionnaire completed by child welfare caseworkers during investigations of child maltreatment resulted in a substantial increase in the identification of families experiencing IPV.[38] Additional research is needed to develop and evaluate appropriate screening and assessment methods and tools to identify those in need of assistance throughout all phases of a family's involvement with the child welfare system, while ensuring that women and children are not placed at risk for additional violence or are not harmed in other ways. If procedures for interviewing children regarding their exposure to parental violence were refined, then the identification of affected children and their families and provision of services to them could be improved.[39]

Our findings showed a strong relationship between female caregivers' major depression and victimization involving both severe and less severe forms of IPV. Notably 41 percent of the women who experienced severe IPV and 30 percent of the women who experienced less severe violence had major depression compared with less than 20 percent of female caregivers who did not report any violence in the preceding year. These results, along with the findings on the relationship between IPV and child behavior, suggest that screening for mental health problems in adult victims and their children, in concert with screening for IPV, is warranted.

As new policies and protocols increase the identification of IPV and co-occurring problems, resources will be needed to meet the service demand. The importance of this issue was highlighted by the recent experience of Minnesota's child welfare system following the state legislature's revision of the definition of child neglect to include exposure to IPV.[40] With the implementation of this change, counties throughout the state saw a large increase in child abuse reports that involved exposure to IPV, and administrators estimated that millions of dollars in new resources would be required to serve these families. After approximately one year, the legislature repealed the revised statute because of the burden on the child welfare system and the lack of funding for new services.

Proper training of child welfare workers is also important. It has been recommended that training should focus on improving the identification of IPV and providing appropriate intervention. In addition, training efforts should involve cross-training with advocates for victims of IPV and other key stakeholders.[41] Some preliminary research suggests that training programs using detailed curricula developed specifically for addressing IPV within the child welfare system may have a positive impact on workers' knowledge and attitudes.[42] The evaluations of these curricula have been limited, however, to pre- and posttest designs that did not use comparison groups. Experimental research that examines the effects of training on actual practice over longer time intervals is needed.[43]

Once IPV has been identified, services with demonstrated efficacy need to be available. Model programs designed to address IPV have recently been implemented in child welfare agencies, many of them involving advocates or specialists who provide training and case consultation on IPV to child welfare staff as well as direct service to families in some cases. However, such programs have yet to be rigorously evaluated.[44] In a review of evaluation research conducted between 1980 and 1996, the National Research Council and the Institute of Medicine identified only three studies that examined supportive interventions (one involving shelter services and two involving advocacy services) for victims of IPV and that used experimental or quasi-experimental designs.[45] Since the publication of this review, promising new findings have been reported for interventions provided to female victims of IPV and their children. These programs have provided varying combinations of services, including advocacy and parenting support for mothers and mentoring and psychoeducational groups for children.[46] There is some evidence of positive effects of these programs on women and children who initially received assistance as they were leaving shelters or who accessed community-based services, as was measured by reductions in the risk of reabuse and improved maternal and child outcomes.[47] However, these interventions have not been tested with families involved with child welfare services. Additional research is needed to improve the outlook for these families in the short and long term.

Statistical Note

Polychotomous logistic regression is used to perform logistic regression analyses with categorical outcome variables that have more than two response categories (that is, severe violence, less severe violence, and no violence, with the latter serving as the reference group).[48]

Notes

1. Richard J. Gelles and Murray A. Straus, *Intimate Violence* (New York: Simon and Schuster, 1988); Patricia Tjaden and Nancy Thoennes, *Full Report of the Prevalence, Incidence, and Consequences of Violence against Women* (Washington: U.S. Department of Justice, Office of Justice Programs, 2000).

2. Lawrence A. Greenfeld and others, *Violence by Intimates: Analysis of Data on Crimes by Current or Former Spouses, Boyfriends, and Girlfriends* (Washington: U.S. Department of Justice, Office of Justice Programs, 1998).

3. John Fantuzzo and others, "Domestic Violence and Children: Prevalence and Risk in Five Major U.S. Cities," *Journal of the American Academy of Child and Adolescent Psychiatry* 36, no. 1 (1997): 116–22.

4. Janis Wolak and David Finkelhor, "Children Exposed to Partner Violence," in *Partner Violence: A Comprehensive Review of 20 Years of Research,* edited by Jana L. Jasinski, Linda M. Williams, and David Finkelhor (Thousand Oaks, Calif.: Sage Publications, 1998), pp. 73–112.

5. Murray A. Straus, Richard J. Gelles, and Suzanne K. Steinmetz, *Behind Closed Doors: Violence in the American Family* (Newbury Park, Calif.: Sage Publications, 1980); Murray A. Straus and Christine Smith, "Family Patterns and Child Abuse," in *Physical Violence in American Families: Risk Factors and Adaptations to Violence in 8,145 Families,* edited by Murray A. Straus and Richard J. Gelles (New Brunswick, N.J.: Transaction Publishers, 1995), pp. 245–61.

6. Murray A. Straus and Christine Smith, "Family Patterns and Child Abuse"; Lisa Avery, Dianne Hutchinson, and Keitha Whitaker, "Domestic Violence and Intergenerational Rates of Child Sexual Abuse: A Case Record Analysis," *Child & Adolescent Social Work Journal* 19, no. 1 (2002): 77–90; Kathryn Bowen, "Child Abuse and Domestic Violence in Families of Children Seen for Suspected Sexual Abuse," *Clinical Pediatrics* 39, no. 1 (2000): 33–40; Nancy D. Kellogg and Shirley W. Menard, "Violence among Family Members of Children and Adolescents Evaluated for Sexual Abuse," *Child Abuse & Neglect* 27, no. 12 (2003): 1367–376; Bonnie D. Kerker and others, "Identification of Violence in the Home: Pediatric and Parental Reports," *Archives of Pediatrics & Adolescent Medicine* 154, no. 5 (2000): 457–62; Susan M. Ross, "Risk of Physical Abuse to Children of Spouse Abusing Parents," *Child Abuse & Neglect* 20, no. 7 (1996): 589–98; Emiko A. Tajima, "The Relative Importance of Wife Abuse as a Risk Factor for Violence against Children," *Child Abuse & Neglect* 24, no. 11 (2000): 1383–398.

7. Anne E. Appel and George W. Holden, "The Co-Occurrence of Spouse and Physical Child Abuse: A Review and Appraisal," *Journal of Family Psychology* 12, no. 4 (1998): 578–99.

8. Ibid.

9. Jeffrey L. Edleson, "The Overlap between Child Maltreatment and Woman Battering," *Violence Against Women* 5, no. 2 (1999): 134–54; Loring P. Jones, Elizabeth Gross, and Irene Becker, "The Characteristics of Domestic Violence Victims in a Child Protective Service Caseload," *Families in Society* 83, no. 4 (2002): 405–15; Randy H. Magen and others, "Identifying Domestic Violence in Child Abuse and Neglect Investigations," *Journal of Interpersonal Violence* 16, no. 6 (2001): 580–60; Melanie Shepard and Michael Raschick, "How Child Welfare Workers Assess and Intervene around Issues of Domestic Violence," *Child Maltreatment* 4, no. 2 (1999): 148–56.

10. June Madsen Clausen and others, "Mental Health Problems of Children in Foster Care," *Journal of Child and Family Studies* 7, no. 3 (1998): 283–96; Daniel J. Pilowsky, "Psychopathology among Children Placed in Family Foster Care," *Psychiatric Services* 46, no. 9 (1995): 906–10.

11. Janis Wolak and David Finkelhor, "Children Exposed to Partner Violence"; Amy Holtzworth-Munroe, A. Natalie Smutzler, and Elizabeth Sandin, "A Brief Review of the Research on Husband Violence. Part II: The Psychological Effects of Husband Violence on Battered Women and Their Children," *Aggression and Violent Behavior* 2, no. 2 (1997): 179–213; Gayla Margolin and Elana B. Gordis, "The Effects of Family and Community Violence on Children," *Annual Review of Psychology* 51 (2000): 445–79; Wanda K. Mohr and others, "Children Exposed to Family Violence: A Review of Empirical Research from a Developmental-Ecological Perspective," *Trauma Violence & Abuse* 1, no. 3 (2000): 264–83.

12. Katherine M. Kitzmann and others, "Child Witnesses to Domestic Violence: A Meta-Analytic Review," *Journal of Consulting & Clinical Psychology* 71, no. 2 (2003): 339–52;

David A. Wolfe and others, "The Effects of Children's Exposure to Domestic Violence: A Meta-Analysis and Critique," *Clinical Child and Family Psychology Review* 6, no. 3 (2003): 171–87.

13. **Internalizing problems:** George W. Holden and Kathy L. Ritchie, "Linking Extreme Marital Discord, Child Rearing, and Child Behavior Problems: Evidence from Battered Women," *Child Development* 62, no. 2 (1991): 311–27; Sara R. Jaffee and others, "Influence of Adult Domestic Violence on Children's Internalizing and Externalizing Problems: An Environmentally Informative Twin Study," *Journal of the American Academy of Child & Adolescent Psychiatry* 41, no. 9 (2002): 1095–103; Alytia A. Levendosky and Sandra A. Graham-Bermann, "The Moderating Effects of Parenting Stress on Children's Adjustment in Woman-Abusing Families," *Journal of Interpersonal Violence* 13, no. 3 (1998): 383–97; Judith M. McFarlane and others, "Behaviors of Children Who Are Exposed and Not Exposed to Intimate Partner Violence: An Analysis of 330 Black, White, and Hispanic Children," *Pediatrics* 112, no. 3, pt. 1 (2003): e202–e207. **Anxiety and depression:** Alan J. Litrownik and others, "Exposure to Family Violence in Young At-Risk Children: A Longitudinal Look at the Effects of Victimization and Witnessed Physical and Psychological Aggression," *Journal of Family Violence* 18, no. 1 (2003): 59–73; Laura Ann McCloskey, Aurelio Jose Figueredo, and Mary P. Koss, "The Effects of Systemic Family Violence on Children's Mental Health," *Child Development* 66, no. 5 (1995): 1239–261. **Externalizing problems:** Sara R. Jaffee and others, "Influence of Adult Domestic Violence on Children's Internalizing and Externalizing Problems"; Judith M. McFarlane and others, "Behaviors of Children Who Are Exposed and Not Exposed to Intimate Partner Violence"; Mary A. Kernic and others, "Behavioral Problems among Children Whose Mothers Are Abused by an Intimate Partner," *Child Abuse & Neglect* 27, no. 11 (2003): 1231–46; Maura O'Keefe, "Adjustment of Children from Maritally Violent Homes," *Families in Society: The Journal of Contemporary Human Services* 75, no. 7 (1994): 403–15. **Aggression, oppositional behaviors, and conduct problems:** George W. Holden and Kathy L. Ritchie, "Linking Extreme Marital Discord, Child Rearing, and Child Behavior Problems"; Laura Ann McCloskey, Aurelio Jose Figueredo, and Mary P. Koss, "The Effects of Systemic Family Violence on Children's Mental Health"; Holly Shinn Ware and others, "Conduct Problems among Children at Battered Women's Shelters: Prevalence and Stability of Maternal Reports," *Journal of Family Violence* 16, no. 3 (2001): 291–307.

14. Katherine M. Kitzmann and others, "Child Witnesses to Domestic Violence."

15. Diana J. English, David B. Marshall, and Angela J. Stewart, "Effects of Family Violence on Child Behavior and Health during Early Childhood," *Journal of Family Violence* 18, no. 1 (2003): 43–57.

16. Gayla Margolin and Elana B. Gordis, "The Effects of Family and Community Violence on Children"; Wanda K. Mohr and others, "Children Exposed to Family Violence"; David A. Wolfe and others, "The Effects of Children's Exposure to Domestic Violence"; Benjamin E. Saunders, "Understanding Children Exposed to Violence: Toward an Integration of Overlapping Fields," *Journal of Interpersonal Violence* 18, no. 4 (2003): 356–76.

17. Ronald J. Prinz and Margaret M. Feerick, "Next Steps in Research on Children Exposed to Domestic Violence," *Clinical Child and Family Psychology Review* 6, no. 4 (2003): 215–19.

18. Katherine M. Kitzmann and others, "Child Witnesses to Domestic Violence."

19. Bridgett A. Besinger and others, "Caregiver Substance Abuse among Maltreated Children Placed in Out-of-Home Care," *Child Welfare* 78, no. 2 (1999): 221–39; Susan D. Phillips and others, "Parental Arrest and Children Involved with Child Welfare Services Agencies," *American Journal of Orthopsychiatry* 74, no. 2 (2004): 174–86.

20. Andrea L. Hazen and others, "Intimate Partner Violence among Female Caregivers of Children Reported for Child Maltreatment," *Child Abuse & Neglect* 28, no. 3 (2004): 301–19.

21. Andrea L. Hazen and others, "Female Caregivers' Experiences with Intimate Partner Violence and Behavior Problems in Children Investigated as Victims of Maltreatment," *Pediatrics* 117, no. 1 (2006): 99–109.

22. Andrea L. Hazen and others, "Intimate Partner Violence among Female Caregivers Reported for Child Maltreatment."

23. U.S. Department of Health and Human Services, *National Survey of Child and Adolescent Well-Being (NSCAW), CPS Sample Component: Wave 1 Data Analysis Report* (Washington: DHHS, Administration for Children and Families, Administration on Children, Youth and Families, Children's Bureau, April 2005).

24. The percentages presented here and elsewhere may not add to 100 because of rounding.

25. An odds ratio indicates the odds of experiencing the outcome in a particular group compared with a reference group. Odds ratios larger than 1 indicate a greater likelihood of the outcome; odds ratios less than 1 indicate a lower likelihood.

26. Andrea L. Hazen and others, "Female Caregivers' Experiences with Intimate Partner Violence and Behavior Problems in Children Investigated as Victims of Maltreatment."

27. Jeffrey L. Edleson, "The Overlap between Child Maltreatment and Woman Battering"; Loring P. Jones, Elizabeth Gross, and Irene Becker, "The Characteristics of Domestic Violence Victims in a Child Protective Service Caseload."

28. **National Family Violence Surveys:** Richard J. Gelles and Murray A. Straus, *Intimate Violence;* Murray A. Straus and Richard J. Gelles, "Societal Change and Change in Family Violence from 1975 to 1985 as Revealed by Two National Surveys," in *Physical Violence in American Families: Risk Factors and Adaptations to Violence in 8,145 Families,* pp. 113–31. **National Violence against Women Survey:** Patricia Tjaden and Nancy Thoennes, *Full Report of the Prevalence, Incidence, and Consequences of Violence against Women.* **National Comorbidity Survey:** Ronald C. Kessler and others, "Patterns and Mental Health Predictors of Domestic Violence in the United States: Results from the National Comorbidity Survey," *International Journal of Law & Psychiatry* 24, nos. 4-5 (2001): 487–508.

29. Lawrence A. Greenfeld and others, *Violence by Intimates;* Jeffrey Fagan and Angela Browne, *Violence between Spouses and Intimates: Physical Aggression between Women and Men in Intimate Relationships* (Washington: National Academy Press, 1994).

30. Therese Zink and others, "What Are Providers' Reporting Requirements for Children Who Witness Domestic Violence?" *Clinical Pediatrics* 43, no. 5 (2004): 449–60.

31. Jeffrey L. Edleson, "Should Childhood Exposure to Adult Domestic Violence Be Defined as Child Maltreatment under the Law?" in *Protecting Children from Domestic Violence,* edited by Peter G. Jaffe, Linda L. Baker, and Alison J. Cunningham (New York: Guilford, 2004), pp. 8–29; Glenda Kaufman Kantor and Liza Little, "Defining the Boundaries of Child Neglect: When Does Domestic Violence Equate with Parental Failure to Protect?" *Journal of Interpersonal Violence* 18, no. 4 (2003): 338–55.

32. Jeffrey L. Edleson, "Should Childhood Exposure to Adult Domestic Violence Be Defined as Child Maltreatment under the Law?"

33. Susan D. Phillips and others, "Parental Arrest and Children Involved with Child Welfare Services Agencies"; Wendy Reich and others, "Psychopathology in Children of Alcoholics," *Journal of the American Academy of Child & Adolescent Psychiatry* 32, no. 5 (1993): 995–1002.

34. Patricia L. Kohl and others, "Child Welfare as a Gateway to Domestic Violence Services," *Children and Youth Services Review* 27, no. 11 (2005): 1203–221.

35. Diana J. English and others, "Characteristics of Repeated Referrals to Child Protective Services in Washington State," *Child Maltreatment* 4, no. 4 (1999): 297–307.

36. Patricia L. Kohl and others, "Child Welfare as a Gateway to Domestic Violence Services."

37. National Council of Juvenile and Family Court Judges, *Effective Intervention in Domestic Violence & Child Maltreatment Cases: Guidelines for Policy and Practice* (Reno, Nev.: NCJFCJ, Family Violence Department, 1999); National Association of Public Child Welfare Administrators, *Guidelines for Public Child Welfare Agencies Serving Children and Families Experiencing Domestic Violence* (Washington: American Public Human Services Association, 2001).

38. Randy H. Magen and others, "Identifying Domestic Violence in Child Abuse and Neglect Investigations"; Randy H. Magen, Kathryn Conroy, and Alisa Del Tufo, "Domestic Violence in Child Welfare Preventative Services: Results from an Intake Screening Questionnaire," *Children and Youth Services Review* 22, nos. 3-4 (2000): 251–74.

39. Kathleen Coulborn Faller, "Research and Practice in Child Interviewing: Implications for Children Exposed to Domestic Violence," *Journal of Interpersonal Violence* 18, no. 4 (2003): 377–89.

40. Jeffrey L. Edleson, "Should Childhood Exposure to Adult Domestic Violence Be Defined as Child Maltreatment under the Law?"; Jeffrey L. Edleson, Jenny Gassman-Pines, and Marissa B. Hill, "Defining Child Exposure to Domestic Violence as Neglect: Minnesota's Difficult Experience," *Social Work* 51, no. 2 (2006): 167–74.

41. National Association of Public Child Welfare Administrators, *Guidelines for Public Child Welfare Agencies Serving Children and Families Experiencing Domestic Violence.*

42. Linda G. Mills and Mieko Yoshihama, "Training Children's Services Workers in Domestic Violence Assessment and Intervention: Research Findings and Implications for Practice," *Children and Youth Services Review* 24, no. 8 (2002): 561–81; Daniel G. Saunders and Deborah Anderson, "Evaluation of a Domestic Violence Training for Child Protection Workers & Supervisors: Initial Results," *Children and Youth Services Review* 22, no. 5 (2000): 373–95.

43. National Council of Juvenile and Family Court Judges, *Effective Intervention in Domestic Violence & Child Maltreatment Cases.*

44. Laudan Y. Aron and Krista K. Olson, *Efforts by Child Welfare Agencies to Address Domestic Violence: The Experiences of Five Communities* (Washington: Urban Institute, 1997); Linda G. Mills and others, "Child Protection and Domestic Violence: Training, Practice, and Policy Issues," *Children & Youth Services Review* 22, no. 5 (2000): 315–32.

45. Rosemary Chalk and Patricia A. King, *Violence in Families: Assessing Prevention and Treatment Programs* (Washington: National Academy Press, 1998).

46. **Advocacy:** Ernest N. Jouriles and others, "Reducing Conduct Problems among Children of Battered Women," *Journal of Consulting and Clinical Psychology* 69, no. 5 (2001): 774–85; Cris M. Sullivan, Deborah I. Bybee, and Nicole E. Allen, "Findings from a Community-Based Program for Battered Women and Their Children," *Journal of Interpersonal Violence* 17, no. 9 (2002): 915–36. **Parenting Support:** Ernest N. Jouriles and others, "Reducing Conduct Problems among Children of Battered Women"; Sandra A. Graham-Bermann, "Designing Intervention Evaluations for Children Exposed to Domestic Violence: Applications of Research and Theory," in *Domestic Violence in the Lives of Children: The Future of Research, Intervention, and Social Policy,* edited by Sandra A. Graham-Berman and Jeffrey L. Edleson (Washington: American Psychological Association, 2001), pp. 237–68. **Mentoring for Children:** Ernest N. Jouriles and others, "Reducing Conduct Problems among Children of Battered Women"; Cris M. Sullivan, Deborah I. Bybee, and Nicole E. Allen, "Findings from a Community-Based Program for Battered Women and Their Children." **Psychoeducational Groups for Children:** Cris M. Sullivan, Deborah I. Bybee, and Nicole E. Allen, "Findings from a Community-Based Program for Battered Women and Their Children"; Sandra A.

Graham-Bermann, "Designing Intervention Evaluations for Children Exposed to Domestic Violence."

47. Ernest N. Jouriles and others, "Reducing Conduct Problems among Children of Battered Women"; Cris M. Sullivan, Deborah I. Bybee, and Nicole E. Allen, "Findings from a Community-Based Program for Battered Women and Their Children"; Sandra A. Graham-Bermann, "Designing Intervention Evaluations for Children Exposed to Domestic Violence."

48. David W. Hosmer and Stanley Lemeshow, *Applied Logistic Regression* (New York: Wiley, 2000).

4

Initial Construction of an Actuarial Risk Assessment Measure Using the National Survey of Child and Adolescent Well-Being

ARON SHLONSKY

C hild welfare workers are charged with making crucial decisions on child placement and service, and they must make these decisions while considering the complex interplay between poverty, parental substance abuse, and domestic violence.[1] In such a decisionmaking context, high error rates are inevitable, despite good intentions. For example, some families that would not have maltreated their child in the future will have their child placed in care (these cases are false positives), while some children will be left with families that will maltreat them (these are false negatives). Indeed, referring to the latter category, of the estimated 879,000 victims of child maltreatment in the United States in 2000, children with a prior history of maltreatment were three times as likely to experience a recurrence of abuse. Even worse, among the 1,200 children who died as a result of abuse or neglect in 2000, 18 percent were previously known to child protective services.[2] Although false positives are more difficult to quantify, there is reason to believe that the overall percentage of false positives is too high and could be reduced with better methods for making placement decisions.[3]

These shortcomings of the child welfare system may stem, in part, from the lack of readily available, reliable, and valid risk assessment instruments with

Special thanks to Dennis Wagner of Children's Research Center for his patience and guidance on this project and to the Center for Intervention and Prevention Research on HIV and Drug Abuse at Columbia University for their generous support.

which to guide pressing decisions encountered during the course of a child protective services case (for example, at an initial screening, during an investigation, and concerning family reunification). Assessment is the foundation of clinical practice. Any movement of the health care[4] and allied fields[5] toward evidence-based practice in all facets of clinical work must begin with accurate assessments. The availability of secondary data from the National Survey of Child and Adolescent Well-Being (NSCAW), the first longitudinal study employing a national probability sample of children and parents coming in contact with child protective services, offers a unique opportunity to develop valid risk assessment tools for use by workers for predicting maltreatment recurrence across the country.

Risk assessment in the child welfare field generally refers to the prediction of whether a child will be reabused. Risk assessment is subject to a host of biases and errors in the decisionmaking process and requires the integration of various kinds of data (for example, from self-report; observation; and agency protocol, such as rules and regulations and third-party reports) that differ in their accuracy, complexity, and predictive value. With respect to predictive value, risk assessment is prone to two key errors: overestimating the true probability of risk to a child and underestimating this risk.[6] Caseworkers must distinguish between child maltreatment and poor parenting before planning a course of action that is most likely to prevent further harm. Yet the instruments used in the field have limited ability to accurately predict which families will maltreat their children in the future.

The many sources of decisionmaking bias suggest the need for procedures that minimize them.[7] Actuarial models are designed to address some of these biases. They are derived from modeling the empirical relationships between certain predictive variables and outcomes. Actuarial models are generally developed by taking a sample population (for example, a sample of children and families involved in the child welfare system), analyzing their paths over time (for example, service history), relating these paths to a set of characteristics or events specific to each family, and identifying events that are highly associated with an outcome of interest (for example, recurrence of abuse or neglect). An event or characteristic becomes predictive if it remains associated with the outcome and adds to the predictive capacity of the risk assessment scale. Actuarial models stand in contrast to simple lists of predictive variables that are not organized around their statistical properties to predict risk or to consensus-based systems in which practitioners assess selected characteristics identified by agreement among experts and then make their own judgment about an outcome, such as risk or clinical intuition, that is not informed by data or expert consensus.

Child welfare agencies have traditionally employed clinical expertise as a basis for assessing risk, despite the fact that this has proven to be less accurate than actuarial prediction.[8] When predictions of experts are compared with statistical models, they are less accurate than models even though the experts may have created the tools themselves.[9] Since 1990 many studies have evaluated the predictive capacity of individual risk factors and risk assessment models used to predict maltreatment recurrence;[10] yet few comparisons have been made between the various risk assessment instruments used in child protective services. A notable exception is Christopher Baird and Dennis Wagner's evaluation of three commonly used risk assessment instruments: Michigan's Family Risk Assessment of Abuse and Neglect (FRAAN), an actuarial approach; the Washington Risk Assessment Matrix (WRAM), a consensus-based approach; and the California Family Assessment Factor Analysis (CFAFA) a consensus-based approach.[11] Not surprisingly, FRAAN's actuarial approach substantially outperformed the other tools in terms of correctly classifying high-risk families that later maltreated their children. In addition to being data-driven, the FRAAN is largely composed of simple (yes and no) questions that make it easy to score reliably. It separately predicts for abuse and neglect (an acknowledgement that these are two very different forms of maltreatment) and calculates an overall risk rating rather than relying on caseworker judgment to assign a level of risk.

Nonetheless, even the very best risk assessment instruments do not predict maltreatment well enough for use as the sole basis of decisionmaking. Rather, these tools can be used to classify families into escalating degrees of risk (low, moderate, high, or very high) with the greatest possible precision, and this information is then combined with clinical assessment skills to formulate a service plan.[12] The hope is that actuarial approaches to such classifications will provide greater consistency of and enhanced predictive validity for decisions through optimal weighting of statistically valid risk indicators. Actuarial instruments and accompanying decisionmaking tools have been developed by the Children's Research Center (CRC), and these have been put into operation with some degree of success.[13] However, the development of these tools tends to be state specific and is not based on national probability samples. Reliable, valid risk assessment instruments applicable in a wide range of child protection settings serving diverse populations are needed to improve the management of risk in child welfare agencies. Now, for the first time, national data exist for the development of such tools.

Methods

This study describes the beginning stages of instrument development using the rich data contained in NSCAW. Since the actuarial approach appears to hold the greatest promise in terms of prediction and in fielding an instrument that works in practice, actuarial strategies were employed throughout.

NSCAW Background and Challenges

NSCAW is the first longitudinal study of investigations by child protective services that employs a national probability sample with data collected from children and families. It is also the first study to relate these data to child and family well-being, service history, community environment, and other characteristics. This rich data set offers opportunities and challenges for the development of actuarial measures to predict the risk of reabuse for children remaining with their parents after an investigation. The abundant child well-being information coupled with case outcome data that are national in scope present the prospect of original and nuanced analyses. Yet the size of NSCAW (over 20,000 variables per subject) and its complexity (multiple waves, weighted sampling design) make the process of distilling predictive information into a manageable instrument a formidable challenge. In addition, the major aim of this study is to develop a practical tool that has the potential to change the way child welfare practice is conducted across the country. For a risk assessment instrument to be useful, the information upon which it is based must be composed of elements that are readily and immediately available to most child protective service workers conducting investigations.

Another challenge in using NSCAW to design a risk assessment measure is that re-reports and resubstantiations may be underestimated as a result of the survey's data collection procedures. After the initial interview, child protective services (CPS) workers were only interviewed at later waves if the family was receiving services at the subsequent wave's interview date, if the family indicated that they had received child welfare services at some point during the prior interview period, or if the family had been oversampled as part of the service group. Since administrative records were not checked for all children at each wave of the study, there is a likelihood that some reports and investigations were missed entirely—those that did not result in placement or that resulted in placement between waves. Unfortunately, there does not appear to be a way to estimate such a bias, and its effect on the construction of the tool will only be hinted at when the final product is cross-validated using another sample.

Design

The overall objective of the study is to construct a risk assessment instrument that predicts recurrence of maltreatment of children who were left in the care of their parents. For the initial stages of instrument development, only items from the NSCAW risk assessment instrument, the age of the child, and a short list of case factors (for example, abuse type, substantiation decision) were used to predict the risk of re-report and risk of resubstantiation at twelve, twenty-four, and thirty-six months.[14] The instrument will be augmented later with information about well-being and other information about the child and the family unique to NSCAW. Longer follow-up periods and risk of entry into foster care will also be explored over time.

Before data analysis, items from a review of CRC actuarial risk assessment instruments were used as an initial template of risk factors for this study. In addition, an extensive review of the literature on risk of re-report and resubstantiation of child maltreatment was conducted. These steps generated a matrix of potential risk factors for an exact or a proximal match with items contained in NSCAW.[15] To derive re-report dates and the period of time between them within a twelve-, twenty-four-, and thirty-six-month framework and to establish whether children were in care at the close of investigation, re-reports, resubstantiations, and child placements in the NSCAW database were restructured into separate, unduplicated events for each child.

Sample

The overall sampling frame included only children in the CPS portion of NSCAW (N = 5,501) who were in the care of their biological parents at the close of the investigation, whose caseworkers completed the NSCAW risk assessment instrument at wave 1, and (because of the nature of the complex survey design and length of follow-up) who had a thirty-six-month follow-up sampling weight. The sample was then randomly divided into construction and validation subgroups. This paper reports on initial results using only the construction sample of 2,401 children.

Analysis

Simple bivariate correlations were initially run between the six outcomes (re-report and resubstantiation at twelve, twenty-four, and thirty-six months), selected case factors, and items from the NSCAW risk assessment. Analysis of covariance between significant factors was then conducted, and either factors that were very highly associated (0.7 or greater) were combined into single factors or only one factor was chosen for subsequent multivariate analyses and scaling. The Burgess method was used to create a simple risk scale by summing significant factors.[16] All factors with simple (bivariate) correlations in the original Burgess scale were maintained in a revised scale, and those that were significant in the regression were then weighted more heavily.[17]

Results

The construction sample contains a substantial portion of infants (19 percent) as well as children aged eleven and older (26 percent) (table 4-1). Children are 46 percent White, followed by 28 percent Black, 19 percent Hispanic, and 8 percent other.[18] About half (49 percent) of the children are male. The largest

Table 4-1. *Characteristics of Children in the Construction Sample*[a]

Characteristic	Percent
Age	
0–2	18.9
3–5	21.0
6–10	34.7
11 and older	25.5
Gender	
Male	48.9
Female	51.6
Race	
Non-Hispanic Black	27.5
Non-Hispanic White	45.7
Hispanic	18.9
Other	7.9
Abuse type	
Physical	27.5
Sexual	11.9
Emotional	7.7
Physical neglect	17.4
Neglect	26.7
Abandonment	0.8
Moral or legal	0.5
Educational	1.6
Exploitation	0.3
Other	4.4
With a re-report by	
Month twelve	15.0
Month twenty-four	22.2
Month thirty-six	26.8
With resubstantiation by	
Month twelve	7.3
Month twenty-four	10.3
Month thirty-six	10.8

Source: Authors' calculation.
a. $N = 2,041$.

single category of maltreatment type is neglect (close to 44 percent), followed by physical abuse (28 percent) and sexual abuse (12 percent). These proportions roughly mirror national percentages for children who were investigated for maltreatment at the time the NSCAW sample was selected, although this construction subset appears to have a lower proportion of very young (aged younger than four years) and Hispanic children, as well as slightly lower levels of neglect and physical abuse.[19] As anticipated, base rates for re-report and resubstantiation in the construction sample are somewhat lower than would be expected when comparing with those rates from other studies. The percentages for re-report (22 percent of the sample) and resubstantiation (10 percent of the sample) at twenty-four months for the construction sample are comparable with reinvestigation and resubstantiation percentages reported in several CRC studies, although there appears to be wide variation across states and counties.[20] Six-month national estimates of revictimization in 2000 (8.6 percent of children reported for subsequent substantiated maltreatment) also indicate that the twelve-month resubstantiation rate of 7 percent in the construction sample is within range but somewhat lower than expected.[21] These lower base rates indicate that the construction sample is either slightly different than the samples generating these other reports or, more likely, that re-report and reinvestigation are somewhat underreported in NSCAW.

The risk assessment instrument contained in NSCAW comprises thirty-four items and is completed by the investigative social worker. Many of the questions are similar to the early CRC Michigan instrument and later CRC iterations, such as the California Family Risk Assessment, both of which have been validated in the field.[22] These items include such case factors as history of prior allegations, investigations, and substantiations; child characteristics, such as severe behavior problems; and caregiver characteristics, such as history of alcohol problems and domestic violence. Also included in the NSCAW version are case-worker assessments of the probability that reabuse will occur within certain follow-up periods conditional on whether services are received or not received.

Each of these factors was placed into a correlation matrix predicting re-report and resubstantiation at all three follow-up periods (twelve, twenty-four, and thirty-six months).[23] Items that were correlated at a prespecified significance level ($p < 0.10$), rather than at the standard level ($p < 0.05$), were selected and ordered by whether they were significant across follow-up periods. The more liberal probability inclusion criterion ($p < 0.10$) was used because of the fairly low base rate of recurrence in this sample and the need to include weakly as well as strongly correlated items in order to create a viable scale.[24] Given that the NSCAW risk assessment instrument contains many items common to a standardized tool, such as the CRC Michigan model, the number of factors correlated with re-report and resubstantiation is fairly small, especially considering the liberal inclusion criteria. Only eight of the thirty factors about the case, family, or child on the NSCAW risk assessment instrument were significant across all follow-up periods, which included

—prior history of child welfare reports,
—prior investigations of maltreatment,
—prior history of child maltreatment,
—child's special needs and behavior problems,
—active alcohol use by parent,

—parent's unrealistic expectations of the child,
—parent's history of abuse and neglect,
—high stress in the family (table 4-2).[25]

Factors commonly predicting reabuse in other studies (for example, low social support and poor parenting skills) were only significant at certain follow-up periods, and other common predictors (for example, parent has a serious mental health problem or parent uses inappropriate or excessive discipline) were not related to recurrence of maltreatment.

One of the important elements to consider when creating a predictive instrument is the degree to which any two items are related to each other. Analysis of covariance among significant predictors revealed that prior report and prior investigation were correlated at 0.94 (that is, if one is present, the other will almost always be present), and prior substantiation was correlated with prior report and prior investigation at about 0.70. As such, all three items were combined into a single factor to increase efficiency and decrease error.[26] All of the items measuring caseworker predictions of future abuse were highly correlated with one another and with key case and risk factors. These items were dropped from subsequent analyses and will be investigated for their predictive utility after the final actuarial model is built. Remaining factors, even those that were highly correlated (for example, parent has poor parenting skills and parent has unreal expectations of the child correlated at 0.52), were retained and make up the first iteration of the scale.[27] Final actuarial models only included twelve-month follow-up data because of potential underreporting of re-reports and reabuse across waves in the NSCAW and because current federal standards are built on six- and twelve-month recurrence rates.

To ascertain which variables are the best predictors and to figure out an optimal weight to assign them in the scale, all significant risk factors were entered into logistic regressions predicting re-report and resubstantiation. Also included in the models were factors of the child (age, gender, and race and ethnicity) and the case (caseworker rating of level of harm to child, whether the original allegation was substantiated, and most serious maltreatment type).[28]

Children in families with a history of reports, investigations, or substantiations (these were combined into a single predictor variable) had more than twice the odds (odds ratio [OR] = 2.24) of being re-reported than children in families without such a history.[29] The presence of another supportive caregiver in the home was inversely related to re-report, with children in such families having close to half the odds (OR = 0.61) of re-report than children in families without another supportive caregiver. High stress in the family was also related to re-report. Children in families that caseworkers rated as having high stress had almost twice the odds (OR = 1.83) of experiencing a re-report as did children in families rated as having less stress. Very young children may also be more likely to have a re-report (OR = 1.69).

Table 4-2. *Correlation between Risk Assessment Items and Re-Report and Resubstantiation across Follow-up Periods*[a]

| | Type of report and time of follow-up (months) | | | | | |
| | Re-report | | | Resubstantiation | | |
Item	Twelve	Twenty-four	Thirty-six	Twelve	Twenty-four	Thirty-six
History of maltreatment reports	*	*	*	*	*	*
Prior investigation of maltreatment	*	*	*	*	*	*
History of child welfare services	*	*	*	*	*	*
Special needs and behavioral problems	*	*	*	*	*	*
Active alcohol use by parent	*	*	*	*	*	*
Parent's unrealistic expectations of child	*	*	*	*	*	*
Parent's history of abuse or neglect	*	*	*	*	*	*
High stress in family	*	*	*	*	*	*
Social worker assessment of the probability of abuse in the next twelve months without services	*	*	*	*	*	*
Social worker assessment of the probability of abuse in the next twenty-four months without services	*	*	*	*	*	*
Another supportive caregiver in home	*	*	*	*	*	
Low social support	*	*	*			
Poor parenting skills				*	*	*
Social worker assessment of the probability of abuse in the next twenty-four months with services				*	*	*
History of domestic violence against parent	*	*				
Reasonable level of parent cooperation					*	*
Prior incident substantiated abuse or neglect			*			*
Parent has recent history of arrests	*					
Parent has intellectual impairment		*				
Parent has physical impairment			*			
Family has trouble paying for basic necessities		*				
Active domestic violence			*			
Social worker assessment of the probability of abuse in the next twelve months with out-of-home placement					*	

Source: Author's calculations.

*$p < 0.10$.

a. The sample is composed of children in the home of the parent at the end of an investigation who completed a risk assessment at wave 1. The following risk assessment items were not significant at any point for either re-report or resubstantiation: child has poor ability to self-protect, active alcohol abuse by secondary caregiver, active drug abuse by parent, active drug abuse by secondary caregiver, parent has serious mental health problem, parent uses inappropriate or excessive discipline, secondary caregiver uses inappropriate or excessive discipline, parent shows motivation to change, history of abuse or neglect in secondary caregiver, parent involvement in nonchild protection services, social worker assessment of the probability of abuse in the next twelve months with services, and social worker assessment of the probability of abuse in the next twenty-four months with out-of-home placement.

The model for resubstantiation had fewer and somewhat different predictive items than the re-report model, which may be a function of their underlying base rates.[30] Similar to re-report, the model for resubstantiation included such items as child aged younger than four years at investigation (OR = 1.54) and high stress in the family (OR = 1.67), and these were of roughly the same strength as in the re-report model. However, the resubstantiation model also included poor parenting skills as a strongly related factor. Children with parents that were rated by social workers as having poor parenting skills had more than twice the odds (OR = 2.22) of having a subsequent substantiated report of maltreatment within twelve months of the close of investigation.

There are various ways to create a risk assessment scale from a set of variables that are found to be predictive of subsequent maltreatment. The items can simply be added together to generate a score (that is, equal weighting is given to all significant factors), or items can be weighted by their relative predictive strength. In this analysis, items that were significant at the $p < 0.10$ level were weighted by a factor of two, while all other factors were assigned a weight of one. Although more precise weights that correspond more closely to the actual coefficient values might produce better estimates, there is a need to simplify weighting schemes for use in the field. For this reason, only whole numbers were used.

The last step was to determine which scale scores should generate a classification of low, medium, or high risk, so that practitioners could accurately establish the degree of risk associated with any given score. Two risk assessment instruments were produced, one for re-report and one for resubstantiation. Cut-off points (specific scores demarcating each of the risk levels) were generated by calculating failure rates for each scale increment and finding natural breakpoints about the base rate. Scale scores of increasing magnitude should reflect increasing risk of subsequent maltreatment. These scores were analyzed with respect to whether there was a re-report or resubstantiation, and cut points were selected that maximized the differences between risk levels (that is, children with scores falling in the "low risk" category would be less likely to experience a re-report or resubstantiation than were those with scores falling in the "moderate risk" range and so on). The resulting models discriminate well between the three risk categories, showing a marked correspondence between increasing risk and maltreatment occurrence.

The initial re-report scale resulted in classifications of low risk for scores ranging from –2 to 1, moderate risk for scores ranging from 2 to 5, and high risk for scores greater than 5 (table 4-3). For the re-report model (figure 4-1), children classified as high risk were about 6 times more likely to have a re-report than children who were classified as low risk (29 percent and 4.7 percent, respectively).[31] The rate of re-report in the high-risk category (0.29) was also more than twice the base rate of report reoccurrence (0.14) within the construction

Table 4-3. *Risk Classification for Twelve-Month Re-report Model*[a]

Score	Number of observations	Number of failures	Percent failure
Low risk			
−2	65	3	4.6
−1	34	1	2.9
0	210	11	5.2
1	136	14	10.3
Moderate risk			
2	204	19	9.3
3	215	26	12.1
4	218	31	14.2
5	203	35	17.2
High risk			
6	184	37	20.1
7	180	26	14.4
8	128	28	21.9
9	111	23	20.7
10	68	11	16.2
11	50	12	24.0
12 or more	35	6	17.1
Total	2,041	283	13.9

Source: Author's calculations.
a. The overall risk of re-report was 13.9 percent.

sample. Both of these ratios are informal indications that an actuarial tool is classifying cases within reasonable parameters. A formal statistical test, corrected for the survey design, also finds significant differences between risk categories.

The initial resubstantiation scale resulted in classifications of low risk for scores ranging from 0 to 3, moderate risk for scores ranging from 4 to 5, and high risk for scores greater than 5 (table 4-4). The resubstantiation model also appears to discriminate between risk levels well, though the low base rate (7 percent) of event recurrence translates into lower proportions of cases classified correctly. Children classified as high risk were almost four times as likely to have a resubstantiation as children classified as low risk (15 percent and 4.2 percent, respectively) (figure 4-2). The rate of resubstantiation in the high risk category (0.15) was also almost twice the base rate of reabuse (0.073). A statistical test finds significant ($p = 0.028$) differences between risk categories.

To test whether two separate models were needed, each of the two instruments was used to predict the outcome of the other. That is, the re-report instrument was used to predict resubstantiation, and the resubstantiation instrument was also used to predict re-report. Both models were far less effective at

Figure 4-1. *Likelihood of Report of Maltreatment for Families Classified as Low, Medium, and High Risk*[a]

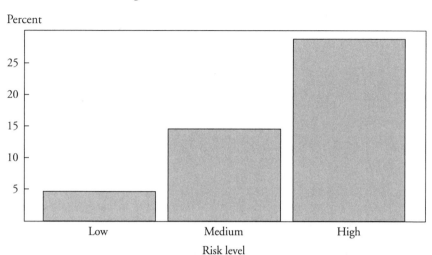

Percent

Source: Authors' calculations.
a. Base rate = 15 percent.

classifying cases correctly, and at this stage of model development, it appears better to maintain separate models for re-report and resubstantiation.

Discussion

Using NSCAW to generate a valid risk assessment instrument that could be widely used by child protection caseworkers and administrators shows some promise. The adaptation of the simple risk assessment tool contained in the survey at wave 1 produced a small set of factors that predicts re-report and resubstantiation for this group of children at rates better than chance. The revised set of factors, when weighted, scored, and parsed into ascending risk levels, classifies children into easily interpretable risk categories at levels of accuracy that approach other actuarial tools used in the field. This is a good beginning.

However, some cautions are in order. While the tool has promise, the most surprising finding is that many of the factors included in the NSCAW risk assessment instrument were not predictive of re-report or resubstantiation, making the number of factors included in the final model somewhat small. Re-report and resubstantiation for children in NSCAW may be underreported, and this may have biased findings on risk. Rather than gathering more reliable administrative data, NSCAW uses caregiver recollection of case activity or services'

Table 4-4. *Risk Classification for Twelve-Month Resubstantiation Model*[a]

Score	Number of observations	Number of failures	Percent failure
Low risk			
0	164	5	3.0
1	125	7	5.6
2	282	13	4.6
3	209	7	3.3
Moderate risk			
4	254	18	7.1
5	237	13	5.5
High risk			
6	225	22	9.8
7	224	23	10.3
8	167	20	12.0
9	104	14	13.5
10 or more	50	5	10.0
Total	2,041	147	7.2

Source: Author's calculations.
a. The overall risk of resubstantiation was 7.2 percent.

receipt at the time of the interview to gather data on re-report and resubstantiation.[32] Given the stigma of such involvement, there is a strong likelihood of underreport. Actuarial risk assessment tools can only be generated when outcomes are reliably known.

In addition, some of the items in the NSCAW risk assessment instrument may not be sufficiently refined to be used as valid risk indicators. For example, CRC items generally weight multiple instances of prior CPS involvement more heavily than single instances. The NSCAW items only included single instances. Another limitation of NSCAW is that many of these items cannot be made more sensitive by adding information from other portions of the survey. In particular, NSCAW modules pertaining to child and family history before the investigation that triggered inclusion into the study are largely missing (that is, family history before the investigation located in the caseworker section contains no information). While child mental health and other outcome indicators are robustly measured in NSCAW, the survey was more limited in its access to traditional administrative outcome data (for example, number, type, length, and duration of prior child welfare services), and these data have been found to predict maltreatment recurrence.

Finally, risk assessment instruments, even those that are reliable and valid, are limited by the nature of the samples upon which they are based. For instance, as with most risk assessment studies, children were only included in this study

Figure 4-2. *Likelihood of Substantiation of Maltreatment for Families Classified as Low, Medium, and High Risk*

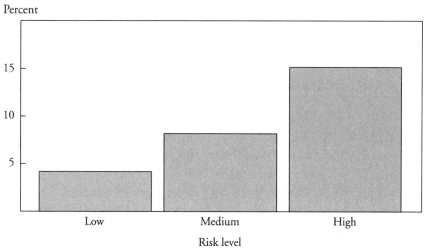

Percent

Source: Authors' calculations.

population if they remained with their parents after the initial investigation.[33] Children who were immediately removed from the care of their parents were probably suffering more obvious and serious maltreatment, which possibly would have put them at greater risk of maltreatment recurrence if left in the home. By removing them from the risk set, instruments may be biased toward less serious cases.[34]

These limitations notwithstanding, some interesting findings emerged with respect to predicting maltreatment recurrence in a nationally representative sample within twelve months of investigation. Children aged three or younger; children in families that had at least one report, investigation, or substantiation; and children with behavior problems were all more likely to experience subsequent maltreatment. In terms of family characteristics and circumstances, caseworker attribution of high stress in the family, parental alcohol problems, parental personal history of maltreatment, poor parenting skills, and unreal expectations of the child by the parent were also linked with a subsequent incidence of child maltreatment. Interestingly, the presence of another supportive caregiver in the home, low social support, history of domestic violence, and parental criminal history were only predictive of re-report. Possibly, re-reports would turn into resubstantiations over time, but the absence of substantiated maltreatment after 12 months raises questions about the use of these constructs to predict actual (not just reported) recurrence.

The models presented here should not be used as risk assessment tools since they are incomplete and have not been validated. The addition of other predictive factors should result in more accurate classification. Indeed simply adding or deleting a factor during this construction phase resulted in substantial differences in predictive capacity, which indicated a degree of instability. Thus there is a strong possibility that, within the larger NSCAW survey, other factors can be included that can substantially improve the models.

The predictive factors contained in the final instruments may be helpful for jurisdictions that are considering building their own risk assessment models. Even validated risk assessment tools should not be used as the sole basis of intervention decisions in child maltreatment cases. When used in the field, actuarial models can enhance decisionmaking, but they are not designed to replace clinical skills or clinical judgment. The instruments do not capture whether there are extenuating circumstances (judgment), nor do they assess the nature or scope of services needed by the family (skills). Rather, they are designed to provide additional information and to help child welfare workers and administrators organize a response that reliably takes risk into account when decisions are made and scarce resources are distributed.[35]

Assessment is the foundation of practice, without which intervention cannot reasonably proceed. Yet most assessments of risk of child maltreatment are based on clinical expertise or consensus-based risk assessment measures. There may be a misperception among some CPS staff that actuarial tools represent a mechanized form of clinical practice and that such tools minimize the importance of clinical judgment. Although any instrument can be misused, actuarial tools are best employed as one source of information among many. Rather than conflating risk assessment with clinical assessment, well-constructed, highly predictive actuarial tools can relieve caseworkers and managers of the burden of trying to guess (and second guess) how risky a case may be. Within a certain margin of error, the risk is pretty well known. Armed with this information, CPS workers can focus on more important matters—namely, how to proceed once the risk level is known.

Notes

1. **Poverty:** Duncan Lindsey, *The Welfare of Children* (Oxford University Press, 1994); Leroy L. Pelton, *For Reasons of Poverty: A Critical Analysis of the Public Child Welfare System in the United States* (New York: Praeger, 1989). **Parental abuse:** Susan J. Kelley, "Child Maltreatment in the Context of Substance Abuse," in *The APSAC Handbook on Child Maltreatment,* 2d ed., edited by John E. B. Myers and Lucy Berliner (Thousand Oaks, Calif.: Sage Publications, 2002), pp. 105–17; Sarah E. Ullman and Leanne R. Brecklin, "Sexual Assault History and Health-Related Outcomes in a National Sample of Women," *Psychology of Women Quarterly* 27, no. 1 (2003): 46–57; Isabel Wolock and Stephen Magura, "Parental Substance Abuse as a Predictor of Child Maltreatment Re-Reports," *Child Abuse & Neglect* 20, no. 12 (1996):

1183–193; Isabel Wolock and others, "Child Abuse and Neglect Referral Patterns: A Longitudinal Study," *Children and Youth Services Review* 23, no. 1 (2001): 21–47. **Domestic violence:** Richard E. Heyman and Amy M. Smith Slep, "Do Child Abuse and Interparental Violence Lead to Adulthood Family Violence?" *Journal of Marriage and the Family* 64, no. 4 (November 2002): 864–70; Amy M. Slep and Richard E. Heyman, "Where Do We Go from Here? Moving toward an Integrated Approach to Family Violence," *Aggression & Violent Behavior* 6, nos. 2-3 (2001): 353–56.

2. U.S. Department of Health and Human Services, Administration on Children, Youth and Families, *Child Maltreatment 2000* (Washington: U.S. Government Printing Office, 2002) (www.acf.hhs.gov/programs/cb/pubs/cm00/chapterthree.htm#child).

3. Duncan Lindsey, "Reliability of the Foster Care Placement Decision: A Review," *Research on Social Work Practice* 2, no. 1 (1992): 65–80; John Ruscio, "Information Integration in Child Welfare Cases: An Introduction to Statistical Decision Making," *Child Maltreatment* 3, no. 2 (1998): 143–56.

4. Cochrane Collaboration, "Preparing, Maintaining, and Promoting the Accessibility of Systematic Reviews of the Effects of Health Care Interventions," (www.cochrane-renal.org/docs/cc_newbroch.pdf [May 1, 2003]); David L. Sackett and others, *Evidence-Based Medicine: How to Practice and Teach EBM,* 2d ed. (New York: Churchill Livingstone, 2000).

5. Campbell Collaboration (www.campbellcollaboration.org [May 1, 2003]); Leonard Gibbs and Eileen Gambrill, "Evidence-Based Practice: Counterarguments to Objections," *Research on Social Work Practice* 12, no. 3 (2002): 452–76; Enola K. Proctor, Aaron Rosen, and Chaie-Won Rhee, "Outcomes in Social Work Practice," *Journal of Social Work Research & Evaluation* 3, no. 2 (2002): 109–23; Enola K. Proctor, "Research to Inform the Development of Social Work Interventions," *Social Work Research* 27, no. 1 (2003): 3–5.

6. Eileen Gambrill and Aron Shlonsky, "Risk Assessment in Context," *Children and Youth Services Review* 22, no. 11 (2000): 813–37.

7. Eileen Gambrill, *Critical Thinking in Clinical Practice: Improving the Accuracy of Judgments and Decisions about Clients* (San Francisco: Jossey-Bass, 1990); Eileen Gambrill, *Social Work Practice: A Critical Thinker's Guide* (Oxford University Press, 1997); Richard Nisbett and Lee Ross, *Human Inference: Strategies and Shortcomings of Social Judgment* (Edgewood Cliffs, N.J.: Prentice-Hall, 1980); Eileen Gambrill and Aron Shlonsky, "Risk Assessment in Context."

8. Christopher Baird and others, "Risk Assessment in Child Protective Services: Consensus and Actuarial Model Reliability," *Child Welfare* 78, no. 6 (1999): 723–48; Peter Pecora, "Investigating Allegations of Child Maltreatment: The Strengths and Limitations of Current Risk Assessment Systems," *Child and Youth Services* 15, no. 2 (1991): 73–92; Michael S. Wald and Maria Woolverton, "Risk Assessment: The Emperor's New Clothes?" *Child Welfare* 69, no. 6 (1990): 483–511; William M. Grove and Paul E. Meehl, "Comparative Efficiency of Informal (Subjective, Impressionistic) and Formal (Mechanical, Algorithmic) Prediction Procedures," *Psychology, Public Policy, and Law* 2, no. 2 (1996): 293–323; Robyn M. Dawes, *House of Cards: Psychology and Psychotherapy Built on Myth* (New York: Free Press, 1994).

9. Robyn Dawes, *House of Cards.*

10. Christopher Baird and Dennis Wagner, "The Relative Validity of Actuarial and Consensus-Based Risk Assessment Systems," *Children and Youth Services Review* 22, nos. 11-12 (2000): 839–71; Michael J. Camasso and Radha Jagannathan, "Prediction Accuracy of the Washington and Illinois Risk Assessment Instruments: An Application of Receiver Operating Characteristic Curve Analysis," *Social Work Research* 19, no. 3 (1995): 174–83; Peter Lyons, Howard J. Doueck, and John Wodarski, "Risk Assessment for Child Protective Services: A Review of the Empirical Literature on Instrument Performance," *Social Work Research* 20, no. 3

(1996): 143–55; Thomas P. McDonald and Jill Marks, "A Review of Risk Factors Assessed in Child Protective Services," *Social Service Review* 65, no. 3 (1991): 112–32; Susan J. Zuravin, John G. Orme, and Rebecca L. Hegar, "Predicting Severity of Child Abuse Injury with Ordinal Probit Regression," *Social Work Research* 18, no. 3 (1994): 131–38.

11. Christopher Baird and Dennis Wagner, "The Relative Validity of Actuarial and Consensus-Based Risk Assessment Systems."

12. For a larger discussion of the psychometric properties of actuarial tools used in child welfare services, see Aron Shlonsky and Dennis Wagner, "The Next Step: Integrating Actuarial Risk Assessment and Clinical Judgment into an Evidence-Based Practice Framework in CPS Case Management," *Children and Youth Services Review* 27, no. 3 (2005): 409–27. This article also discusses the appropriate use of such tools given their substantial limitations and the complexities of providing services within a child protection framework.

13. Christopher Baird, "Risk Assessment and Decision-Making in Child Welfare Services" (Madison, Wisc.: Children's Research Center, April 2004); (Will Johnson, "Effectiveness of California's Child Welfare Structured Decision-Making (SDM) Model: A Prospective Study of the Validity of the California Family Risk Assessment" (Oakland, Calif.: Alameda County Social Services Agency, February 16, 2004); Dennis Wagner, Kristen Johnson, and Rod Caskey, "Evaluation of Michigan's Foster Care Structured Decision Making Case Management System" (Madison, Wisc.: Children's Research Center, September 2002).

14. The NSCAW risk assessment instrument was completed by the caseworker as part of the initial wave 1 interview. Final risk models were limited to twelve months of follow-up.

15. The initial construction of the actuarial instrument described in this paper makes limited use of this matrix. The next stages of development involve the testing and possible integration of these other factors.

16. Ernest W. Burgess, "Factors Determining Success or Failure on Parole," in *The Workings of the Indeterminate-Sentence Law and the Parole System in Illinois,* edited by Andrew A. Bruce, Albert J. Harno, and Ernest W. Burgess (Springfield: Parole Board of Illinois, 1928), pp. 221–34. Although methods other than the process outlined by Burgess may have slightly better predictive capacity in construction samples, the tools they produce may be less predictive when cross-validated on other samples because of "overfitting." For a comparison of scale construction methods, see Eric Silver, William R. Smith, and Steven Banks, "Constructing Actuarial Devices for Predicting Recidivism," *Criminal Justice and Behavior* 27, no. 6 (2000): 733–64.

17. To maximize predictive capacity and to avoid overfitting the model to the construction sample (and being subject to shrinkage during cross-validation), regressions were used to identify and weight factors having strong independent associations with re-report or resubstantiation. In other words, factors that had greater predictive value factored more prominently in the final risk assessment models, but all of the other factors with less independent predictive value were still included.

18. Figures may not add to 100 because of rounding.

19. U.S. Department of Health and Human Services, Administration on Children, Youth and Families, *Child Maltreatment 2000* (Washington: U.S. Government Printing Office, 2002).(www.acf.hhs.gov/programs/cb/pubs/cm00/chapterthree.htm#child).

20. Kristin Johnson and Dennis Wagner, "Colorado Department of Human Services: Risk Validation Study" (Madison, Wisc.: Children's Research Center, 2000); Dennis Wagner and Kristin Johnson, "California Structured Decision Making, Risk Assessment Revalidation: A Prospective Study" (Madison, Wisc.: Children's Research Center, 2003).

21. U.S. Department of Health and Human Services, Administration on Children, Youth and Families, *Child Maltreatment 2003* (Washington: U.S. Government Printing Office, 2005).

22. **CRC Michigan instrument:** See, for example, Dennis Wagner, Sue Hull, and Julie Luttrell, "The Michigan Department of Social Services Risk Based Structured Decision Making System: An Evaluation of Its Impact on Child Protection Service Cases," in *The 9th National Roundtable on Child Protective Services Risk Assessment: Summary of Proceedings* (Denver, Colo.: American Humane Association, 1995), pp. 167–91. **California Family Risk Assessment:** See, for example, Will Johnson, "Effectiveness of California's Child Welfare Structured Decision-Making (SDM) Model." **Field validation:** Christopher Baird and Dennis Wagner, "The Relative Validity of Actuarial and Consensus-Based Risk Assessment Systems."

23. The variation in timing of interviews at each wave (that is, interviews did not occur exactly eighteen months after investigation closure) necessitated the restructuring of NSCAW reabuse data into an event-level table (that is, each instance of re-report or resubstantiation represented a separate row for each date so exact time periods between maltreatment incidents could be calculated). After such a restructuring, any follow-up period can be easily calculated. Follow-up periods for this study (twelve, twenty-four, and thirty-six months) differ from NSCAW waves of child interviews (baseline, eighteen, and thirty-six months after the close of the initial investigation) so that these periods could better match other studies of risk assessment instruments.

24. This more liberal standard of significance is used throughout the paper, and items that are referred to as "significant" conform to this level of probability. Although this author does not normally endorse such an approach, it appears that the low base rate and complexity of the data require such a tactic. Restricting probabilities to the $p < 0.05$ level results in too few items to construct a scale.

25. Two other factors were also predictive across time periods: "Social worker assessment of the probability of abuse in the next twelve months without services" and "Social worker assessment of the probability of abuse in the next twenty-four months without services." However, these two are not characteristics based on the case, family, or child and were not explored further in this analysis.

26. A tool should be both efficient and accurate. If items are highly related, they are essentially measuring the same construct and including them in an instrument creates a level of redundancy that is inefficient and that increases error (that is, if each item is included, the same construct would essentially be counted twice).

27. Despite the need for parsimony in actuarial tools, some built-in redundancy is required to construct a valid tool. There is reason to believe that the inclusion of moderately correlated (redundant) items in a predictive scale will not adversely harm predictive validity and may actually enhance it. This may be because despite efforts to include only items that can be readily known, it is unlikely that all factors in all cases will be known to caseworkers.

28. All variables were entered into the models for re-report and resubstantiation simultaneously, and insignificant variables were manually removed according to the largest p-value. Original models for each outcome included all final scale items, child age, child gender, child race and ethnicity, level of harm to child, status of substantiation of the allegation, and most serious maltreatment type.

29. Logistic regression produces coefficients that can be translated into odds ratios, which are a relatively quick and easy form of expressing relative probabilities. The magnitude and direction of odds ratios are determined in the following manner: an odds ratio of 1 means that there is no difference in the probability of an event occurring (in this case, re-report); an odds ratio falling between 0 and 1 means that the event is less likely to occur in this group; and an odds ratio greater than 1 means that the event is more likely to occur in this group. The further the numbers are from 1 (that is, closer to 0 or further from 1), the greater the magnitude of the effect.

30. A lower base rate results in fewer events (in this case, reports or substantiated reports), in effect diminishing the power of the logistic regression to detect predictive variables.

31. One of the factors ("another supportive caregiver in home") was actually a strength that, if present, decreased the overall risk score. In some instances, this resulted in an overall risk score that was less than 0.

32. NSCAW uses caregiver recollection of case activity or services' receipt unless the child was in foster care at a given NSCAW wave of data collection or they entered the study as part of the services' sample, in which case the caseworker was asked to provide such information.

33. See, for example, Christopher Baird and Dennis Wagner, "The Relative Validity of Actuarial and Consensus-Based Risk Assessment Systems."

34. For a more detailed discussion of this and other methodological limitations, see Eileen Gambrill and Aron Shlonsky, "Risk Assessment in Context."

35. Aron Shlonsky and Dennis Wagner, "The Next Step: Integrating Actuarial Risk Assessment and Clinical Judgment into an Evidence-Based Practice Framework in CPS Case Management."

5

Building on Strengths: Current Status and Opportunities for Improvement of Parent Training for Families in Child Welfare

MICHAEL S. HURLBURT, RICHARD P. BARTH,
LAUREL K. LESLIE, JOHN A. LANDSVERK,
AND JULIE S. McCRAE

The purpose of this paper is to understand in greater detail recent trends in the use of parent training for families involved with child welfare and to propose promising directions for development and research of parent training services relevant to child welfare, using data from the National Survey of Child and Adolescent Well-Being (NSCAW) and the Caring for Children in Child Welfare (CCCW) study. This paper focuses specifically on parent training services delivered to families who receive child welfare services, or services initiated

Contributing authors had the following affiliations during the development of this paper: Michael S. Hurlburt, Rady Children's Hospital, San Diego; Richard P. Barth, University of North Carolina, School of Social Work; Laurel K. Leslie, Rady Children's Hospital, San Diego; John A. Landsverk, Rady Children's Hospital, San Diego; and Julie S. McCrae, University of North Carolina, School of Social Work. The Caring for Children in Child Welfare (CCCW) project was a collaborative effort between the Child and Adolescent Services Research Center (CASRC) at Rady Children's Hospital in San Diego, the Department of Psychiatry at the University of Pittsburgh, the Columbus Children's Hospital, the Services Effectiveness Research Program at Duke University, and the Research Triangle Institute (RTI). The study was funded by the National Institute of Mental Health (MH59672). A complete description of the study and a list of key personnel are available at www.casrc.org/projects/CCCW/index.htm. It should be noted that this document also includes data from the National Survey of Child and Adolescent Well-Being (NSCAW), which was developed under contract to RTI from the Administration on Children, Youth and Families, U.S. Department of Health and Human Services (ACYF/DHHS). The CCCW also maintains ongoing collaboration with the NSCAW Research Group. The information and opinions expressed herein reflect solely the position of the authors. Nothing herein should be construed to indicate the support or endorsement of its content by ACYF/DHHS.

by child welfare, and whose children remain at home after they come into contact with the child welfare system because of allegations of abuse or neglect.

In addition to putting children at risk of physical harm, harmful parenting practices can place children at risk for disruption of normal development across a range of developmental domains.[1] Parent training services are especially significant because they have the potential to reduce the likelihood of child maltreatment and affect children's development and well-being, an increasingly important focus in child welfare policy.[2]

Child welfare services are predicated on the notion that child welfare agencies will make reasonable efforts to help maltreating parents retain or resume the care of their children. Almost certainly, the most common service that parents are provided at this time, and are expected to complete, is parent training.[3]

Historical Perspective on Parent Training in Child Welfare Services

Despite the frequency with which parent training is delivered to families, a historical review of child welfare services suggests that the development and refinement of parent training programs in the child welfare field has not received a level of focus comparable with that of parent training programs designed principally to reduce child behavioral difficulties. Steven Schlossman traces the policy roots of parent education back to the early part of the twentieth century, when parent education was intended to be a universal approach to teaching new mothers about child development and good parenting.[4] Beginning with the development of federal poverty programs in the mid-1960s, parent training programs were used to address the shortcomings of poor families. However, the impact of these programs was moderate and did not justify significant expansion.[5] At that time, the policy debate about parent training did not focus on the appropriateness of using this approach with the population of families involved with child welfare.

In an update to an authoritative textbook on child welfare services published during this same period, Alfred Kadushin described delivery of family life education programs in the context of Family Service Agencies of America, a national organization of local agencies that provided counseling and in-home services for families. For an author known for his encyclopedic knowledge and precision, Kadushin was quite vague about the ways, if any, that these general parenting classes were restructured or modified for families involved with child maltreatment. The impression that emerged from Kadushin's descriptions was that parent training for families involved with child welfare services largely remained in a mold cast in the fifties and rested on a range of general methods of preventive parent education.[6] Even in recent years, parent training continues to receive relatively little attention in important comprehensive volumes on the organization and delivery of child welfare services.[7]

From a research perspective, evidence regarding the impact of parent training in the child welfare arena has also been relatively limited. Only a small body of research has accumulated regarding the impacts of different parent training programs on parenting skills and maltreatment recurrence rates among families involved with child welfare services.[8]

Parent Training from a Behavioral Health Perspective

In contrast to the relatively limited research conducted on parent training of maltreating parents, a stronger body of research has focused on preventing or treating conduct disorders in children.[9] Over the last three decades, clinical researchers have developed and tested a number of different approaches to structured parent training that rely primarily on modifying parenting practices thought to influence child conduct problem trajectories, including parental warmth and play, limit setting, discipline consistency, and harsh or critical discipline. Although child behavioral difficulties are often viewed as the impetus for these interventions, they have substantial relevance to child welfare as evidenced by ongoing research with child welfare populations and by reviews of such programs from a child welfare perspective conducted by Richard Barth and others, and by the Chadwick Center for Children and Families at Rady Children's Hospital in San Diego.[10] These reviews concluded that the aims of evidence-based models of parent training in the behavioral health domain have much in common with the aims of parent training in the child welfare field. However, for a number of reasons, assessing the relevance of such programs to child welfare still requires work.

As a group, families of children referred to child welfare may present more complex constellations of challenges and concerns than might families seen in most studies of parent training. These challenges include increased frequency of mental health problems; parental incarceration, antisocial behavior, or both; social isolation; domestic violence; unusually neglectful or punitive parenting practices; and poverty.[11] Although these are substantial challenges, parent-child interactions have been found amenable to change, even among families with these additional risk characteristics.[12]

Thus despite the gap between what is known about well-established parent training programs that are focused on child behavioral health and the relative lack of knowledge about their impacts on children and parents involved with child welfare, it seems appropriate to examine some of the lessons learned from these well-established programs in behavioral health and to consider their structure relative to the current state of parent training delivered to families in contact with the child welfare system.

Three Examples of Well-Established Parent Training Models

Three parent training programs that have consistently been identified as having strong empirical support, as determined by randomized clinical trials, can usefully be considered as reference points with which to compare parent training services delivered to families receiving child welfare services. These programs include Parent-Child Interaction Therapy (PCIT), Parent Management Training (PMT), and the Incredible Years (IY).[13] All three have relatively extensive data from randomized trials that support their effectiveness in changing parenting practices (and thereby child behavior), and in the literature, all three are routinely identified as models having extensive empirical support.[14] Although each program has its own specific methods and objectives, strong similarities exist across the three regarding the components of the intervention models themselves and the conditions under which positive outcomes have been observed in controlled studies.

All three emerge from a social learning framework, with foundations in basic research on coercive family interaction patterns.[15] All three begin with a focus on strengthening positive dimensions of the parent-child relationship. Techniques include training in special playtime, in which parents learn to follow their children's leads and play with their children at their current developmental levels. Other program modules focus on effectively using praise and rewards to increase desired child behavior and ignoring to decrease undesirable child behavior; decreasing the use of parental directives and commands; and using precise, nonviolent, behavioral approaches to managing challenging child behavior, such as structured procedures for the use of time-out, loss of privileges or other consequences, and brief work chores for older children.

The three models also share much in common regarding the way they are delivered. All three models have detailed materials to support parental skill building each week, specific practice-based homework assignments for parents, and methods for monitoring changes in parenting practices of parents receiving services. All rely heavily on having parents take an active role in learning and practicing new skills, such as role-playing parent-child interactions with other parents or receiving in vivo coached practice with their child. Finally, these programs seem to require a minimum of fifteen hours of intervention for the individually delivered PCIT and twenty-five hours for the group format training programs (IY and PMT) just to complete the basic program components that are focused on the range of skills discussed above.

Beyond specific model components, existing randomized trials of parent training programs related to child behavioral health also tend to have unique features that may not be present in many applied parent training programs serving child welfare settings. For example, randomized trials of these programs have often included relatively intensive initial training for the professionals delivering the program and then supervision before and during program delivery. Supervision has often involved verifying that particular content was covered appropriately, systematically reviewing areas of strength and weakness with cotherapists in the group-based IY and PMT models, and having supervisors view videotapes of group facilitators or therapists to provide feedback about the way in which they delivered a program.

Methods

The similarities among these well-established parent training programs are sufficient for them to serve as a useful collection of reference points against which to compare parent training services as delivered in the community. This paper uses data from NSCAW and the CCCW study to characterize variability in and common approaches to the organization, financing, and delivery of parent training services around the United States for parents of children involved in child welfare, using well-established programs from behavioral health as a reference point.

Overview

The present analyses rely on data on children from NSCAW and CCCW. The CCCW study gathered data about policies and practices in each of the ninety-six counties in which NSCAW collected data on children. The data about child welfare and other service systems from the CCCW study have provided important complementary contextual data to data available from NSCAW.

Sample

Information about the receipt of parent training and other child welfare services was analyzed for families in which the index NSCAW child remained at home and the family received some type of child welfare services ($N = 2,308$). Some analyses used subsets of this sample because certain study measures applied only to children of specific ages.

Complementary information about the delivery of parent training services from the CCCW study was gathered from key informants knowledgeable about parent training for families in their local public child welfare agency. Specifically, questions were asked about delivery of parent training services for families involved in child welfare services in the key informant's county. In NSCAW, counties were the primary sampling units, even within states in which child welfare agencies span broader regions than a single county. In most cases, a local child welfare agency had the same geographic boundaries as a county. Therefore, the terms "county" and "child welfare agency" will be used interchangeably throughout this chapter. Because NSCAW sampled geographic areas at the county level and questions about parent training were asked about families involved with child welfare services in the county, the NSCAW county-level weighting provides appropriate estimates of the number of counties having particular characteristics regarding the delivery of parent training, even if some counties exist within the service delivery area of child welfare agencies with broader jurisdiction.

Interviews about parent training were completed in seventy-eight counties, and interviews in three more counties were partially completed. In counties in which the interview module on parent training was not completed, the child welfare director or the research review committee of the local child welfare agency refused the study's request for participation or did not respond to repeated contact attempts.

Procedures

In the CCCW study, interview data about parent training were collected from child welfare key informants from February 2003 to March 2004. Names of key informants were obtained from the NSCAW contact in each county. Information about the CCCW study, a summary of the interview, and a copy of the informed consent agreement were sent to each identified informant. Trained research assistants at Rady Children's Hospital in San Diego then contacted each informant by telephone to complete the interview. Completion of an interview module typically required no more than forty-five minutes. Most study respondents were administrators within the child welfare organization having responsibility for oversight of parent training programs delivered by child welfare or served as a liaison to organizations delivering parent training services. In situations where identified respondents were not able to answer some or all of the questions, they were encouraged to identify alternate informants who could provide the relevant information.

The data on the child and the family from NSCAW were drawn from initial and follow-up interviews with child welfare workers and caregivers. Trained field representatives collected data from these individuals during face-to-face interviews.

Current caregivers were most often the child's biological parent. On average, initial interviews of the current caregiver were completed 5.3 months after the referral of the index child to child welfare that led to eligibility for inclusion into NSCAW. Follow-up interviews at wave 2 with current caregivers were conducted on average 13.8 months after the referral to child welfare services.

Initial interviews with child welfare workers were scheduled to be completed as soon after the close of the child welfare investigation as possible and were completed 5.0 months on average after referral. Follow-up interviews at wave 2 with child welfare workers were conducted on average 14.6 months after the referral.

Measures

County-level key informant information. In CCCW interview modules, questions were asked about policy and financing, program implementation, and parent training models used in each county. Key informants reported on parent training programs conducted by up to three organizations in their county that had been identified as delivering the most parent training to families receiving child welfare services whose children remained at home following a child welfare investigation. Specific questions asked during this interview are described in more detail in the results section and in tables 5-1 and 5-2.

Parent training and other services. In NSCAW, questions about services that might encompass significant elements of parent training were asked of child welfare workers and caregivers at waves 1 and 2. Reports by parents and child welfare workers were used to confirm whether the caregiver had received parent training. (See table 5-3 for a description of the questions used to define parent training.) The use of intensive family preservation services and family counseling were identified from reports of child welfare workers and parents during wave 2 interviews, which referred to the period since the child's contact date with child welfare. Specifically, child welfare workers reported about the use of intensive family preservation services or other "home-based or community-based child welfare services that are designed specifically to prevent out-of-home placement of a child." Caregivers and child welfare workers were asked whether "the family was counseled together as a group."

Maltreatment. Child welfare workers were asked to identify the types of maltreatment that had been alleged using a modified Maltreatment Classification Scale.[16] Six indicator variables for maltreatment history were created: physical abuse, sexual abuse, emotional abuse, supervisory neglect, physical neglect, and abandonment.

Parenting risk factors. Several risk factors were examined for their relationship with receipt of parent training services. These risk factors consisted of a summative score based on several questions to child welfare workers about parenting risks (described in notes to table 5-4); a score associated with the perceptions of the child welfare worker concerning the severity of the maltreatment that led to referral (described in notes to table 5-4); and a number of individual questions to the child welfare worker from the NSCAW maltreatment risk assessment section, including questions about the presence of substance use, domestic violence, difficulty in paying for necessities, and any prior report of maltreatment.

Contextual variables. Several contextual variables were also considered for their relationship with receipt of parent training services. In the NSCAW data, counties were categorized as urban or nonurban, according to the 1990 Census data. Counties with greater than 50 percent of the population in urban areas were classified as urban, all others as rural. Using the target sample of in-home cases receiving some child welfare services, the percentage of families receiving intensive family preservation services was computed for each county. Finally, a variable reflecting the state in which the county is located was entered to understand whether there is significant variation between states in the delivery of parent training services.

Child behavior. The Child Behavior Checklist (CBCL), a widely used and psychometrically established measure, was used to estimate emotional and behavioral problems among youth.[17] Two caregiver report forms of the CBCL were employed, one for children aged two to three and another for children aged four to eighteen. Children falling at or above the clinical cut-point on the externalizing scale were categorized as having clinically significant behavioral problems.

Living environment. The Home Observation for Measurement of the Environment–Short Form (HOME-SF) was used to assess the quality of the child's caregiving environment. The HOME-SF is a modification of the HOME Inventory, which has been used in more than 200 published studies, has been used to develop norms on young children of varying races and socioeconomic levels, and has good reliability and validity for families of different racial and ethnic backgrounds and for families living in impoverished urban environments.[18] The HOME-SF provides a total score and scores for cognitive and verbal stimulation and for emotional support and nurturing. Half of the items are caregiver reports, and half are observational. A higher score indicates the presence of more positive characteristics in the home environment. HOME-SF scores were computed separately for children less than three years of age (eighteen total items), aged three to five (twenty-six total items), and aged six to ten (twenty-seven total items). The HOME-SF applies only to children who are younger than eleven-years-old.

Analyses

Analyses used key informant responses from the CCCW study to characterize child welfare approaches to providing parent training services at the county level. Descriptive statistics incorporated county-level sampling weights; therefore, the estimates reported apply to the population of U.S. counties, with estimates pertaining to percentages of counties having various characteristics.

Further analyses used NSCAW data of the child and the family to characterize the number of parent training sessions received by caregivers according to reports of parents and child welfare workers. Descriptive statistics and logistic regression were used to understand variation in and predictors of the receipt of parent training services through twelve months following referral to child welfare services.

Results

Results of analyses are first presented for information derived from CCCW surveys of key informants and then for information emerging from NSCAW interviews of parents and caregivers.

Results from County-Level Key Informant Surveys

County child welfare respondents confirmed the high frequency with which parent training services are considered part of the family case plan. In more than 90 percent of counties, child welfare representatives reported that parent training is part of the case plan for half or more of the families receiving some child welfare services whose children remain at home (table 5-1). Nearly 50 percent of counties reported that parent training is part of the case plan most or all of the time. In most counties, key informants also reported that parent training services are ordered on the basis of an assessment of need and are not mandated as part of a general child welfare policy.

Implementation

Counties appear to vary somewhat regarding the settings in which parent training services are delivered and the individuals who deliver these services (table 5-1). Most key informants reported that parent training services are delivered in community settings and in families' homes. A slightly larger proportion of counties (50 percent) reported that families' homes are the primary location for parent training than the proportion that reported community-based locations as the primary location (46 percent).

Most counties reported that parent training services are delivered in part by community-based organizations (CBOs) contracting with the child welfare system or by other CBOs, such as family service agencies or YMCAs. In just less than one-third of counties, child welfare agency staff are the primary providers of parent training.

In just 30 percent of counties, families involved with child welfare services have a priority for admission to parent training services. Almost all counties reported receiving information back about caregivers' participation in parent training, including whether they completed training, the number of hours completed, and in most counties, some information about caregivers' performances in training.

Specifics of Parent Training Service Delivery

In addition to information about the location and providers of parent training, counties described the specific features of parent training programs. Most counties (84 percent) reported that families in contact with child welfare services frequently received parent training services in groups that included families not in

Table 5-1. *Percentages of Counties Reporting Various Policy, Financing, and Implementation Characteristics for Parent Training Services*[a]

Characteristic	Counties reporting
Policy	
Policy requiring all families to receive parent training	3.2
Parent training included in case plan	
Never	0.0
Sometimes	8.6
About half of the time	43.7
Most of the time	41.6
Always	6.1
Parent training delivered to	
All families	5.7
Some families (with identified need)	94.3
Financing	
Provided at least in part by community organizations at no cost to child welfare[b]	61.4
Implementation	
Locations where parent training services are delivered (more than one can be selected)	
Family's home	89.0
CWS agency	44.9
Mental health agency	57.3
Other community locations	86.7
Primary location where parent training services are delivered	
Family's home	49.9
CWS agency	4.1
Mental health agency	10.0
Other community locations	36.0
Providers of parent training services (more than one can be selected)	
Public child welfare agency staff	49.7
Providers contracted by the CWS	85.8
Community-based organizations	82.6
Mental health agency	63.3
Other community locations	7.9
Primary providers of parent training services	
Child welfare agency staff	29.8
Providers contracted by the CWS, community-based organizations, or mental health agencies	35.0
Community-based organizations not contracted by the CWS	27.2
Mental health agency not contracted by the CWS	5.5
Other	2.5
Families involved with child welfare have priority for admission	29.7

Characteristic	Counties reporting
Child welfare receives information from parent training programs about (more than one can be selected)	
Completion status	98.0
Hours completed	83.4
Performance in training	80.6

Source: Authors' calculations.

CWS = child welfare system.

a. Based on seventy-eight counties weighted to represent the population of counties in the United States using county-level NSCAW weights. Percentages may not sum to 100 percent because of rounding.

b. Other public or community-based agencies pay for parent training through their own funding mechanisms.

contact with child welfare services (table 5-2). When parent training was delivered in a group format, families were most commonly grouped by the age of the child (70 percent of counties). Grouping based on type of maltreatment and on other specific issues was less common but did occur in some counties.

The number of hours of parent training services that caregivers could expect to receive varied by county. Some two-thirds of counties reported the maximum number of hours as twenty or fewer, and one-quarter reported it as ten or fewer.

When queried about specific programs used for parent training in child welfare settings, the counties reported a diverse array of parenting programs. Many counties reported that each contracted provider used its own program. The five most commonly reported programs were, in descending order of use: Active Parenting, Nurturing Parenting, STEP, Parents as Teachers, and Tough Love. In total, 41.2 percent of counties reported using one or more of these five programs. Another 26.7 percent reported (not shown in table 5-2) using only programs other than these five, and 32.1 percent reported not using a standardized program.

The three model programs discussed above were not among the five most commonly used programs: the Incredible Years program was used in only 1.4 percent of counties, Parent-Child Interaction Therapy in 0.2 percent of counties, and Parent Management Training was not explicitly noted to be in use at all. Other programs were mentioned even less, including those that might be considered as promising because of their relatively rigorous evaluations or because they were strongly based in social learning theory—including Project 12 Ways in 0.2 percent of counties, and Triple P, which was not mentioned at all.[19]

Parent Training Results from NSCAW

Data from child welfare workers and caregivers for the sample of cases participating in NSCAW help to place these survey results of key informants in the

Table 5-2. *Percentage of Counties Reporting Various Parent Training Program Characteristics*[a]

Characteristic	Counties reporting
Parenting group organization	
Families involved with child welfare services in groups with other families not involved with child welfare services	
Yes	84.4
No	7.9
Other[b]	7.7
Groups frequently organized by (more than one can be selected)	
Child's age	69.7
Maltreatment type	7.1
Racial and ethnic group	0.4
Language	6.8
Other[c]	40.9
Hours	
Minimum hours of parent training parents complete on average	
Less than 10	31.1
11–20	44.5
21–30	15.2
31–50	7.9
More than 50	1.4
Maximum hours of parent training parents complete on average	
Less than 10	25.0
11–20	42.2
21–30	16.9
31–50	3.6
More than 50	12.2
Specific parent training programs in use (more than one can be selected)	
Active Parenting	21.4
Nurturing Parenting	9.6
STEP	8.9
Parents as Teachers	5.2
Tough Love	5.0
No specific or standardized program in use	32.1

Source: Authors' calculations.

a. Percentages may not sum to 100 percent because of rounding.

b. A small proportion of agencies (8 percent) specifically noted that inclusion in the same parent training groups of families that were or were not involved with child welfare services depended on the provider delivering the services. In these counties, contracted providers typically served only child welfare clients, whereas community-based organizations not contracted with child welfare services served a broader range of families.

c. Other methods for grouping included focusing on children with disabilities, religion, teen mothers, domestic violence, and parents with mental health problems.

context of other existing services that might address similar aims. In the target NSCAW sample of families receiving some child welfare services whose child remained at home, 39 percent of parents received parent training services within twelve months of contact with a child welfare agency according to reports of child welfare workers or caregivers. Further analyses showed that an additional 11 percent of families received parent training if the time window was expanded to thirty-six months. Through twelve months, the time when most parent training was initiated, a total of 28 percent of families received parent training in conjunction with intensive family preservation services, family counseling, or both, whereas only 11 percent received parent training services alone. Another 19 percent of families reported receiving family preservation or family counseling and not parent training, and 43 percent of families reported receiving none of these three types of services.

The combined responses of parents and child welfare workers in NSCAW confirm at the client level what key informants in the CCCW study reported at the county level about parents' receipt of parent training services. However, child welfare workers and caregivers had notable differences concerning the extent of parent training services received by caregivers. Among families in this sample, for which a child welfare worker and a caregiver were interviewed at twelve months (N = 928), 25 percent of caregivers reported having received some type of parent training, whereas child welfare workers reported that 42 percent of primary caregivers had received such services. In total, child welfare workers reported that 13 percent of families received one to ten sessions, 6 percent received eleven to fifteen sessions, and 24 percent had received sixteen or more sessions of parent training. In contrast, 10 percent of caregivers reported receiving one to ten sessions, 4 percent reported eleven to fifteen, and 12 percent reported sixteen or more. Some of this discrepancy could be due to caregiver reports that covered the period from wave 1 to wave 2, whereas child welfare worker reports extended from a family's contact date with child welfare up to the wave 2 interview.

Characteristics of Families Receiving Parent Training in Child Welfare Services

Data from NSCAW help provide context to the characteristics of families receiving child welfare services while their children remained at home, and the factors associated with whether families receive parent training services. Table 5-3 summarizes characteristics of all families receiving any child welfare services whose children remain at home and the characteristics of the subset of families that received at least some parent training. A review of the relationships between baseline characteristics and receipt of parent training suggests only a few significant associations among those examined. Significant correlations included several variables reported by child welfare workers, including poor parenting

Table 5-3. *Comparison of Families that Received Child Welfare Services while Their Child Remained at Home with the Subgroup of Families Receiving Parent Training*[a]

Percentage with each characteristic

Baseline characteristic	Families receiving any child welfare services[b]	Families receiving parent training[c]
Children		
Age of index child		
0–2	18.5	22.1
3–5	22.9	25.8
6–10	31.6	30.4
Older than 10	27.1	21.7
Number of children in household		
One	26.3	27.4
Two	25.2	23.8
Three	26.1	24.2
Four or more	22.4	24.6
CBCL[d]		
Greater than or equal to 64 (clinical range)	37.5	36.7
Less than 64 (normal or borderline)	62.5	63.3
Primary caregivers		
Age		
Younger than 25	19.6	22.5
25–34	40.1	44.7
35–44	31.5	25.9
45–54	6.8	5.9
45–54	2.0	1.0
Race and ethnicity		
Non-Hispanic Black	30.9	26.2
Non-Hispanic White	45.2	47.2
Hispanic	16.6	21.0
Other	7.2	5.6
Marital status		
Married	28.2	26.9
Separated, divorced, or widowed	38.6	38.2
Never married	33.2	34.9
Risk factors of parent or family		
Parenting practices[e]	0.8	1.4**
Active substance use[f]	27.9	37.2**
Active domestic violence[f]	15.5	19.2*
Trouble paying for necessities[f]	34.0	38.2
Prior report of maltreatment[f]	58.5	58.6
Maltreatment		
Physical abuse	32.5	31.4
Sexual abuse	12.7	9.2
Emotional abuse	11.2	9.3
Neglect (failure to provide)	28.9	29.2

Percentage with each characteristic

Baseline characteristic	Families receiving any child welfare services[b]	Families receiving parent training[c]
Neglect (failure to supervise)	41.3	47.9*
Abandonment	1.6	2.7
Maltreatment score: risk, harm, evidence[g]	8.2***	. . .
Contextual variables		
Urbanicity		
Urban	78.6	78.1
Nonurban	21.4	21.9
Receiving intensive family preservation services[h]	33.2***	. . .
State		
California	12.3	11.9
Florida	16.2	11.4
Illinois	2.1	2.7
Michigan	6.0	5.2
New York	2.4	3.5
Ohio	2.9	2.7
Pennsylvania	4.6	6.1
Texas	5.5	9.8
Remainder	48.0	46.6

Source: Authors' calculations.

*p < 0.05, **p < 0.01, ***p < 0.001.

. . . Not applicable.

a. Analysis used wave 1 NSCAW child-level weights. The number of cases included in analyses for each variable differs somewhat depending upon rates of missing data. Families receiving parent training are a subset of those receiving any child welfare services. Percentages across categories may not sum to 100 percent because of rounding. Parent training is defined as having received parent training services according to the report of the parent or child welfare worker.

b. Based on NSCAW data, our estimate of the annual number of families that receive some kind of child welfare services following an investigation of child abuse or neglect in which the target child remains at home is 573,961.

c. Based on NSCAW data, our estimate of the annual number of families that receive parent training services delivered or arranged by child welfare services following an investigation of child abuse or neglect in which the target child remains at home is 223,844.

d. CBCL (Child Behavior Checklist) available for children aged 2 and older with caregiver interview completed.

e. Parenting practices defined as the sum of three dichotomous parenting risk factors as reported by child welfare worker: poor parenting, unrealistic expectations of child, and excessive or inappropriate discipline. Score range: 0–3.

f. Risk factors reported as present by child welfare worker. Substance use includes active use by primary or secondary caregiver or both in the home.

g. The maltreatment composite of risk and harm and evidence is defined as the sum of three variables reported by the child welfare worker: level of severity of risk to child (1–4 score), level of harm to child of abuse leading to index report of maltreatment (1–4 score), and level of evidence available to substantiate the case (1–5 score). Average risk score was 8.2, with a total score range of 3–13. For every point increase in the risk score, odds of receiving parent training were 1.2 times higher.

h. The average percentage of families receiving family preservation services in a county for the target population for this paper was 33.2 percent. For every percentage point increase in a county's delivery of family preservation services, odds of receiving parent training were 1.02 times higher.

practices; substance use by a primary caregiver; presence of domestic violence; a composite indicator of maltreatment: risk, harm, and evidence; and referral for failure to supervise.[20] Several contextual variables also predicted receipt of parent training services (table 5-3). Caregivers in counties with higher rates of use of intensive family preservation services were more likely to receive parent training. For every percentage point increase in a county's delivery of family preservation services, the odds of receiving parent training were 1.02 times higher. Substantial variation also existed at the state level, with caregivers in some states receiving parent training at higher rates than did caregivers in others. These differences are more easily understood in the context of a multivariate model.

Multivariate Models of Use of Parent Training Services

Several multivariate models were used to analyze the independent association of predictor variables with receipt of parent training services. The odds ratios emerging from the multivariate models also provided a clear representation of how much more likely caregivers were to receive parent training services as a function of different predictors. The model in table 5-4 reflects the predictors having relatively consistent relationships with receipt of parent training services across tested models. This core multivariate model was estimated for families of children aged two and older, for whom CBCL data were available. Other significant predictors that appeared in separate models are described later in the text after considering the results presented in table 5-4.

With the exception of substance use by a primary caregiver and types of maltreatment, significant predictors of parent training were consistent with those having a univariate relationship with parent training. In particular, parental risk factors were associated with higher levels of use of parent training services. For example, a parenting risk score based on the child welfare worker's assessment of the caregiver's parenting practices predicted receipt of parent training services. On this 0–3 scale, every additional risk reported by the child welfare worker was associated with a 1.39 times increase in the likelihood of receiving parent training. A composite indicator consisting of risk associated with the maltreatment, of worker-reported harm to the child, and of evidence supporting maltreatment also was strongly associated with parent training. A caregiver with a score 3 points (approximately 1 standard deviation) above the mean on this composite variable had a 1.6 times greater chance of receiving parent training than a caregiver with an average risk composite (average = 8.2 on the 3–13 scale).

The core multivariate model was extended by stratifying by age and by adding two primary scales from the Home Observation for Measurement of the Environment Inventory, cognitive stimulation and emotional support.[21] In a model focused on the youngest age group (ages 0 to 2, not shown in the table), parents with less cognitively stimulating home environments were more likely to

Table 5-4. *Logistic Regression Predicting Receipt of Parent Training Services by Twelve Months for Caregiver of Index Child Aged Two or Older at the Time of Investigation*[a]

Characteristic	Beta	Odds ratio
Children		
Age of index child		
2–5 (reference group)	. . .	. . .
6–10	−0.67	0.51
Older than 10	−0.39	0.68
Race and ethnicity		
Non-Hispanic Black	−0.20	0.82
Non-Hispanic White (reference group)	. . .	. . .
Hispanic	0.47	1.59
Other	0.12	1.13
CBCL externalizing score[b]	0.01	1.01
Number of children in household		
One (reference group)	. . .	. . .
Two	−0.20	0.82
Three	−0.14	0.87
Four or more	0.20	1.22
Primary caregiver		
Age		
Younger than 25 (reference group)	. . .	. . .
25–34	−0.05	0.96
35–44	−0.27	0.77
45–54	−0.19	0.83
Older than 54	−0.85	0.43
Marital status		
Separated, divorced, or widowed (reference group)	. . .	. . .
Never married	−0.01	0.99
Married	0.04	1.04
Risk factors of parent and family		
Parenting practices[c]	0.33	1.39*
Active substance use[d]	0.16	1.17
Active domestic violence[d]	0.63	1.88*
Trouble paying for necessities[d]	−0.04	0.96
Prior report of maltreatment[d]	0.10	1.11
Maltreatment		
Physical abuse	−0.11	0.89
Sexual abuse	−0.14	0.87
Emotional abuse	−0.60	0.55
Neglect (failure to provide)	−0.17	0.85
Neglect (failure to supervise)	0.22	1.25
Abandonment	1.92	6.85*
Maltreatment composite: risk, harm, evidence[e]	0.16	1.17*

(continued)

Table 5-4 *(continued)*

Characteristic	Beta	Odds ratio
Contextual variables		
Urban	0.41	1.51*
Percentage of families receiving intensive family preservation services	0.02	1.02*
State		
California	−0.91	0.40
Florida	−1.71	0.18*
Illinois	−1.39	0.25*
Michigan	−0.90	0.40
New York	−0.56	0.57
Ohio	−0.88	0.41
Pennsylvania	−0.08	0.92
Texas	. . .	. . .
Remainder	−1.20	0.30*

Source: Authors' calculations.

CBCL = Child Behavior Checklist.

*$p < 0.05$.

a. Analysis used wave 1 NSCAW child-level weights. Parent training is defined as having received parent training services according to the report of the parent or child welfare worker. Odds ratios are transformations of the beta estimates from logistic regression. The model is limited to children aged 2 years and older so that a CBCL score could be included in the analysis. Differences in results for models including all children are described in the discussion of results in the text, although the pattern of findings for variables other than the CBCL was very similar.

b. CBCL externalizing t score was entered as a continuous variable.

c. Parenting practices were defined as the sum of three dichotomous parenting risk factors as reported by the child welfare worker: poor parenting, unrealistic expectations of child, and excessive or inappropriate discipline. Score range: 0–3; higher scores are for presence of more risk factors.

d. Risk factors reported as present by the child welfare worker. Substance use included active use by primary or secondary caregiver or both in the home.

e. The maltreatment composite composed of risk and harm and evidence is defined as the sum of three variables reported by the child welfare worker: level of severity of risk to child (1–4 score), level of harm to child of abuse leading to index report of maltreatment (1–4 score), and level of evidence available to substantiate the case (1–5 score). Total score range: 3–13; higher scores are for higher levels of risk, harm, and evidence.

receive parent training services (odds ratio = 0.78, $p < 0.01$). In a model of children aged three to five, the two additional HOME scores did not predict receipt of parent training services. Finally, in a model of children aged six to ten, poor cognitive stimulation was once again associated with an increased likelihood of receiving parent training services (odds ratio = 0.83, $p < 0.05$).

Discussion

In the introduction to this chapter, it was suggested that parent training, which focuses on changing parents' knowledge, skills, and behavior, might be a promising avenue for reducing future maltreatment among families receiving child welfare services. Yet there is substantial room for enhancing the impact of parent training services, which is consistent with data from this nationally representative survey as well as with several well-studied parent training models. However, improvement of parent training likely will require more than adopting model parent training programs.

At a broad level, parent training is a compelling area for improvement because it is already a common service. Results from the CCCW key informant surveys and data on caregivers from the NSCAW show that almost 40 percent of families receiving child welfare services whose children remain at home receive parent training services, although the overall prevalence of use varies from state to state.

Results from studies of parent training in the child behavioral health arena provide solid evidence that highly structured parenting programs that focus on parental skill development can change key parenting practices such as warmth, consistency of limit setting, and use of nonviolent alternatives in challenging disciplinary situations. Many studies have had such findings, some conducted with target groups with substantial numbers of families having prior involvement with child welfare or significant risk factors associated with abuse and neglect, although few have focused explicitly on families in contact with child welfare.[22]

The work of Mark Chaffin and others is one exception that provides an important link between the theoretical underpinnings of evidence-based parent training programs from the behavioral health literature and maltreatment reduction among families receiving child welfare services.[23] Their randomized trial of Parent-Child Interaction Therapy revealed that reductions in re-reports of physical abuse to child welfare that occurred among families receiving PCIT were partially explained by changes in the parenting behaviors targeted by PCIT. The parenting behaviors are very similar to those targeted by other evidence-based parent training programs, such as the Incredible Years and Parent Management Training. Furthermore, a trend in Chaffin's PCIT study cited above suggested that parents with a higher mastery of targeted parenting skills had lower maltreatment recurrence, providing further support for the argument that key parenting practices targeted in well-established parent training programs have direct relevance to maltreatment reduction in child welfare.

Although parent training is a common service, it appears that in many areas of the country it may not yet be responding to the needs of families involved with child welfare. One indication of this problem is the number of hours of parent training families can expect to receive. With most counties reporting that parents receive a maximum of twenty hours of group-based parent training, and many reporting that families receive fewer hours than that, it seems likely that current parent training efforts often underestimate the time required to generate changes in caregivers' parenting practices. In addition to the time allocated for parent training, reports of key informants reveal that child welfare programs are not using the parent training models that have the strongest base of empirical research showing their effectiveness. According to recent reviews of the parent training literature, several of the most frequently used parent training programs reported on by CCCW key informants have little evidence to support their effectiveness in changing parenting practices.[24]

Data about the current state of parent training is increasing as is collective evidence about the effects of model programs. Nonetheless it remains difficult to make specific recommendations on how to improve the state of parent training. In addition, few studies of parent training models focus directly on reducing child maltreatment or relate to large groups of families referred to child welfare, despite the growing body of evidence that seems increasingly relevant to the child welfare field. The multivariate model presented in this chapter also gives some indication that families receiving parent training services tend to have an unusually high number of risk factors that may impair parenting practices. Parent training is more likely to be prescribed for families perceived as having additional risks, such as poor parenting practices, more severe maltreatment with more conclusive evidence to support its presence according to the child welfare worker, and high levels of substance use and domestic violence. Independent observational data regarding the home environment also show, in two of three age groups, that the home environments of families receiving parent training tend to be particularly low in cognitive stimulation, even relative to other families involved with child welfare services.

The diverse types and causes of maltreatment raise questions about whether different parent training programs may be more responsive to some kinds of maltreatment than to other kinds. For example, PCIT seems particularly targeted to reduce physical abuse, which was observed in the trial by Chaffin and others, but its potential for reducing the number of neglect cases is less clear. Safecare, a promising model for neglect, does not have the depth of focus on alternatives to physical discipline that such programs as PCIT, IY, and PMT do. Also it may be more responsive to neglect than to physical abuse. Thus a child welfare agency considering improvement of parent training services should consider whether any single parent training program can respond to different kinds of maltreatment. In addition to the varying effects it has on different types of maltreatment, parent training may vary substantially for children at different developmental levels. These considerations suggest that combinations of programs, or methods for assessing and directing caregivers to the most relevant parent training services, may also be as important to the overall effectiveness of efforts to improve the outcomes of parent training as efforts simply focused on implementation of specific model programs.

In addition to conceptual questions about the evidence supporting the effects of model parent training programs, other issues arise around the structure of parent training services. The structure of parent training models from the mental health field do not necessarily correspond well with the locations and methods used to deliver parent training to families receiving child welfare services. For example, although many behavioral health–focused parent training services are delivered in group format in the community, half of counties primarily offer parent training to families involved with child welfare services in home settings. If there are other compelling reasons from a service-system perspective for carrying out home-based service delivery in a particular child welfare agency, improvements in parent training might need to rely more on the principles and materials of effective parenting programs, or on significant adaptations of those programs, rather than on the precise delivery format of the model programs. As indicated by the growing number of websites cataloging evidence-based interventions, the current approach to interpreting scientific evidence places much greater emphasis on the faithful replication of existing program models in their entirety rather than drawing upon the common principles and materials of well-established parent training models with strong core similarities, despite the fact that child welfare–focused service agencies may have strong and valid reasons to adapt the structure of different models to fit within their own system.

Another important structural issue in the delivery of parent training services involves supervision of parent training. As noted, one of the common features of well-studied parent training models is that close supervision ensures quality delivery of program content and methods. The contribution of close supervision to positive client outcomes is not well understood because it has typically been an integral component of randomized trials rather than tested explicitly in study designs. However, the integral role that supervision plays in randomized trials to ensure delivery of programs with high fidelity suggests that it may also play a key role in the level of outcomes achieved when programs are implemented in the community. For parent training delivered at home and in group settings, our anecdotal experience is that resources for supervision are limited in community-based service settings. The concern about support for implementation is further highlighted by evidence from this study suggesting that many counties rely on contractors to deliver parent training services and that such services often are delivered to a broader array of families than just those involved with child welfare or mental health services. Parent training programs for broader populations suggests that support for close supervision of how parent training is delivered in child welfare settings is less likely than in mental health settings where some supervision (although often limited) is the norm. Furthermore, counties reported relying at least in part on parent training services delivered by other community-based programs at no cost to child welfare agencies, suggesting that in a substantial number of counties and cases, child welfare agencies had limited control over the way in which parent training services were delivered.

The issues noted above naturally lead to questions about the costs and benefits associated with efforts to improve parent training services as a strategy for reducing subsequent maltreatment. Unfortunately, evidence is limited regarding the costs and benefits of implementing parent training programs in child welfare services. Chaffin and others reported that delivery of PCIT, if taken to larger scales, could be cost effective for reducing recurrence of physical abuse, but those data arose from a controlled environment in which factors that often undermine implementation of new programs, such as staff turnover and quality supervision, were less significant issues than they would be in the field.[25]

Given the tension between growing evidence of the effectiveness of parent training models and the limitations of that evidence, what courses of action seem prudent? The current state of evidence is sufficient to recommend that to understand the potential for quality improvement child welfare agencies need to devote careful attention to evaluating how the current structure of parent training services within counties (or within broader regional child welfare jurisdictions) relates to the extensively tested parent training models. A child welfare agency could elect to carefully monitor participation levels, topics covered, and learning approaches used in training programs for a subset of families referred to parent training for the purpose of understanding how parent training approaches received by families compare with features of other reference parent training models, as described in this chapter. Ideally one would expect to see features such as active parent participation in role-playing parent-child interactions or methods for direct coaching of parents, thorough coverage of specific topics common to evidence-based parenting models, structured homework, and methods for assessing parent progress on key outcomes. In addition, child welfare agencies could track key outcome measures, such as the parent-child conflict tactics scale, injury occurrences, re-referral to child welfare, or structured observations of parent-child interactions, to estimate overall changes in parenting practices after the family has been referred to child welfare.[26] Once again, this approach could take place with a subset of parents to track trends in changes in parenting practices following referral to parent training. Such monitoring could serve as an anchor for efforts to understand changes in these indicators following efforts to improve the quality of training. Finally counties could experiment with ways to enhance parent training. Depending on how such services are already delivered in a region, this approach might involve implementation of a well-established parent training program for a subset of families referred to parent training. It could also involve efforts to incorporate elements of well-established programs into the structure of existing services to test their effectiveness (for example, supervision, structured homework for parents, active parent learning methods that require problem solving of problematic parent-child interactions), which ideally would be initiated in a pilot fashion so as to provide opportunities to understand potential costs and benefits of such changes.

The choice of whether to adopt existing model programs or to experiment with specific features of those programs depends on how one interprets the evidence from well-established programs in the mental health arena relative to existing services available to a child welfare agency. This paper attempts to provide some guidance about the evidence supporting existing model programs and components of such programs when trying to improve the quality of parent training services.

Overall, this is a time of transformation both for child welfare services and for evidence-based parent training.[27] Evidence-based parent training models from the mental health arena are emerging from a long developmental phase. They have increasing relevance to the child welfare setting and reduction of maltreatment. At the same time, the child welfare field is showing new awareness of the importance of evidence-based methods, shown by special issues of *Child Welfare* and *Research on Social Work Practice* devoted to using evidence-based knowledge to improve policies, practices, and outcomes in child welfare systems.[28] Given the relatively limited number of studies that include extensive numbers of families involved with child welfare, development of effective methods for tracking whether changes in parent training services result in positive changes in key indicators (for example, parental attendance or targeted parenting behaviors) is now as important as the incorporation of new parent training programs or their principles into efforts to improve services.

Notes

1. Many studies have documented developmental differences that arise between children living in circumstances that do and do not include maltreatment of one form or another. Maltreated children experience problems across many dimensions, including antisocial behavior, peer relationships, social functioning, withdrawal, persistence in complex tasks, self-esteem, academic performance, and grade retention. A selection of references describing such findings includes Dante Cicchetti and Sheree L. Toth, "A Developmental Psychopathology Perspective on Child Abuse and Neglect," *Journal of the American Academy of Child and Adolescent Psychiatry* 34, no. 5 (1995): 541–65; Kenneth A. Dodge, Gregory S. Pettit, and John E. Bates, "Effects of Physical Maltreatment on the Development of Peer Relations," *Developmental Psychopathology* 6, no. 1 (1994): 43–55; John Eckenrode, Molly Laird, and John Doris, "School Performance and Disciplinary Problems among Abused and Neglected Children," *Developmental Psychology* 29, no. 1 (1993): 53–62; Byron Egeland, Alan L. Sroufe, and Martha F. Erickson, "The Developmental Consequences of Different Patterns of Maltreatment," *Child Abuse & Neglect* 7, no. 4 (1983): 459–69; Byron Egeland and others, "The Long-Term Consequences of Maltreatment in the Early Years: A Developmental Pathway Model to Antisocial Behavior," *Children's Services: Social Policy, Research, and Practice* 5, no. 4 (2002): 249–60; Martha F. Erickson, Byron Egeland, and Robert Pianta, "The Effects of Maltreatment on the Development of Young Children," in *Child Maltreatment: Theory and Research on the Causes and Consequences of Child Abuse and Neglect,* edited by Dante Cicchetti and Vicki Carlson (Cambridge University Press, 1989), pp. 647–84; Mary E. Haskett and Janet A. Kistner, "Social Interactions and Peer Perceptions of Young Physically Abused

Children," *Child Development* 62, no. 5 (1991): 979–90; Debbie Hoffman-Plotkin and Craig Twentyman, "A Multimodal Assessment of Behavioral and Cognitive Deficits in Abused and Neglected Preschoolers," *Child Development* 55, no. 3 (1984): 794–802; Edward Mueller and Nancy Silverman, "Peer Relations in Maltreated Children," in *Child Maltreatment: Theory and Research on the Causes and Consequences of Child Abuse and Neglect,* pp. 529–78; National Research Council, *Understanding Child Abuse and Neglect* (Washington: National Academy Press, 1993), chapter 6; Susan M. Shonk and Dante Cicchetti, "Maltreatment, Competency Deficits, and Risk for Academic and Behavioral Maladjustment," *Developmental Psychology* 37, no. 1 (2001): 3–17.

2. The Keeping Children and Families Safe Act in 2003 (Public Law [PL] 108-36) amended the Child Abuse Prevention and Treatment Act. One significant focus of the amendments contained in the act was directed at increasing the likelihood that children and families in contact with child welfare services would be linked to health, mental health, and developmental services designed to improve developmental outcomes for children.

3. Richard P. Barth and others, "Parent-Training Programs in Child Welfare Services: Planning for a More Evidence-Based Approach to Serving Biological Parents," *Research on Social Work Practice* 15, no. 5 (2005): 353–54.

4. Steven L. Schlossman, "The Formative Era in American Parent Education: Overview and Interpretation," in *Parent Education and Public Policy,* edited by Ron Haskins and Diane Adams (Norwood, N.J.: Ablex, 1983), pp. 346–73.

5. Ron Haskins and Diane Adams, "Parent Education and Public Policy: Synthesis and Recommendations," in *Parent Education and Public Policy,* pp. 346–73.

6. Alfred Kadushin, *Child Welfare Services,* 3d ed. (New York: Prentice Hall, 1980); Alfred Kadushin and Judith A. Martin, *Child Welfare Services,* 2d ed. (New York: Prentice Hall, 1988).

7. Charmaine R. Brittain and Deborah E. Hunt, eds., *Helping in Child Protective Services: A Competency-Based Casework Handbook,* 2d ed. (Oxford University Press, 2004).

8. Mark Chaffin and Bill Friedrich, "Evidence-Based Treatments in Child Abuse and Neglect," *Children and Youth Services Review* 26, no. 11 (2004): 1097–113.

9. A number of different papers reviewing treatment models with strong empirical support have reached this conclusion. Examples of such reviews, conducted from different perspectives, include Richard P. Barth and others, "Parent-Training Programs in Child Welfare Services"; Elizabeth V. Brestan and Sheila M. Eyberg, "Effective Psychosocial Treatments of Conduct-Disordered Children and Adolescents: 29 Years, 82 Studies, 5,272 Kids," *Journal of Clinical Child Psychology* 27, no. 2 (1998): 180–89; Bruce F. Chorpita and others, "Toward Large-Scale Implementation of Empirically Supported Treatments for Children: A Review and Observations by the Hawaii Empirical Basis to Services Task Force," *Clinical Psychology, Science and Practice* 9, no. 2 (2002): 165–90.

10. Mark Chaffin and others, "Parent-Child Interaction Therapy with Physically Abusive Parents: Efficacy for Reducing Future Abuse Reports," *Journal of Consulting and Clinical Psychology* 72, no. 3 (2004): 500–10; Richard P. Barth and others, "Parent-Training Programs in Child Welfare Services"; see also the California Evidence-Based Clearinghouse for Child Welfare website (www.cachildwelfareclearinghouse.org).

11. U.S. Department of Health and Human Services, *National Survey of Child and Adolescent Well-Being (NSCAW), CPS Sample Component: Wave 1 Data Analysis Report* (Washington: DHHS, Administration on Children, Youth and Families, Children's Bureau, 2005), chapter 6.

12. Nazli Baydar, Jamila M. Reid, and Carolyn Webster-Stratton, "The Role of Mental Health Factors and Program Engagement in the Effectiveness of a Preventive Parenting Pro-

gram for Head Start Mothers," *Child Development* 74, no. 5 (2003): 1433–453; Mark Chaffin and others, "Parent-Child Interaction Therapy with Physically Abusive Parents."

13. **PCIT:** Toni Eisenstadt and others, "Parent-Child Interaction Therapy with Behavior Problem Children: Relative Effectiveness of Two Stages and Overall Treatment Outcomes," *Journal of Clinical Child Psychology* 22, no. 1 (1993): 42–51; Sheila M. Eyberg and others, "Parent-Child Interaction Therapy with Behavior Problem Children: One and Two Year Maintenance of Treatment Effects in the Family," *Child and Family Behavior Therapy* 23, no. 4 (2001): 1–20; Toni L. Hembree-Kigin and Cheryl B. McNeil, *Parent-Child Interaction Therapy* (New York: Plenum Press, 1995). **PMT:** Lew Bank and others, "A Comparative Evaluation of Parent-Training Interventions for Families of Chronic Delinquents," *Journal of Abnormal Child Psychology* 19, no. 1 (1991): 15–33; Martha E. Bernal and others, "Outcome Evaluation of Behavioral Parent Training and Client-Centered Parent Counseling for Children with Conduct Problems," *Journal of Applied Behavior Analysis* 13, no. 4 (1980): 677–91; Rex L. Forehand and Robert J. McMahon, *Helping the Noncompliant Child: A Clinician's Guide to Parent Training* (New York: Guilford Press, 1981); Gerald R. Patterson and others, "A Comparative Evaluation of a Parent Training Program," *Behavior Therapy* 13, no. 5 (1982): 638–50; Steve Peed and others, "Evaluation of the Effectiveness of a Standardized Parent Training Program in Altering the Interaction of Mothers and Their Noncompliant Children," *Behavior Modification* 1 (1977): 323–50; Alan E. Kazdin and others, "Effects of Parent Management Training and Problem-Solving Skills Training Combined in the Treatment of Antisocial Child Behavior," *Journal of the American Academy of Child & Adolescent Psychiatry* 26, no. 3 (1987): 416–24. **IY:** Carolyn Webster-Stratton, "Long-Term Follow-Up of Families with Young Conduct Problem Children: From Preschool to Grade School," *Journal of Clinical Child Psychology* 19, no. 2 (1990): 144–49; Carolyn Webster-Stratton and Mary A. Hammond, "Treating Children with Early-Onset Conduct Problems: A Comparison of Child and Parent Training Interventions," *Journal of Consulting and Clinical Psychology* 65, no. 1 (1997): 93–109; Carolyn Webster-Stratton and others, "Preventing Conduct Problems, Promoting Social Competence: A Parent and Teacher Training Partnership in Head Start," *Journal of Clinical Child Psychology* 30, no. 3 (2001): 283–302; Carolyn Webster-Stratton and others, "Treating Children with Early-Onset Conduct Problems: Intervention Outcomes for Parent, Child, and Teacher Training," *Journal of Clinical Child and Adolescent Psychology* 33, no. 1 (2004): 105–24.

14. Several examples of reviews that have identified these as model programs for reducing mental health problems include "Blueprints for Violence Prevention Overview," Center for the Study and Prevention of Violence, Boulder, Colorado (www.colorado.edu/cspv/blueprints); Elizabeth V. Brestan and Sheila M. Eyberg, "Effective Psychosocial Treatments of Conduct-Disordered Children and Adolescents"; Bruce F. Chorpita and others, "Toward Large-Scale Implementation of Empirically Supported Treatments for Children"; John R. Weisz, Kristin M. Hawley, and Amanda Jensen Doss, "Evidence Update: Empirically Tested Psychotherapies for Youth Internalizing and Externalizing Problems and Disorders," *Psychiatric Clinics of North America* 13, no. 4 (2004): 729–815.

15. Constance Hanf, "A Two-Stage Program for Modifying Maternal Controlling during Mother-Child (M-C) Interaction," paper presented at the meeting of the Western Psychological Association, Vancouver, British Columbia, Canada, April 1969.

16. Jody Manly and others, "The Impact of Subtype, Frequency, Chronicity and Severity of Child Maltreatment on Social Competence and Behavior Problems," *Developmental Psychopathology* 6, no. 1 (1994): 121–43.

17. Thomas M. Achenbach, *Manual for the Child Behavior Checklist/4–18 and 1991 Profile* (Burlington: University of Vermont, Department of Psychiatry, 1991).

18. Robert H. Bradley and Bettye M. Caldwell, "The Relation of Infants' Home Environments to Achievement Test Performance in First Grade: A Follow-Up Study," *Child Development* 55, no. 3 (1984): 803–09; Frank L. Mott, "The Utility of the Home-SF Scale for Child Development Research in a Large National Longitudinal Survey: The National Longitudinal Survey of Youth 1979 Cohort," *Parenting: Science and Practice* 4, nos. 2-3 (2004): 259–70.

19. Project 12 Ways is also known as SafeCare. See John R. Lutzker and Kathryn M. Bigelow, *Reducing Child Maltreatment: A Guidebook for Parent Services* (New York: Guilford Press, 2002); Matthew R. Sanders and others, "The Triple P—Positive Parenting Program: A Comparison of Enhanced, Standard, and Self-Directed Behavioral Family Intervention," *Journal of Consulting and Clinical Psychology* 68, no. 4 (2000): 624–40.

20. The composite indicator of maltreatment—risk, harm, and evidence—is defined as the sum of three variables reported by child welfare workers: level of severity of risk to child (on a scale of 1 to 4), level of harm to child of abuse that leads to an index report of maltreatment (1–4 scale), and level of evidence available to substantiate the case (1–5 scale).

21. Robert H. Bradley and Bettye M. Caldwell, "The Relation of Infants' Home Environments to Achievement Test Performance in First Grade."

22. Carolyn Webster-Stratton and Mary A. Hammond, "Treating Children with Early-Onset Conduct Problems."

23. Mark Chaffin and others, "Parent-Child Interaction Therapy with Physically Abusive Parents."

24. See the California Evidence-Based Clearinghouse for Child Welfare website (www.cachildwelfareclearinghouse.org); Richard P. Barth and others, "Parent-Training Programs in Child Welfare Services."

25. U.S. Department of Health and Human Services, "Physical Abuse Treatment Outcome Project: Application of Parent-Child Interaction Therapy (PCIT) to Physically Abusive Parents" (Washington: DHHS, Administration on Children, Youth and Families, Children's Bureau, Office on Child Abuse and Neglect, 2000).

26. Murray Straus and others, "Identification of Child Maltreatment with the Parent-Child Conflict Tactics Scales: Development and Psychometric Data for a National Sample of American Parents," *Child Abuse & Neglect* 22, no. 4 (1998): 249–70.

27. Mark Chaffin and Bill Friedrich, "Evidence-Based Treatments in Child Abuse and Neglect"; Kauffman Best Practices Project, *Closing the Quality Chasm in Child Abuse Treatment: Identifying and Disseminating Best Practices,* Findings of the Kauffman Best Practices Project to Help Children Heal from the Effects of Child Abuse (Kansas City, Mo.: Kauffman Foundation, 2004).

28. Barbara Thomlison, "Characteristics of Evidence-Based Child Maltreatment Interventions," *Child Welfare* 82, no. 5 (2003): 541–69; Barbara Thomlison, "Using Evidence-Based Knowledge to Improve Policies and Practices in Child Welfare: Current Thinking and Continuing Challenges Research on Social Work Practice," *Research on Social Work Practice* 15, no. 5 (2005): 321–22.

6

Alcohol, Drug, and Mental Health Service Need for Caregivers and Children Involved with Child Welfare

ANNE M. LIBBY, HEATHER D. ORTON,
RICHARD P. BARTH, AND BARBARA J. BURNS

Mental health and substance use disorders are major public health problems affecting millions of American families, with estimated annual costs in the billions of dollars borne by individuals and society.[1] Many adults who suffer from these problems are also parents, a situation that possibly places their children at risk for the negative consequences associated with mental health and substance abuse problems. Studies have shown poorer developmental outcomes on physical, cognitive, and social dimensions for children of parents with substance or mental health problems and increased risk of these children for emotional problems and substance use themselves.[2] This paper draws on the National Survey of Child and Adolescent Well-Being (NSCAW), a nationally representative sample of children involved with local child welfare systems and their caregivers, to estimate the prevalence and severity of mental health and substance abuse problems in parents and children.

The child welfare system is charged to ensure child safety, but it is also a source of services for children and parents who have mental health or substance abuse problems.[3] Several studies have estimated the rate of substance abuse problems for families involved with the child welfare system at 40 to 80 percent, although to date there have been no comprehensive studies conducted to provide

This paper was prepared for presentation at the Child Protection Conference, July 21, 2005, Washington, D.C. The authors gratefully acknowledge the William T. Grant Foundation for partial support of this work.

107

national estimates.[4] In a previous study using NSCAW data, caregivers' need for and receipt of mental health and substance abuse assessment and treatment was described and compared by ethnic groups.[5] These families were similar on many dimensions of risk for unmet need, and they faced substantial gaps between measured need and access to treatment services. For example, although nearly all the American Indian caregivers who were assessed showed serious or moderate impairment in mental health and were often reported by the caseworkers as having a serious mental or emotional problem, only 19 percent were referred for mental health services provided or paid for by the child welfare agency. Substantially fewer (3.2 percent) actually received mental health services as a result of the referral. This pattern of unmet need for mental health services was reflected in other racial and ethnic groups, although unequally. Among those shown to have need, only 26 percent of Whites, 11 percent of Blacks, and 24 percent of Hispanics received services.

Children involved with child welfare systems have long been known to be at risk for emotional and behavioral problems, in part because of negative life experiences before removal or investigation, a common history of poor access to health care, and possible separation from their family.[6] Compared with children from similar socioeconomic backgrounds, youths in foster care exhibit significantly higher rates of serious emotional and behavioral problems, chronic physical disabilities, developmental delays, and poorer school achievement.[7] Psychiatric epidemiological studies estimate that about 5 to 9 percent of youths aged nine to seventeen years in a typical community will have extreme functional impairment. This figure compares with estimates of children in foster care in need of psychiatric services that range between 35 and 85 percent.[8] Neglected, physically abused, or sexually abused youth are at high risk for conduct problems, depression, anxiety, and social withdrawal, and they lag behind their same-aged peers in social skills and adjustment.[9] Studies have shown that maltreatment interrupts cognitive development and attentional capacities, so it is not surprising that youths in foster care are more likely than their counterparts who are not involved with child welfare to have lower academic achievement.[10]

Much less evidence about behavioral and emotional problems is available to describe the well-being of youths still living at home who are involved with child welfare systems. Community studies showing the effects of poverty on the need for services suggest that this population would be at elevated risk compared with the general population.[11] In a recent study based on NSCAW of behavioral problems of children involved with child welfare services, the rate of behavioral problems, indicated by a score in the clinical range of the Child Behavior Checklist, was 48 percent of children aged two- to fourteen-years-old at the time of the investigation.[12]

This paper assesses family mental health and substance abuse problems by measuring the co-occurrence of caregivers' alcohol, drug, and mental health problems with children's behavioral problems. The relationships between children's behavioral problems and services received by their caregivers for their specific alcohol, drug abuse, and mental health (ADM) problems are also examined, with results having implications for receipt of services for and improvement of problem behaviors for caregivers and their children.

Methods

Children in the NSCAW child protective services sample who were aged two to fourteen years at baseline were included. Children younger than age two were not included because behavioral measures were not available for them. Data from interviews at baseline and month eighteen (wave 3) of the child, current caregiver, and the child welfare worker were used. Since caregiver measures from the interviews at baseline and month eighteen were used, only children whose caregivers remained constant during this time frame were included in the study. The final sample consisted of 1,876 children and their caregivers. Data were drawn from the twelve-month interview to fill in missing eighteen-month responses if the same caregiver responded to both interviews. Descriptions of measures used in this study follow.

Caregiver substance use and mental health problems and risk factors

At baseline, caregivers were administered a structured clinical interview using the Composite International Diagnostic Interview–Short Form (CIDI-SF) to assess substance dependence (drug or alcohol dependence separately) and to detect the occurrence of a major depressive episode in the past year.[13] Also at baseline, the child welfare worker was asked to identify, via a checklist, caregiver risk factors, which included "serious problems with alcohol or drugs" (aggregated to substance use problem) and "serious mental health or emotional problems." These items gathered from the caregiver and child welfare worker were combined into a variable indicating whether the caregiver had any of the above ADM problems. Other assessed risk items included cognitive impairment, physical impairment, impaired parenting (that is, poor parenting skills, inappropriate or excessive discipline), monetary problems (that is, problems paying for basic necessities), and current domestic violence.

Youth behavior problems

The Child Behavior Checklist (CBCL), which was completed by caregivers for children as young as two years, was used to estimate emotional and behavioral problems for youths.[14] Indicator variables were created for scores in the clinical range of sixty-four and higher on the internalizing and externalizing subscales and the total score, as has been done in other studies of this child welfare population.[15] Overall mental health problems for youths (substance abuse was not assessed) were indicated by a score in the clinical range for at least one of these three measures (internalizing, externalizing, or total CBCL score).

Youth characteristics

The sample of children and adolescents aged two to fourteen years at baseline was divided into three age groups: two to five, six to ten, and eleven to fourteen, with the youngest two groups being compared with the oldest group. The child's placement at baseline was categorized as "in-home" or "out-of-home." Gender was also reported for the child and caregiver. The race and ethnicity of both were identified as mutually exclusive categories: non-Hispanic White, non-Hispanic Black, Hispanic, and other or unknown.

The type of maltreatment that instigated the initial investigation was identified by the child welfare worker using a modified Maltreatment Classification Scale.[16] Categories included physical, sexual, and emotional abuse; failure to provide; failure to supervise; abandonment; moral or legal maltreatment; educational maltreatment; exploitation; and other types of neglect. For these analyses, physical, sexual, and emotional abuse were grouped and compared with all other types of maltreatment.

Caregiver assessments, referrals, and service receipt

At the twelve- and eighteen-month assessments, the child welfare worker was asked questions regarding referrals made for the caregiver and services received by the caregiver since the last interview. The child welfare worker also indicated if a referral was made for an ADM problem. If a referral was made, the child welfare worker indicated whether the caregiver received the services and, if so, whether they were services for substance use or mental health problems. If a referral was not made, the worker indicated the reasons why, which included that the parent was already receiving the service.

If a child and his or her family were not receiving any type of child welfare services after baseline, no interview of the child welfare worker was done for that wave. In these instances, it was assumed that no referrals were made through the child welfare system and that no services were received for an ADM problem. Although unlikely, it is possible that caregivers received services outside the child welfare system.

Data Analysis

Weighted descriptive statistics for the sample of 1,876 children and their caregivers were estimated. Statistical analysis was then used to estimate: relationships between baseline characteristics of the child and caregiver and caregiver ADM problems, relationships between risk factors for the child and caregiver and caregiver receipt of services for substance use problems at eighteen months, and relationships between risk factors for the child and caregiver and caregiver receipt of services for mental health problems at eighteen months. Only caregivers from the sample who had a mental health or substance use problem at baseline ($n = 745$) were included in the models of caregiver service receipt at eighteen months because service receipt was assumed to be conditional on need. Mental health and substance use problems were combined because of the comorbidity between these disorders.

For baseline child and caregiver characteristics, the entire sample of 1,876 child-caregiver pairs was compared with the sample of children aged two to fourteen years whose caregiver had changed between baseline and the eighteen-month assessment ($n = 1,038$). The purpose of this comparison was to assess possible bias that may have been introduced by dropping from the sample those children who had changed caregivers. The two groups were not significantly different with respect to their respective distributions on age, race and ethnicity, and gender. Baseline measurements of behavioral problems also did not differ significantly between the two groups. However, the children whose caregivers were the same at baseline and at eighteen months were significantly less likely to have been in an out-of-home placement at baseline (3.4 percent) than children whose caregivers had changed (12.3 percent). The group of children whose caregivers had changed was also more likely to have caregivers at baseline with ADM problems (50 percent compared with 41 percent). Therefore, the sample used in these analyses was slightly less severe because the children were less likely to be in an out-of-home placement and were less likely to have caregivers with baseline ADM problems than the entire NSCAW sample.

Results

Table 6-1 presents demographic characteristics of the 1,876 children at baseline according to whether their caregivers had a baseline ADM problem or not. The majority of the children were in the two youngest age groups (two- to ten-years-old). Nearly half of the children were White, with 27 percent Black and 20 percent Hispanic. Overall, slightly less than half were boys (49 percent). Slightly less than half entered into child welfare systems because of physical, sexual, or emotional abuse, and 97 percent were at home at baseline rather than in an out-of-home placement.

Table 6-2 presents children's behavioral problems by caregivers' ADM problems at baseline. Prevalence of children's baseline behavioral problems ("Overall ADM") ranged from 46.5 to 65.7 percent across the groups of caregivers with baseline substance use or mental health problems. The prevalence of children's baseline behavioral problems among those whose caregivers did not have a baseline ADM problem (28.6 percent) was significantly lower than that among those caregivers who did have an ADM problem (54.8 percent). The highest prevalence of children's behavioral problems at baseline (65.7 percent) was seen

Table 6-1. *Characteristics of Children and Caregivers in the Sample,*
by Caregiver ADM Problem at Baseline[a]

| Characteristic | Caregiver ADM Problem at Baseline | | |
	Yes (n = 1,018) percent	No (n = 858) percent	Total (N = 1,876) percent
Child's age			
2–5	29.0	30.1	29.6
6–10	42.7	46.4	44.9
11–14	28.4	23.5	25.5
Child's gender			
Female	47.5	53.5	51.0
Male	52.5	46.5	49.0
Child's race and ethnicity			
Non-Hispanic White	47.9	45.6	46.5
Non-Hispanic Black	29.4	24.9	26.7
Hispanic	15.7	22.3	19.6
Other	7.0	7.3	7.2
Caregiver's race and ethnicity			
Non-Hispanic White	53.8	49.5	51.3
Non-Hispanic Black	26.7	22.2	24.0
Hispanic	13.5	21.2	18.0
Other	6.0	7.2	6.7
Maltreatment type			
Abuse	45.2	51.6	49.0
Neglect or other maltreatment	54.8	48.4	51.0
Child's placement at baseline			
In-home	91.7	100.0	96.6
Out-of-home	8.3	0.0	3.4

Source: Authors' calculations using NSCAW.

ADM = Alcohol, drug, or mental health problem.

a. Sample sizes are unweighted; percentages are weighted and may not total to 100 because of rounding.

for the group of caregivers who had substance dependence at baseline, as measured by the CIDI-SF. For children in this group of caregivers, 57.9 percent had clinically significant externalizing CBCL scores. Clinically significant externalizing behavior problems were also high (51.9 percent) among youths with a depressed caregiver, as measured by the CIDI-SF. The group of caregivers with serious mental health problems at baseline, as judged by the child welfare worker, had the highest prevalence of children with clinically significant internalizing scores (34.0 percent). There were no significant relationships between active substance use by the caregiver, as judged by the child welfare worker, and any of the baseline problems reported for children. There were significant

Table 6-2. *Child Behavior Problems, by Caregiver ADM Problems at Baseline*[a]

| | Caregiver ADM problems at baseline | | | | | | | | | | | |
| | Substance abuse per CW | | Substance dependence per CIDI-SF | | MH problems per CW | | Major depression per CIDI-SF | | Overall ADM[c] | | No ADM[c] | |
Child behavior problems at baseline	Number	Percent	Number	Percent	Number	Percent	Number	Percent	Number	Percent	Number	Percent
Clinically significant CBCL score												
Externalizing	90	38.4	29	57.9*	143	48.7*	229	51.9*	363	46.6*	162	20.0*
Internalizing	62	20.2	24	23.4	109	34.0*	161	28.8*	257	27.7*	127	13.7*
Total	102	38.5	34	60.3*	164	54.2*	239	51.6*	391	48.1*	191	23.4*
Overall ADM[b]	120	46.5	38	65.7*	181	59.0*	272	58.9*	447	54.8*	233	28.6*
No overall ADM[b]	161	53.5	29	34.3*	159	41.1*	181	41.1*	409	45.2*	473	71.4*
Total[d]	281	100.0	67	100.0	340	100.0	453	100.0	856	100.0	706	100.0

Source: Authors' calculations using NSCAW.

ADM = Alcohol, drug, or mental health problem; CBCL = Child Behavior Checklist; CIDI-SF = Composite International Diagnostic Interview–Short Form; CW = child welfare worker; MH = mental health.

*$p < 0.001$: significant difference between value for caregiver with reported problem and caregiver without the same problem.

a. Sample sizes are unweighted, and column percents are weighted.

b. Overall ADM for children includes clinically significant externalizing, internalizing, or total CBCL scores.

c. Overall ADM for caregivers includes substance abuse per CW, substance dependence per CIDI-SF, MH problems per CW, or major depression per CIDI-SF.

d. Because of missing data, only 1,562 children and their caregivers are represented in this table.

relationships between having a caregiver with substance dependence as measured by the CIDI-SF and all of the child's baseline problems except for internalizing behavior problems. There were also significant relationships for both caregiver mental health problems as judged by a child welfare worker and caregiver major depression as measured by the CIDI-SF with all child behavior problems at baseline.

Results from the multivariate analyses are presented in table 6-3. The first column presents the results of the model used to assess the relationships between child and caregiver baseline characteristics and caregiver ADM problems at baseline. Children with a clinically significant externalizing score at baseline were more than three times as likely to have a caregiver with an ADM problem at baseline (odds ratio [OR] = 3.4). Children in the youngest age group (two- to five-years-old) were 80 percent more likely (OR = 1.8) to have a caregiver with a baseline ADM problem than children in the oldest age group (eleven to fourteen years). Neither child's gender nor caregiver's race and ethnicity had significant associations with caregiver ADM problems at baseline. With respect to baseline risk factors of the caregiver as assessed by the caseworker, caregivers who had impaired parenting skills were significantly more likely to have a baseline ADM problem (OR = 3.4).

The second and third columns of table 6-3 present the results of the models used to estimate the likelihood of service receipt for substance use problems and mental health problems, respectively, by the caregiver between baseline and wave 3. Only children whose caregivers had a baseline ADM problem were included in these models. There were no significant relationships between internalizing or externalizing problems in the children and caregiver receipt of services for substance use problems. However, caregivers of children with externalizing problems were more than three times as likely to receive mental health services (OR = 3.2). The caregivers of children who were maltreated or neglected were significantly more likely to receive both kinds of services than caregivers of children who were abused. Caregivers whose children were in-home at baseline were 70 percent less likely to receive services for substance use problems (OR = 0.3). Caregivers of the youngest group of children were significantly less likely to receive substance abuse services (OR = 0.2), but not mental health services. Caregivers of female children were significantly less likely to receive mental health services (OR = 0.5) but not substance abuse services. Hispanic caregivers were significantly more likely than other ethnic groups to receive substance abuse services (OR = 11.0), and Black caregivers were significantly less likely than other ethnic groups to receive mental health services (OR = 0.2). Caregiver risk factors such as monetary problems and parenting impairment had no significant effect on either kind of service receipt.

Table 6-3. *Relationships between Child ADM Problems and Caregiver ADM Problems at Baseline and between Child ADM Problems at Baseline and Caregiver ADM Service Receipt at Wave 3*

	Caregiver ADM problem at baseline [a]	Caregiver received services at wave 3 for—[b]	
		Substance abuse problem	Mental health problem
Caregiver baseline characteristics			
Clinically significant CBCL score			
Externalizing	3.4**	1.0	3.2**
Internalizing	1.3	0.4	0.9
Maltreatment type			
Neglect or other maltreatment	1.1	7.4**	3.0*
Abuse (reference group)	1.0	1.0	1.0
Child placement [c]			
In-home	n.a.	0.3*	0.5
Out-of-home	n.a.	1.0	1.0
Child's age			
2–5	1.8*	0.2*	2.1
6–10	1.2	2.8	1.0
11–14 (reference group)	1.0	1.0	1.0
Child's gender			
Female	1.1	1.0	0.5*
Male (reference group)	1.0	1.0	1.0
Caregiver baseline characteristics			
Race and ethnicity			
Non-Hispanic Black	1.4	2.5	0.2**
Hispanic	0.8	11.0**	1.3
Other	0.8	2.0	0.5
Non-Hispanic White (reference group)	1.0	1.0	1.0
Caregiver risk factors			
Physical impairment	1.5	0.6	1.0
Impaired parenting skills	3.4**	1.3	1.8
Monetary problems	1.6	1.1	0.7
Domestic violence	1.5	1.0	0.8

Source: Authors' calculations using NSCAW.

n.a. Not applicable.

ADM = Alcohol, drug, or mental health problem; CBCL = Child Behavior Checklist.

**$p < 0.01$, *$p < 0.05$.

a. Caregivers with an ADM problem at baseline: $N = 1,413$.

b. Only caregivers with an ADM problem at baseline ($N = 745$) were included in these models.

c. All children with a caregiver with an ADM problem at baseline had an out-of-home placement at baseline; therefore, this variable was not included in the model predicting caregiver ADM problems at baseline.

Discussion

This study showed a consistent association between clinically significant child problems and caregiver ADM problems, especially for child externalizing behavior problems and caregiver receipt of services for mental health problems. The children of caregivers with substance use or mental health problems at baseline were twice as likely to have clinically significant externalizing symptoms as children whose parents did not have substance use or mental health problems at baseline.

Even after adjusting for many covarying factors that could explain the relationship between substance abuse of the caregivers and externalizing problems of the child, the relationship still held. Children with clinically significant externalizing behavior problems were more likely to have a caregiver with ADM problems than children without clinically significant externalizing problems. This finding is very likely to have clinical significance. Further, the multivariate models offer a direct, albeit general, explanation of this finding. Caregiver ADM problems were significantly associated with child welfare workers' assessments of the presence of impaired parenting. This finding from a national probability survey supports similar findings from local intervention studies that the parenting of substance-involved mothers is often substandard and has serious consequences for their children.[17]

Parenting programs and substance abuse programs, however, remain largely disconnected. Even though the ostensible reason for concern about parental ADM problems is the risk of inadequate parenting, the treatment approaches for parenting problems and those for substance abuse typically follow different and independent courses. Nancy Suchman and others have argued that these interventions generally have not strengthened family bonds at the same time as they have improved some child behaviors. They encourage interventions that also focus on maternal responsiveness and the development of the parent-child relationship.[18] Indeed, with the exception of the rare substance abuse programs that allow mothers to remain with one or two young children in group care, there are almost no programs that expressly address the needs of substance-involved mothers to improve their parenting skills so that they can better manage the behavior problems of their children.[19] Only a few clinical studies have focused on parent training with substance-involved parents, but they show promising effects—especially for addressing children's externalizing problems.[20] One program that addressed parenting along with substance abuse is the Parents Under Pressure program, designed for mothers on methadone in Australia. This small study showed positive benefits on child behavior in a pre- and postevaluation.[21]

Children's externalizing behavior problems were significantly associated with caregiver receipt of mental health services at eighteen months following the case investigation. This result raises questions about child placement if caregivers have ADM problems that impair their parenting but are not linked to appropriate treatment services by child welfare systems. In our study, neglect and out-of-home placement were significant predictors of receipt of mental health or substance abuse services. Given that 97 percent of children were in-home at baseline, this association does not bode well for child placement or case outcomes for the many families in which caregivers with ADM problems did not receive intervention and their children remained in their custody. In addition to ensuring child safety, one could argue that caregiver functioning may be a second critical component of the decision on whether to leave children with their caregivers. The aim of achieving permanency could be hampered by gaps in services for caregivers.

Just as caregiver ADM problems are considered a risk factor for child behavioral problems, so may the reverse be true. Child behavior problems could be an indication that a caregiver may also need treatment. Of course, other work suggests that front-end detection of problems may not be the biggest barrier in family functioning; nevertheless, these findings suggest that risk factors for children's safety and well-being may manifest themselves in caregiver ADM problems. Thus family-based interventions may offer special value for families in child welfare systems in a way not well studied in the treatment literature. Future research will progress from the examination of caregiver ADM problems toward recognition of child ADM problems and the development and testing of ways to improve access to treatment services for families involved with child welfare systems.

Statistical Note

To obtain population-based estimates to describe the sample, weighted descriptive statistics and weighted odds ratio estimates that are nationally representative were obtained using the analysis weights and Stata svy procedures.

Notes

1. U.S. Department of Health and Human Services, "Mental Health: A Report of the Surgeon General" (Rockville, Md.: DHHS, 1999); DHHS, "Blending Perspectives and Building Common Ground: A Report to Congress on Substance Abuse and Child Protection" (Washington: DHHS, Administration for Children and Families, Substance Abuse and Mental Health Services Administration, Office of the Assistant Secretary for Planning and Evaluation, 1999).

2. U.S. Department of Health and Human Services, "Blending Perspectives and Building Common Ground"; Joseph Semidei and others, "Substance Abuse and Child Welfare: Clear Linkages and Promising Responses," *Child Welfare* 80, no. 2 (2001): 109–28; Christine Walsh and others, "The Relationship between Parental Substance Abuse and Child Maltreatment: Findings from the Ontario Health Supplement," *Child Abuse & Neglect* 27, no. 12 (2003): 1409–425.

3. U.S. General Accounting Office, "Child Welfare and Juvenile Justice: Federal Agencies Could Play a Stronger Role in Helping States Reduce the Number of Children Placed Solely to Obtain Mental Health Services," GAO-03-397 (Washington, 2003).

4. U.S. Department of Health and Human Services, "Blending Perspectives and Building Common Ground"; J. Semidei and others, "Substance Abuse and Child Welfare"; Marc Mannes, "Seeking the Balance between Child Protection and Family Preservation in Indian Child Welfare," *Child Welfare League of America* 72, no. 2 (1993): 141–52.

5. Anne M. Libby and others, "Alcohol, Drug and Mental Health Specialty Treatment Services by Race/Ethnicity: A National Study of Children and Parents Involved with Child Welfare," *American Journal of Public Health* 96, no. 4 (2006): 628–31.

6. Linnea Klee and others, "Implementing Critical Health Services for Children in Foster Care," *Child Welfare* 71, no. 2 (1992): 63–74.

7. Neal Halfon and others, "Mental Health Service Utilization by Children in Foster Care in California," *Pediatrics* 6, pt. 2 (1992): 1238–244; Sarah M. Horowitz and others, "Impact of Developmental Problems on Young Children's Exits from Foster Care," *Child Abuse & Neglect* 15, no. 2 (1994): 53–62; Mark D. Simms and Neal Halfon, "The Health Care Needs of Children in Foster Care: A Research Agenda," *Child Welfare* 73, no. 5 (1994): 505–24.

8. Robert M. Friedman and others, "Prevalence of Serious Emotional Disturbance in Children and Adolescents: Technical Report," in *Mental Health, United States,* edited by Ronald W. Manderscheid and Mary A. Sonnerschein (Washington: U.S. Department of Health and Human Services, Substance Abuse and Mental Health Services Administration, Center for Mental Health Services, 1996), pp. 71–89; John Landsverk and Anne Garland, "Foster Care and Pathways into Mental Health Services," in *The Foster Care Crisis: Translating Research into Practice and Policy,* edited by Patrick Curtis and Grady Dale (University of Nebraska Press, 1999), pp. 193–210.

9. Mimi V. Chapman and others, "Children's Voices: The Perceptions of Children in Foster Care," *American Journal of Orthopsychiatry* 74, no. 3 (2004): 293–304.

10. Tara Kelley-Baker and others, *In the Wake of Childhood Maltreatment* (Washington: U.S. Department of Justice, Office of Juvenile Justice Delinquency Prevention, 1997); E. Milling Kinard, "Perceived and Actual Academic Competence in Maltreated Children," *Child Abuse & Neglect* 25, no. 1 (2001): 33–45.

11. Elizabeth J. Costello and others, "The Great Smokey Mountains Study of Youth: Goals, Design, and Prevalence of DSM-III-R Disorders," *Archives of General Psychiatry* 53, no. 12 (1996): 1129–136.

12. Barbara J. Burns and others, "Mental Health Need and Access to Mental Health Services by Youths Involved with Child Welfare: A National Survey," *Journal of the American Academy of Child & Adolescent Psychiatry* 43, no. 8 (2004): 960–70.

13. World Health Organization, Composite International Diagnostic Interview (CIDI), version 1.0 (Geneva, 1990).

14. Thomas M. Achenbach, *Integrative Guide for the 1991 CBCL 4-18, YSR, and TRF Profiles* (Burlington: University of Vermont, Department of Psychiatry, 1991).

15. Barbara J. Burns and others, "Mental Health Need and Access to Mental Health Services by Youths Involved with Child Welfare."

16. Jody T. Manly and others, "The Impact of Subtype, Frequency, Chronicity, and Severity of Child Maltreatment on Social Competence and Behavior Problems," *Development and Psychopathology* 6, no. 1 (1994): 121–43.

17. MaryLouise Kerwin, "Collaboration between Child Welfare and Substance-Abuse Fields: Combined Treatment Programs for Mothers," *Journal of Pediatric Psychology* 30, no. 7 (2005): 581–97.

18. Nancy Suchman and others, "Rethinking Parenting Interventions for Drug-Dependent Mothers: From Behavior Management to Fostering Emotional Bonds," *Journal of Substance Abuse Treatment* 27, no. 3 (2004): 179–85.

19. Harry Clark, "Residential Substance Abuse Treatment for Pregnant and Postpartum Women and Their Children: Treatment and Policy Implications," *Child Welfare* 80, no. 2 (2001): 179–98; Lawrence Greenfield and others, "Effectiveness of Long-term Residential Substance Abuse Treatment for Women: Findings from Three National Studies," *American Journal of Drug and Alcohol Abuse* 30, no. 3 (2004): 537–50.

20. Marina Barnard and Neil McKeganey, "The Impact of Parental Problem Drug Use on Children: What Is the Problem and What Can Be Done to Help?" *Addiction* 99, no. 5 (2004): 552–59; Richard Catalano and others, "An Experimental Intervention with Families of Substance Abusers: One-Year Follow-Up of the Focus on Families Project," *Addiction* 94, no. 2 (1999): 241–54.

21. Sharon Dawe and others, "Improving Family Functioning and Child Outcome in Methadone Maintained Families: The Parents under Pressure Programme," *Drug and Alcohol Review* 22, no. 3 (2003): 299–307.

7

Medicaid and Mental Health Care for Children in the Child Welfare System

RAMESH RAGHAVAN AND ARLEEN LEIBOWITZ

C hild welfare policymakers are greatly concerned with ensuring the emotional well-being of maltreated children through the delivery of adequate and appropriate mental health services and with finding financial resources to support such services. In fiscal year 2004, child welfare agencies nationwide investigated the families of around 3 million children for alleged child abuse or neglect.[1] Of these, approximately 872,000 children were determined to be victims of maltreatment. Maltreated children have high needs for, and high use of, mental health services, and states have increasingly come to depend upon Medicaid to fund these services.[2] In recent years, however, Medicaid has undergone significant changes, chief of which is the development of Medicaid managed

This study was supported by the Agency for Healthcare Research and Quality (1 RO3 HS013611-01) and the Centers for Disease Control and Prevention (U48/CCU915773). Dr. Raghavan is an investigator with the Center for Mental Health Services Research at the George Warren Brown School of Social Work, Washington University in St. Louis, and was supported through an award from the National Institute of Mental Health (5P30 MH068579).

The authors thank Mark Schuster, Ronald Andersen, Bonnie Zima, John Landsverk, Roshan Bastani, Susan Ettner, and four reviewers for thoughtful comments on earlier versions of this chapter; Michael Hurlburt for suggestions on use of Area Resource File variables; Michael Mitchell, Christine Wells, and Xiao Chen for statistical consultation; Dave Goldin, Patsy Wood, and Jinjin Zhang for assistance with data management; and Preston Finley for assistance with the references.

The Caring for Children in Child Welfare project (CCCW) is a collaborative effort between the Child and Adolescent Services Research Group (CASRC) at Rady's Children's Hospital in San Diego, the care. These changes are likely to expand and intensify as efforts designed to reduce Medicaid spending accelerate at national and state levels.[3] The extent to which Medicaid managed care has affected mental health care use among children in the child welfare system is not well understood. This chapter examines the effects of several county-level Medicaid managed care policies concerning access to ambulatory and inpatient mental health services by a national sample of children who have come into contact with child welfare agencies. As a result of this analysis, we develop policy recommendations that can guide agencies involved with child welfare, mental health, and child health on how best to ensure the emotional well-being of children in the child welfare system who receive care within Medicaid managed care environments.

A Brief History of the Medicaid–Child Welfare Interface

Before the 1980s, children usually entered the child welfare system because of neglect resulting from parental and social problems, such as poverty, homelessness, incarceration, or mental illness. These children principally needed to be protected, and the child welfare system was oriented toward providing these children with a secure dwelling. The introduction of crack cocaine in the 1980s, and the rise of HIV/AIDS a few years later, produced dramatic changes in the number and type of child welfare cases. Child welfare workers began to encounter increasing numbers of children with complex medical needs stemming from parental substance abuse and HIV. These conditions were expensive to treat and required a broad range of new types of services, a task for which child welfare agencies found themselves unprepared both financially and organizationally.[4]

Previously federal funding streams had usually provided fiscal support to the work of state child welfare agencies; these were, however, inadequate to deal with these new and expensive medical needs. The primary source of federal payments for services was Title IV Part B (Child and Family Services) of the Social Security Act. Although these federal payments provided states with flexibility in spending, funds were capped and usually did not grow from year to year. Bereft

Department of Psychiatry at the University of Pittsburgh (Pittsburgh), the Columbus Children's Hospital, the Epidemiology and Services Research Group at Duke University, and the Research Triangle Institute (RTI). The study is funded by the National Institute of Mental Health (MH59672). A complete description of the study and a list of key personnel are available at www.casrc.org/projects/CCCW/index.htm.

This document also includes data from the National Survey of Child and Adolescent Well-Being (NSCAW), which was developed under contract to RTI from the Administration on Children, Youth and Families, U.S. Department of Health and Human Services (ACYF/DHHS). The CCCW also maintains ongoing collaboration with the NSCAW research group.

The information and opinions expressed herein reflect solely the position of the authors. Nothing herein should be construed to indicate the support or endorsement of its content by ACYF/DHHS.

of federal support for services, states did not have sufficient general revenues to pay for all the services that children needed.

States began to explore alternative funding sources for services and soon recognized the potential of Medicaid. From the states' perspective, Medicaid offered several advantages. Because of the federal match, states could leverage more than a dollar of services for a dollar of state spending. Medicaid was also an entitlement program not subject to funding vicissitudes. Finally, as a state-administered program, Medicaid offered a great degree of flexibility in implementation and control, and, within broad federal boundaries, it offered a great deal of flexibility in the types of services that could be covered.

By the 1990s states began passing legislation designed to expand Medicaid as a significant funding stream to handle child welfare caseloads.[5] The increasing reliance by state child welfare systems on Medicaid to fund services for children in their system is a direct consequence of these efforts. Medicaid rapidly became, and remains, the most important source of financing for mental health services for children in the child welfare system.

Medicaid Coverage for Children in the Child Welfare System

Medicaid coverage today seems to be ensured mostly for children placed in out-of-home care. Around 75 percent of these children are covered under federal categorical eligibility regulations, and the rest are covered through some other criteria (related to disability, income, or other state and county eligibility standards), resulting in 99 percent coverage by Medicaid of children in foster care.[6] In fact, so successful are states in covering children in child welfare under Medicaid that some low-income parents are known to relinquish custody of their children to child welfare agencies so that their child can obtain needed mental health services.[7]

Coverage of children who stayed in their own homes following an investigation is less certain, with reportedly 84 percent of in-home children being eligible for Medicaid coverage.[8] Private insurance, philanthropy, monies from child welfare budgets, and state and local funds provide a patchwork of care for in-home children.

Since the 1980s Medicaid has undergone significant structural changes, perhaps the most salient of which are Medicaid expansions and the rise of Medicaid managed care. Medicaid expansions were enacted through a series of federal laws beginning in the mid-1980s, which separated eligibility for cash assistance (Aid to Families with Dependent Children, or AFDC) from Medicaid. Because AFDC's income eligibility levels were very low, this separation made more families with incomes above AFDC levels eligible for Medicaid. Also, by eliminating the requirement that states obtain federal waivers before enrolling their residents in managed care plans, federal legislation in 1997 moved increasing numbers of these newly insured children into managed care plans. As of 1999, eighteen states mandated the enrollment of children in foster care in managed care plans, and another thirty states permitted such enrollment; 74 percent of all managed care systems covered Medicaid-eligible children in the child welfare system.[9] Today almost every state uses Medicaid managed care to deliver physical health services; 80 percent of all state Medicaid agencies use managed care to deliver mental health or substance abuse services (either all services or a part of these services) to their populations.[10]

From a primary care perspective, managed care offers significant advantages for enrollees, including a focus on prevention, coordination of care, smaller co-pays, and expanded benefit structures.[11] However, children in the child welfare system are a large group of high-need individuals who utilize a considerable proportion of child mental health services. Lacking a way to adequately cover the costs of services to their high-need populations and faced with high variability in these costs due to the relatively smaller number of enrollees, health plans have strong incentives to control the use of mental health services. In addition, commercial managed care organizations may be unfamiliar with the unique needs of children in the child welfare system. Many states have multiple managed care organizations, which may affect continuity of services, and not all child welfare agencies are familiar with the process of accessing care in a managed environment—all of which have the potential to adversely affect care for child welfare populations within managed care environments.[12]

Many managed care organizations contract for—or "carve out"—behavioral health services separately from physical health services.[13] Mental health carve outs are usually managed by specialized behavioral health organizations, which presumably have greater expertise in delivering mental health services.[14] Carve outs have been reported to increase access to services for children with special health care needs.[15] Anecdotal evidence from eight states suggests that children needing behavioral health services within carved-out systems receive care that is consistent with system of care principles, has a wider array of services, has more home- and community-based services, is more flexible in service delivery, has greater involvement of child welfare stakeholders in planning, and has greater interagency systems and processes to implement and monitor care compared with care delivered to children in systems that do not deploy mental health carve outs.[16] Although carving out behavioral health care has resulted in increased initial access to services, access to inpatient and extended care has been problematic because of restrictions on hospitalization and reduced lengths of stay.[17] In contrast, other data suggest that carve outs increase inpatient mental health service use among adolescents.[18]

Managed care also differs from non–managed care settings in mental health provider reimbursement. In contrast to traditional Medicaid, where discounted fee-for-service payment systems predominate, managed care introduces capitated systems of reimbursement, which have been shown to reduce inpatient services and increase ambulatory services for youth in the child welfare system in at least one state, Colorado.[19]

In our prior work using data from the National Survey of Child and Adolescent Well-Being (NSCAW), carve outs reduced use of inpatient mental health services but did not have any effects on ambulatory care.[20] Enrollment into managed care plans or variations in types of provider reimbursement plans did not have any effects on either ambulatory or inpatient service use. Other characteristics of Medicaid's organizational structure that are not directly related to Medicaid managed care but that may affect mental health service delivery—such as variations in recertification intervals, policies that permit children placed out-of-home to "buy into" the State Child Health Insurance Program (SCHIP), and the construction of separate Medicaid programs for children in the child welfare system—have not been subject to analysis at a national level. Therefore, national efforts that have resulted in the enrollment of increasing numbers of children in the child welfare system into Medicaid managed care plans have proceeded for the most part without the benefit of empirical policy guidance based on data on children.

This chapter attempts to address this gap in knowledge by expanding our previous work to analyze effects of additional Medicaid policies on the delivery of mental health services for children in the child welfare system. The Medicaid policies analyzed are related to both Medicaid managed care and other policies not directly linked to Medicaid managed care, such as the level at which Medicaid is organized (for example, state versus local), recertification intervals for Medicaid eligibility, and variations in coverage under Medicaid for children placed in-home and out-of-home. The effects of these policies on the use of both ambulatory and inpatient mental health services are examined. Together, these findings present a comprehensive picture of the effects of Medicaid policies on providing mental health services to a national sample of children in the child welfare system and suggest policies that may improve such services to this highly vulnerable population.

Methods

Data on children were obtained from the child protective services (CPS) sample of NSCAW drawn from child protective services agencies. Independent variables were generated from the baseline wave (from October 1999 to December 2000), and dependent variables related to the use of ambulatory and inpatient mental health services were generated from data from the twelve-month follow-up wave (fielded between October 2000 and March 2002).

Policy data were obtained from the Caring for Children in Child Welfare (CCCW) study—a telephone interview of NSCAW contact persons in each of

NSCAW's primary sampling units (PSU).[21] These key informants provided detailed contextual information regarding the organization and financing of services within county mental health and child welfare agencies, linkages between the mental health and Medicaid agencies, training of child welfare workers, and placement policies. Data on health care providers were obtained from the 1999 Area Resource File (ARF), which lists health resources within each county in the United States.[22]

These sources of data were merged into an integrated data set. From this data set, we excluded children younger than two years of age because the indicator of clinical need, the Child Behavior Checklist (CBCL), used in NSCAW cannot be used with children aged younger than two. We also dropped four children of indeterminate race and ethnicity. Because NSCAW PSUs and Area Resource File counties are not always identical, we had to exclude 300 children because we could not definitively identify their county of residence. Medicaid managed care policies may affect care for not only children enrolled in Medicaid but also for uninsured children (by changing eligibility policies that make it easier or harder to be insured, for example) and for privately insured children (by altering the supply of providers, thus making it easier or harder to obtain services). Therefore, we did not confine the sample to only children insured through Medicaid but included all children. Sample means were substituted for data missing at random. We thus obtained a dataset of variables on individuals containing 3,460 children from NSCAW, with variables on the county characteristics (policies on service use and health resources availability) from CCCW and the Area Resource File.

Variables for the Study

Variable selection was guided by the well-established behavioral model of access to services, which analyzes service use as a function of predisposing, enabling, and need variables.[23] According to this model, individuals use services because they need those services. However, this relationship is affected by sociodemographic and other characteristics of the individual needing services (called predisposing characteristics) and by the financial as well as other resources that individuals have to access those services (called enabling resources). The predisposing characteristics included child age, gender, and race and ethnicity (extracted from NSCAW's caregiver interviews). Maltreatment history, obtained from NSCAW's interviews of child welfare workers, is based on a modified Maltreatment Classification Scale.[24]

Children's placement status was aggregated into two mutually exclusive categories: "in-home" (living with their permanent primary caregiver, usually their birth parent) and "out-of-home" (in foster care with either a relative or a nonrelative or in a group home or residential treatment shelter). We categorized children into insurance categories of "public insurance" (Medicaid), "private insurance," "federal" (CHAMPUS), and "uninsured." Because only 39 children had a federal health insurance policy, we grouped the privately and federally insured into a single category.

Policy variables were obtained from interviews conducted with child welfare and Medicaid agencies. Informants from county child welfare agencies were asked about managed care services for children and adolescents in the county's Medicaid program and whether any children in the child welfare system were covered under a Medicaid managed care plan on either a mandatory or voluntary basis. Informants from the county Medicaid programs were queried on whether Medicaid mental health services were carved out from Medicaid physical health services and on reimbursements to service providers. Reimbursement mechanisms of traditional fee-for-service, discounted fee-for-service, and primary care case management were grouped into a single category of "some type of fee-for-service."

Provider ratios at the county level were constructed by dividing adult psychiatrists by total county population and pediatricians and child psychiatrists by total county child population. Each ratio was multiplied by 10,000 to obtain an average count per 10,000 individuals or children.

Our variable for need was based on the identification of a probable behavioral disorder if the child scored in the clinical range (greater than 63) on the total problem subscale of the Child Behavior Checklist.[25] The CBCL is a well-established measure of childhood behavior problems that has been successfully used in child welfare populations, with moderately high reliability and validity.[26] We also used an additional need variable—the child welfare worker's evaluation of the need for mental health services.

Data from NSCAW's twelve-month follow-up wave were used to construct measures of use of ambulatory and inpatient mental health services.[27] Children were coded as having used ambulatory mental health services if they had seen a mental health professional or someone other than a mental health professional, or if they had been seen in a mental health or community health center, for "emotional, behavioral, learning, attentional, or substance-abuse problems" in the preceding six months. Following Barbara Burns and others, we constructed our variable of any inpatient service use for children who had been to a medical hospital, psychiatric hospital, a psychiatric unit in a medical hospital, a detox unit, or inpatient drug or alcohol unit for "emotional, behavioral, learning, attentional, or substance-abuse problems" in the preceding six months.[28]

Our data analysis strategy was to examine the effects of the county Medicaid policy variables on use of ambulatory and inpatient mental health services by children, controlling for variables at the individual level (predisposing, enabling, and need) and variables on county-level health resources. Ambulatory and inpatient use were analyzed separately, and policy variables were introduced in stages so that the effects of individual policies could be studied. Further details are available in the Statistical Note section.

Results

Results of this study are displayed in tables 7-1 through 7-3.

Sample Characteristics

Children in our sample had a mean age of eight years and were equally divided by gender. The largest proportion was White (46 percent), followed by Black (29 percent) and Hispanic (19 percent) (all percentages weighted). The commonest form of maltreatment was physical abuse (34 percent), followed by sexual abuse (17 percent).[29] A third (36 percent) had scores in the clinical range on the CBCL, while child welfare workers evaluated 14 percent as needing mental health care. Half of the children had Medicaid coverage (51 percent), and 8 percent were uninsured. Most of the children (92 percent) lived in their own homes. A third of caregivers (30 percent) had less than a high school education, 43 percent had completed high school, and 26 percent had gone to college.

The majority of children (71 percent) lived in counties where Medicaid offered managed behavioral health plans, 64 percent in counties that covered child welfare children under such plans, 68 percent in counties that carve outs behavioral health from physical health, and 80 percent in counties that reimbursed mental health providers using some type of fee-for-service. Counties had an average of 1.1 child psychiatrists and 8.6 pediatricians per 10,000 children and 0.9 adult psychiatrists per 10,000 residents. A total of 18 percent of children in the sample obtained ambulatory mental health services, and 2 percent obtained inpatient care.

Bivariate Results

Male gender, older age, out-of-home placement, coverage through public insurance, higher levels of caregiver education, child welfare worker's assessment of need, and a score in the clinical range on the CBCL were all significantly correlated with the use of ambulatory mental health services (table 7-1, ambulatory services). Around 20 percent of boys and 16 percent of girls in our sample used ambulatory mental health services. Proportions of ambulatory service use increased with age: with 9 percent of two- to five-year-olds used ambulatory services compared with 20 percent of six- to eleven-year-olds and 26 percent of twelve- to sixteen-year-olds. Greater proportions of physically abused and abandoned children obtained ambulatory mental health care (21 percent and 44 percent, respectively) than did sexually abused or neglected children (19 percent and 14 percent, respectively). Compared with the proportion of those insured, a smaller proportion of uninsured children were successful in obtaining ambulatory mental health care. Children had slightly higher odds of obtaining ambulatory care if they lived in counties with higher concentrations of child psychiatrists and pediatricians (data not shown).

Similar to the analysis of ambulatory use, older age, history of physical abuse, coverage through public insurance, higher levels of caregiver education, a score in the clinical range on the CBCL, and child welfare worker's assessment of need were all associated with use of inpatient mental health services (table 7-1, inpatient services). In addition, children who lived in counties with greater concentrations of adult psychiatrists had higher odds of inpatient service use (data not shown).

Medicaid variables were not associated with use of ambulatory mental health services in bivariate analyses (table 7-2). With respect to inpatient services, only 0.2 percent of children who lived in counties that offered a separate Medicaid program for children in the child welfare system obtained inpatient care compared with 2 percent of children who lived in counties that enrolled child welfare children into regular Medicaid plans ($p < 0.001$). Other Medicaid variables were not associated with use of inpatient services in bivariate analyses.

Multivariate Results

Multivariate analyses were conducted to identify relationships between two variables, controlling for all other variables in the statistical model. Many, but not all, of the variables significantly associated with use of mental health services in bivariate analyses retained their significance in multivariate analyses using only child-level characteristics (table 7-3). Older children with scores in the clinical range on the CBCL, placed out-of-home with college-educated caregivers, and whose caseworkers felt they needed mental health care had higher odds of using ambulatory mental health services. Compared with those insured, uninsured children had only half the odds of using ambulatory care. Older age, higher levels of caregiver education, clinical scores on the CBCL, and caseworker's assessment of need for services were also significantly associated with use of inpatient care.

When contextual variables are added to the individual model estimating use of ambulatory services, level of Medicaid administration, specific Medicaid programs for children in the child welfare system, managed behavioral carve outs, and other Medicaid variables are not significantly associated with the use of services. However, when controlling for individual characteristics and state health policies, children resident in counties with greater numbers of child psychiatrists have twice the odds of obtaining ambulatory services (odds ratios [OR] between 2.1 and 2.5, all with $p < 0.05$; data not shown).

In terms of inpatient care for mental health, children who live in counties that carve out mental health services have half the odds of inpatient mental

Table 7-1. *Bivariate Associations between Background Variables
and Receipt of Ambulatory Services and Inpatient Services*[a]

Predictor variables	Ambulatory services		Inpatient services	
	Unweighted n	Weighted percent	Unweighted n	Weighted percent
Gender				
Male	454*	19.6*	55	2.1
Female	417*	15.6*	43	1.8
Age				
2–5	146*	9.1*	5*	0.004*
6–11	447*	19.5*	44*	1.7*
12–16	276*	25.5*	49*	4.6*
Race and ethnicity				
Non-Hispanic Black	190	13.9	27	1.2
Non-Hispanic White	502	21.4	55	2.5
Hispanic	107	12.8	12	1.9
Native American and mixed race	71	19.0	4	0.5
Type of maltreatment				
Physical	293*	21.4*	31*	3.2*
Sexual	192	19.2	22	2.8
Neglect	105	14.4	16	1.3
Abandonment	53*	43.8*	7	4.7
CBCL score				
Less than or equal to 63	297*	9.3*	19*	0.7*
Greater than 63	574*	32.7*	79*	4.2*
Child welfare worker assessment of need				
Services required	468*	40.5*	69*	8.6*
Services not required	403*	14.1*	29*	0.9*
Placement				
In-home	581*	15.9*	63	1.8
Out-of-home	290*	38.4*	35	3.0
Insurance status				
Public	660*	24.8*	80*	2.9*
Private and federal	167	19.0	14	1.4
Uninsured	42*	9.4*	4	1.9
Caregiver's educational level				
Less than high school	181*	15.3*	27*	3.0*
High school or equivalent	377*	13.9*	43*	1.8*
College educated	279*	25.1*	21*	0.01*
Total number and percent in service[a]	871	17.6	98	1.9

Source: Authors' calculations.
CBCL = Child Behavior Checklist.
*$p < 0.05$.
a. The total sample size is 3,460. The unweighted number and the weighted percent refer to the number and the weighted percentages of the entire sample that were in ambulatory service or inpatient service.

Table 7-2. *Bivariate Associations between Medicaid Variables
and Receipt of Ambulatory and Independent Inpatient Services*[a]

	Ambulatory services		Inpatient services	
Predictor variable	Unweighted n	Weighted percent	Unweighted n	Weighted percent
State-administered Medicaid	740	17.4	87	2.0
Duration of Medicaid eligibility before recertification required				
Three months	10	47.0	1	6.4
Six months	105	15.4	15	1.9
Twelve months	361	17.5	45	2.6
Some other interval	223	16.8	25	1.6
Children's health insurance status				
Children placed out-of-home eligible to participate in SCHIP	496	17.1	47	1.6
All children placed out-of-home covered under Medicaid	490	17.0	67	2.1
All children placed in-home covered under Medicaid	206	...	31	...
Separate Medicaid program for children in the child welfare system	30	25.7	5	0.2***
Presence of managed behavioral health plans for children and adolescents				
Yes	575	16.6	68	1.6
No	296	20.0	30	2.6
Covered child welfare children under managed behavioral health plans				
Yes	559	17.4	69	1.6
No	312	18.1	29	2.5
Organization of managed behavioral health services				
Carve outs	562	18.1	65	1.4
No carve outs	309	16.7	33	3.0
Provider reimbursement for mental health services				
Some type of fee-for-service	658	17.2	73	1.9
Capitated	213	19.2	25	1.9

Source: Authors' calculations.
SCHIP = State Child Health Insurance Program.
***$p < 0.001$.
a. Weighted model cannot be estimated because all children belong to same stratum.

health care, controlling for child characteristics, provider ratios, and the child's enrollment into managed behavioral health care plans (OR= 0.4, $p < 0.05$). Carve outs are also associated with significantly reduced odds of inpatient care among children insured through Medicaid (not shown). Other variables of policy and provider ratios were not significantly associated with inpatient service use.

Table 7-3. *Odds Ratios of Association between Child or Case Characteristics and Ambulatory Service and Inpatient Service*[a]

Child or case characteristic	Ambulatory service	Inpatient service
Gender		
Male	1.2	1.5
Female (reference group)	1	1
Age	1.1***	1.3**
Race and ethnicity		
Non-Hispanic Black	0.6	0.5
Hispanic	0.6	0.9
Native American and mixed race	0.9	0.2*
Non-Hispanic White (reference group)	1	1
Positive abuse (physical and sexual)	1.3	2.0
Placement		
Out-of-home	1.9**	0.6
In-home (reference group)	1	1
Insurance status		
Private and federal	1.1	1.0
Uninsured	0.4**	0.9
Public (reference group)	1	1
Caregiver's educational level		
Less than high school	1.1	1.6
College educated	1.8**	0.2**
High school or equivalent (reference group)	1	1
CBCL score		
Greater than 63	3.8***	4.6*
Less than or equal to 63 (reference group)	1	1
Child welfare worker assessment of need		
Services required	2.5***	7.7***
Services not required (reference group)	1	1

Source: Authors' calculatons.

CBCL = Child Behavior Checklist.

$p < 0.001$ for ambulatory service; and $F(13, 72) = 10.0$, $p < 0.001$ for inpatient service.

***$p < 0.001$, **$p < 0.01$, *$p < 0.05$.

a. $N = 3,460$. Survey-weighted logistic regressions with $F(13, 72) = 28.87$ (ambulatory service); and $F(13, 72) = 10.0$ (inpatient service); both $p < 0.01$.

Simulation of Carve Out Effects

To study the likely effects of policy changes on the use of inpatient services, we conducted a simple simulation (see Statistical Note for details). If none of the counties carved out mental health care, 3 percent of children would have used inpatient services. If all counties carved out mental health care, 1.6 percent of children would have used inpatient services. If counties that did not previously carve out mental health care began to carve out such services, children in the county's child welfare system would be 50 percent less likely to use inpatient services, controlling for all the variables in the model.

Discussion

We present a comprehensive analysis of the effects of several Medicaid policies on access to ambulatory and inpatient mental health services among a nationally representative sample of children in child welfare systems. Despite the incentives inherent in managed care to limit services, we found no systematic relationship between managed care policies and access to ambulatory mental health services. As previously reported, however, we found that behavioral health carve outs were associated with significant decreases in inpatient mental health service use.[30] Children in counties with behavioral carve outs were 50 percent less likely to be admitted for a mental disorder, controlling for such variables as child sociodemographic characteristics, insurance type, and need. If the mental health needs of children in carve out counties are being addressed on an outpatient basis with less need for inpatient services, behavioral carve outs may be advantageous for children in the child welfare system, as some have argued they are for children needing physical health services.[31] This finding may suggest, then, that carve outs steer children toward ambulatory rather than inpatient settings. However, while the analysis does control for CBCL scores and the child welfare worker's assessment of need for services, the lack of diagnostic information in the data and the inability of the analysis to assess outcomes of children following services limits our ability to draw conclusions regarding the appropriateness of this reduction in inpatient use. Other Medicaid policies, such as the mere presence of Medicaid managed care in the county and variations in provider reimbursement, do not seem to be associated with the use of either ambulatory or inpatient mental health services.

A number of child-level characteristics are associated with access to services. Children who are placed out-of-home have greater odds of ambulatory service use. This finding may reflect access of the out-of-home child to the most appropriate venue of care, because such access is determined by the collective expertise of the child's support network: the child welfare worker, the foster family, and other caregivers. It is also likely that the children with histories of maltreatment that warrant out-of-home placement have the greatest needs for mental health services. This greater need may not be fully captured by the CBCL measure and our analysis, being a selection effect. Being uninsured lowers the odds of ambulatory use more than it does for use of inpatient services, perhaps reflecting the relative inelasticity and urgency of the kinds of needs for which a child requires hospitalization. It is interesting to note that children who have highly educated caregivers are more likely to obtain services in an ambulatory rather than in an inpatient setting, perhaps reflecting the greater resources that highly educated caregivers can deploy to obtain treatment for the child. All of these variables continue to be important even when policy variables are added to the individual model. These findings underline the need for child welfare agencies to focus on children placed out-of-home and give support to efforts by the government to bring more children under an insurance umbrella (such as Insure Kids Now).[32]

Despite the limited numbers of child psychiatrists in absolute and relative terms, the supply of child psychiatrists in a county has a strong association with the use of ambulatory mental health care services. In counties that have one additional child psychiatrist for every 10,000 children, children in the child welfare system have more than twice the odds of obtaining ambulatory mental health services, which perhaps reflects the influence of provider supply on access.[33] It is interesting that the availability of pediatricians and adult psychiatrists has no significant effect on either inpatient or outpatient mental health care. This result could be either a statistical effect reflecting less variability across counties for these specialties than there is for child psychiatrists or a substantive finding reflecting the fact that, because pediatricians and adult psychiatrists are not dependent upon the child mental health market for a major portion of their income, they have less incentive to cause supplier-induced demand.[34] Either of these explanations make it harder to elicit the effects of the supply of these two service providers on inpatient care because only 2 percent of the children in the sample were admitted.

Taken together, the above findings suggest that policymakers in the fields of child welfare and health should consider the role of four agents—caregivers, caseworkers, insurance statutes, and medical providers—that are in position to help children in the child welfare system obtain needed mental health care services. Educated caregivers, aware and activist caseworkers, some type of insurance coverage, and the availability of child psychiatrists all promote the use of services by these children. Out-of-home placement, perhaps by putting caseworkers in charge of children whose parents are unable or unwilling to act as their agents, may also exert an influening role. Medicaid policies, then, seem to be one among a set of interconnected and interdependent factors that ensure mental health care for children in the child welfare system. The development of health policy for children in the child welfare system needs to include these agents if care is to be effectively coordinated. Such an inclusive policy framework has concrete applications. On the supply side, policies that increase the availability of child psychiatrists are likely to affect an increase in the utilization of services by children. On the demand side, caseworker training and universal insurance coverage may also ensure that children receive appropriate care in the child welfare system.

These implications for practice and policy are qualified by a few limitations of this study. First, Medicaid coverage for a child in the child welfare system varies by the child's location and placement status. In all jurisdictions, children become ineligible for Medicaid (and therefore ineligible for Medicaid managed care) if they are detained or incarcerated, because federal law prohibits use of Medicaid funds to serve incarcerated individuals. Within the child welfare system, children who enter residential treatment centers, or who are placed out-of-home, may be removed from Medicaid managed care and covered under traditional Medicaid.[35] These variations in stability of coverage and location are not well captured by the data. Second, primary sampling units within NSCAW and CCCW are not always identical with counties as defined by the Area Resource File. This problem was addressed by matching each of NSCAW's primary sampling units to the appropriate county, but data from 300 children had to be discarded because of persistent and unresolved uncertainty about the health resources environment in which they lived. Finally, because a diagnostic measure within these data sets was lacking, CBCL scores and caseworker assessments were used as measures of need for mental health services. The study's findings, therefore, may not generalize to children with mental and behavioral disorders within the child welfare system, and they are not indicative of the appropriateness of the effects of managed care policies on service use.

In summary, these findings seem to suggest that the majority of Medicaid managed care policies may not have significant consequences, either adverse or positive, for children in the child welfare system. Behavioral carve outs may restrict inpatient mental health care; therefore, states and counties adopting carve out models of Medicaid managed care should pay close attention to service use by children in the child welfare system. Medicaid policy variables, moreover, seem to act in interdependent ways with the actions and attributes of caseworkers, providers, and caregivers. Decisions at the local level about how best to meet the mental health needs of these children should be integrative, taking into account the roles and responsibilities of all of these individuals who care for children. Such an integrative approach to practice and policy may provide the best way for children in the child welfare system to obtain the care they require for their considerable mental health needs.

Statistical Note

All analyses were weighted to account for the complex sampling design of NSCAW that involved stratification and sampling within PSUs (stratum and PSU weights) as well as varying probabilities of selection. We assessed all bivariate associations between predictors and outcomes with simple logistic regression for continuous variables and chi-square analyses of homogeneity for categorical variables. Design-based F statistics were used to assess significance levels.

Two separate sets of survey-weighted multivariate logistic regressions were conducted to examine the relationship between Medicaid policy variables and outcomes of use of ambulatory and inpatient mental health services. First, we constructed and refined a model on the individual by regressing our outcome variables on predisposing, enabling, and need variables using only NSCAW data. We then added policy variables (from CCCW) and health resources variables (from the ARF) to this individual model to conduct our contextual analyses.

For each of these analyses, policy variables were introduced in staged sets to avoid collinearities among policy predictors. A total of seven models were constructed as follows:

—introduction of the variable of whether Medicaid is state or county administered

—examination of the effects of varying recertification intervals for Medicaid

—examination of the SCHIP participation among children in foster care

—examination of the effects of separate Medicaid programs for children in the child welfare system

—examination of the presence of Medicaid managed care in the county

—addition of enrollment of child welfare children into managed care plans and carve outs of mental health services

—introduction of enrollment of child welfare children into managed care plans and type of provider reimbursement

For each of these models, we retained health resources variables and individual covariates.

Significant policy variables were subject to microsimulation modeling. We first estimated existing probabilities of the use of services using the model in which the policy variable was significant. Retaining the specification of this model, we changed the value of the significant variable to 0, indicating that none of the children were subject to that policy, to obtain a probability of the use of services for children not subject to the policy. We then changed the value of the variable to 1 to estimate the probability of service for a set of children with identical characteristics but subject to the policy. We divided the former probability by the latter to determine the effects of adopting the given policy on the use of services; that is, we constructed a relative risk measure of policy adoption.

Only variables significant at the 0.05 level were considered statistically significant in final multivariate models. Standard errors were appropriately corrected for weighting and clustering. We conducted all analyses with Stata version 8.[36]

Notes

1. U.S. Department of Health and Human Services (DHHS), Administration for Children and Families, *Child Maltreatment 2004* (Washington: U.S. Government Printing Office, 2006). (www.acf.hhs.gov/programs/cb/pubs/cm04/index.htm).

2. A wealth of literature, much of it focused on children in foster care, suggests that children in the child welfare system are heavy users of expensive mental health services. A sampling of this literature includes June M. Clausen and others, "Mental Health Problems of

Children in Foster Care," *Journal of Child and Family Studies* 7, no. 3 (September 1998): 283–96; Daniel Pilowsky, "Psychopathology among Children Placed in Family Foster Care," *Psychiatric Services* 46, no. 9 (September 1995): 906–10; Neal Halfon, Ana Mendonca, and Gale Berkowitz, "Health Status of Children in Foster Care: The Experience of the Center for the Vulnerable Child," *Archives of Pediatrics and Adolescent Medicine* 149, no. 4 (April 1995): 386–92; John Landsverk, Ann F. Garland, and Laurel K. Leslie, "Mental Health Services for Children Reported to Child Protective Services," in *APSAC Handbook on Child Maltreatment,* 2d ed., edited by John E. B. Myers and others (Thousand Oaks, Calif.: Sage Publications, 2002), pp. 487–507; Charles Glisson, "Judicial and Service Decisions for Children Entering State Custody: The Limited Role of Mental Health," *Social Science Review* 70, no. 2 (June 1996): 257–81; Neal Halfon, Gale Berkowitz, and Linnea Klee, "Children in Foster Care in California: An Examination of Medicaid Reimbursed Health Services Utilization," *Pediatrics* 89, no. 6, pt. 2 (June 1992): 1230–237; John Takayama, Abraham B. Bergman, and Frederick A. Connell, "Children in Foster Care in the State of Washington: Health Care Utilization and Expenditures," *Journal of the American Medical Association* 271, no. 23 (June 15, 1994) 1850–855; Jeffrey S. Harman, George E. Childs, and Kelly J. Kelleher, "Mental Health Care Utilization and Expenditures by Children in Foster Care," *Archives of Pediatrics and Adolescent Medicine* 154, no. 11 (November 2000): 1114–117; Ann F. Garland and others, "Type of Maltreatment as a Predictor of Mental Health Service Use for Children in Foster Care," *Child Abuse & Neglect* 20, no. 8 (August 1996): 675–88; Barbara J. Burns and others, "Mental Health Need and Access to Mental Health Services by Youths Involved with Child Welfare: A National Survey," *Journal of the American Academy of Child & Adolescent Psychiatry* 43, no. 8 (August 2004): 960–70; Ramesh Raghavan and others, "Psychotropic Medication Use in a National Probability Sample of Children in the Child Welfare System," *Journal of Child and Adolescent Psychopharmacology* 15, no. 1 (February 2005): 97–106.

3. A variety of approaches to, and possible consequences of, Medicaid cost containment are discussed in these three reports: Victoria Wachino, Andy Schneider, and Leighton Ku, "Medicaid Budget Proposals Would Shift Costs to States and Be Likely to Cause Reductions in Health Coverage" (Washington: Center on Budget and Policy Priorities, February 18, 2005); David Rubin and others, "Protecting Children in Foster Care: Why Proposed Medicaid Cuts Harm Our Nation's Most Vulnerable Youth" (Seattle, Wash.: Casey Family Programs, 2005); Families USA, "President's Medicaid Budget Shifts Huge Financial Burden to States" (Washington, February 7, 2005) (www.familiesusa.org/issues/medicaid/medicaid-action/useful-info.html).

4. Abigail English and Madelyn D. Freundlich, "Medicaid: A Key to Health Care for Foster Children and Adopted Children with Special Needs," *Clearinghouse Review* 31 (July-August 1997): 109–31.

5. Ibid.

6. Laurel K. Leslie and others, "Foster Care and Medicaid Managed Care," *Child Welfare* 82, no. 3 (May-June 2003): 367–92.

7. Jan McCarthy and Carl Valentine, "Child Welfare Impact Analysis 1999" (Washington: National Technical Assistance Center for Children's Mental Health, 2000); U.S. General Accounting Office, "Child Welfare and Juvenile Justice: Federal Agencies Could Play a Stronger Role in Helping States Reduce the Number of Children Placed Solely to Obtain Mental Health Services," GAO-03-397 (Washington, 2003) (www.gao.gov/new.items/d03397.pdf).

8. Anne M. Libby and others, "Influences on Medicaid Health Insurance for Children Involved with Child Welfare Services: A National Study" (Denver: University of Colorado, Health Sciences Center, March 21, 2005).

9. Ruth A. Almeida and Harriette B. Fox, "State Medicaid Managed Care Policies Affecting Children" (Washington: Maternal and Child Health Policy Research Center, 1998); Neva Kaye and Cynthia Pernice, *Medicaid Managed Care: A Guide for States,* 4th ed. (Portland, Maine: National Academy for State Health Policy, 1999); Jan McCarthy, "Child Welfare Special Analysis," in Beth A. Stroul, Sheila A. Pires, and Mary I. Armstrong, *Health Care Reform Tracking Project: Tracking State Managed Care Systems as They Affect Children and Adolescents with Behavioral Health Disorders and Their Families—2003 State Survey,* FMHI Publication 212-4 (Tampa, Fla.: Research and Training Center for Children's Mental Health, Department of Child and Family Studies, Division of State and Local Support, Louis de la Parte Florida Mental Health Institute, University of South Florida, 2003), pp. 129–47 (rtckids. fmhi.usf.edu/rtcpubs/hctrking/pubs/2003_statesurvey/default.cfm).

10. U.S. Department of Health and Human Services, "State Profiles of Mental Health and Substance Abuse Services in Medicaid" (Washington: DHHS, Substance Abuse and Mental Health Services Administration, Center for Mental Health Services, 2005).

11. Arleen Leibowitz, Joan Buchanan, and Joyce Mann, "A Randomized Trial to Evaluate the Effectiveness of a Medicaid HMO," *Journal of Health Economics* 11, no. 3 (October 1992): 235–57; Kelly J. Kelleher and Sarah H. Scholle, "Children with Chronic Medical Conditions II: Managed Care Opportunities and Threats," *Ambulatory Child Health* 1, no. 2 (June 1995): 139–46; Sarah H. Scholle and Kelly J. Kelleher, "Children with Chronic Medical Conditions I: Looking for a Medical Home," *Ambulatory Child Health* 1, no. 2 (June 1995): 130–38.

12. Jan McCarthy and Carl Valentine, "Child Welfare Impact Analysis 1999," pp. 6–11.

13. Carve outs are a way to organize service contracts. In a partial carve out, the Medicaid agency might contract with one organization for both physical and mental health services, and this organization then subcontracts with another organization to provide mental health services. In a full carve out, which is the more common model given the consolidation in the mental health plan market, the Medicaid agency contracts with two separate organizations— one for physical health and the other for mental health services.

14. Richard G. Frank and others, "Some Economics of Mental Health 'Carve-outs'," *Archives of General Psychiatry* 53, no. 10 (October 1996): 933–37; Anne E. Brisson and others, "Impact of a Managed Behavioral Health Care Carve-out: A Case Study of One HMO," Working Paper 6242 (Cambridge, Mass.: National Bureau of Economic Research, October 1997).

15. Moira Inkelas, "Incentives in a Medicaid Carve-Out: Impact on Children with Special Health Care Needs," *Health Services Research* 40, no. 1 (February 2005): 79–99.

16. Jan McCarthy and Carl Valentine, "Child Welfare Impact Analysis 1999," p. 8.

17. Ibid., p. 13.

18. Carole R. Gresenz, Xiaofeng Liu, and Roland Sturm, "Managed Behavioral Health Services for Children under Carve-Out Contracts," *Psychiatric Services* 49, no. 8 (August 1998): 1054–058.

19. In a fee-for-service system, the provider bills the health plan for a specified service. The amount billed is usually based on a fee schedule negotiated between the provider and the health plan, and the fee is smaller than (or "discounted" from) the amount the provider would charge a patient who was not part of the plan. This is called discounted fee-for-service and is the most common type of payment mechanism for mental health services. In a capitated model, the health plan pays a provider group a fixed sum of money each month to manage the patient's care—a sum of money that is based on the number of enrollees but is not related to any provided services. Because providers save money when they do not deliver services, they may have an incentive to restrict care. See also Alison Cuellar, Anne Libby, and

Lonnie Snowden, "How Capitated Mental Health Care Affects Utilization by Youth in the Juvenile Justice and Child Welfare Systems," *Mental Health Services Research* 3, no. 2 (June 2001): 61–72.

20. Ramesh Raghavan and others, "Effects of Medicaid Managed Care Policies on Mental Health Service Use among a National Probability Sample of Children in the Child Welfare System," *Children and Youth Services Review* 28, no. 12 (December 2006): 1482–496.

21. John Landsverk and others, "Overview, Design, and Field Experience of 'Caring for Children in Child Welfare': A National Study of the Impact of Organization and Financing Policy on Mental Health Service Provision" (Children's Hospital in San Diego, Child and Adolescent Services Research Center, March 21, 2005).

22. The Area Resource File (ARF) is available from Quality Resource Systems, Fairfax, Virginia (www.arfsys.com).

23. Ronald M. Andersen and Pamela L. Davidson, "Improving Access to Care in America: Individual and Contextual Indicators," in *Changing the U.S. Health Care System,* 2d ed., edited by Ronald M. Andersen, Thomas H. Rice, and Gerald F. Kominski (San Francisco, Calif.: Jossey-Bass, 2001), pp. 3–30.

24. Jody T. Manly, Dante Cicchetti, and Douglas Barnett, "The Impact of Subtype, Frequency, Chronicity, and Severity of Child Maltreatment on Social Competence and Behavior Problems," *Development and Psychopathology* 6, no. 2 (1994): 121–43.

25. Thomas M. Achenbach and Craig Edelbrock, *Manual for the Child Behavior Checklist and Revised Child Behavior Profile* (Burlington: University of Vermont, Department of Psychiatry, 1983).

26. Ann F. Garland and others, "Type of Maltreatment as a Predictor of Mental Health Service Use for Children in Foster Care"; Bonnie T. Zima and others, "Help-Seeking Steps and Service Use for Children in Foster Care," *Journal of Behavioral Health Services and Research* 27, no. 3 (August 2000): 271–85; David J. Kolko, Barbara L. Baumann, and Nicola Caldwell, "Child Abuse Victims' Involvement in Community Agency Treatment: Service Correlates, Short-Term Outcomes, and Relationship to Reabuse," *Child Maltreatment* 8, no. 4 (November 2003): 273-87.

27. Barbara J. Burns and others, *The Child and Adolescent Services Assessment (CASA), Parent Interview and Child Interview* (Durham, N.C.: Developmental Epidemiology Program, Department of Psychiatry, Duke University Medical Center, 1994); Barbara H. Ascher and others, "The Child and Adolescent Services Assessment (CASA): Description and Psychometrics," *Journal of Emotional and Behavioral Disorders* 4, no. 1 (January 1996): 12–20.

28. Barbara J. Burns and others, "Mental Health Need and Access to Mental Health Services by Youths Involved with Child Welfare: A National Survey."

29. These findings differ from other studies using NSCAW data that suggest that neglect is the most common type of abuse. This is because we disaggregate this variable and only code for neglect if it is at least "moderate." We do this because many of the "mild" forms of neglect listed in NSCAW are indistinguishable from circumstances faced by children in poverty. Also the extent to which caregivers can be held responsible when a child lacks "adequate medical, dental, and mental health care" (an indicator of neglect in NSCAW) is unclear, given our contemporary health care system.

30. Ramesh Raghavan and others, "Effects of Medicaid Managed Care Policies on Mental Health Service Use among a National Probability Sample of Children in the Child Welfare System."

31. Arleen Leibowitz, Joan Buchanan, and Joyce Mann, "A Randomized Trial to Evaluate the Effectiveness of a Medicaid HMO"; Kelly J. Kelleher and Sarah H. Scholle, "Children with Chronic Medical Conditions II: Managed Care Opportunities and Threats"; Sarah

Scholle and Kelly J. Kelleher, "Children with Chronic Medical Conditions I: Looking for a Medical Home."

32. Richard Barth, Jill D. Berrick, and Neil Gilbert, *Child Welfare Research Review: Volume 1* (Columbia University Press, 1994); Insure Kids Now (www.insurekidsnow.gov [June 2005]).

33. Donald Pathman, Thomas Ricketts III, and Thomas R. Konrad, "How Adults' Access to Outpatient Physician Services Relates to the Local Supply of Primary Care Physicians in the Rural Southeast," *Health Services Research* 41, no. 1 (2006): 79–102; Lanis Hicks, "Availability and Accessibility of Rural Health Care," *Journal of Rural Health* 6, no. 4 (1990): 485–505; Donald Patrick and others, "Poverty, Health Services, and Health Status in Rural America," *Milbank Quarterly* 66, no. 1 (1988): 105–36.

34. John Wennberg, "On Patient Need, Equity, Supplier-Induced Demand, and the Need to Assess the Outcome of Common Medical Practices," *Medical Care* 23, no. 5 (1985): 512–20.

35. Jan McCarthy, "Child Welfare Special Analysis," p. 141.

36. StataCorp, Stata, version 8 (College Station, Texas, 2003).

8

Systems Integration and Access to Mental Health Care

JOHN A. LANDSVERK, MICHAEL S. HURLBURT, AND LAUREL K. LESLIE

Since the mid-1980s, there has been a significant increase in research and understanding of mental health services for children and adolescents. The initial impetus came from the publication in 1982 of Jane Knitzer's *Unclaimed Children,* which critiqued the lack of integration in mental health services for children and adolescents.[1] The impetus was further stimulated by Beth Stroul and Robert Friedman's 1986 response to Knitzer's work, *A System of Care for Children and Youth with Severe Emotional Disturbances,* presenting principles for delivery of mental health care for children and adolescents.[2] It is now well recognized that children and adolescents with significant mental health needs are found and cared for in multiple sectors of care beyond the specialty mental health sector, including child welfare, juvenile justice, education, general health care and primary care, and alcohol and drug services. In fact, research suggests that more mental health services are delivered to youth in nonspecialty mental health sector services than in the specialty mental health sector.[3] This reality has driven policy efforts to better integrate services across service sectors as reflected by the national Child and Adolescent Service System Program (CASSP) principles, which have been very influential in shaping service delivery policies and funding demonstration models.[4] The positive impact of this integration effort on access to mental health care and better client-level outcomes was assumed in the system-of-care model. However, Leonard Bickman's well-designed landmark studies in Fort Bragg and Stark County, Ohio, found no evidence for positive mental health clinical outcomes following the implementation of system-of-care models, even though both studies demonstrated improved access to a full continuum of specialty mental health care and increased use of outpatient services as opposed to inpatient care.[5] The Fort Bragg and Stark County studies did not address the provision of mental health care for children involved in the child welfare system.

Prior published findings from the National Survey of Child and Adolescent Well-Being (NSCAW) demonstrate high rates of need for mental health services to deal with emotional and behavioral problems assessed in children and adolescents entering the child welfare system. For example, in a study of mental health service use, Barbara Burns and her colleagues reported that "nearly half (48 percent or 960) of the youths aged 2 to 14 years with completed child welfare investigations had clinically significant emotional or behavioral problems," as measured by Thomas M. Achenbach's Child Behavior Checklist (CBCL).[6] Burns and her colleagues further examined the use of specialty mental health services among children involved with child welfare in both in-home and out-of-home settings and found that youths with mental health needs (defined by a clinical range score on the CBCL) were much more likely to receive mental health services than were lower-scoring youths but that only a quarter of such youths received any specialty mental health care during the twelve months surrounding early involvement with the child welfare service system. Furthermore, Laurel K. Leslie and her colleagues examined an additional NSCAW sample of children who had been in out-of-home care for at least twelve months and found that over half of the children ages two to fifteen had received an outpatient mental health service since the time of investigation leading to placement in foster care.[7] Therefore, we now know from the NSCAW study that there are high rates of need for mental health services as well as high rates of use of these services. Even so, these same papers have shown significant levels of unmet need because of the extreme levels of trauma, developmental delay, emotional disorders, and behavioral problems that occur among these youths.

In this chapter we discuss findings from a number of empirical studies that have used data from the National Survey of Child and Adolescent Well-Being and the linked study Caring for Children in Child Welfare (CCCW) to examine access to specialty mental health care for children and youths involved in child welfare. A specific focus of the paper, based on system-of-care principles, is whether access to care increases when there is greater integration between the child welfare and mental health systems, as demonstrated by the number of linkages that have been forged between systems within communities.[8] We also consider whether integration decreases disparities in access to specialty mental health services for youths who are members of racial and ethnic minorities. Thus this paper discusses two of the six mechanisms for improving the quality of health care in the United States set forth in the Institute of Medicine report *Crossing the Quality Chasm,* efficiency and equity.[9]

The need for integrated mental health care for children and adolescents involved with the child welfare system is best framed within the broad goals of the child welfare system: safety, permanence, and well-being. Protecting children (safety) and preserving families (permanence) are the primary responsibilities of the child welfare system. In contrast, the well-being of children served within child welfare requires access to services most often delivered by agencies outside child welfare such as those designed to deliver physical and mental health services, developmental services, and education.[10] Therefore, referral of children and adolescents involved with child welfare to these other service delivery systems and use of their services are critical for attaining the child well-being goal.

Whether the services needed to meet the well-being needs of children in the child welfare system are provided depends on a number of factors. In this chapter we examine the number of system linkages and hypothesize that increased referral to and use of mental health services are related to how well the two systems are connected. Our findings draw on a NSCAW study of policies and procedures related to mental health care, including organizational linkages within communities involved in the NSCAW study. The paper reports on community variations in organizational linkages between child welfare and mental health services as well as screening and assessment protocols used by child welfare systems to identify children in need of mental health care. We also report findings from an initial test of the hypothesis that the degree of cross-system linkage is positively related to the use of mental health care by children and adolescents involved with child welfare services. Finally, we integrate the information from these findings to suggest policy and practice recommendations. We do not report on outcomes for children. We do, however, note that improved access to coordinated mental health does not necessarily equate with better outcomes for the children served if the care provided is ineffective.

Method

NSCAW is a rich source of information for understanding the use of mental health care in child welfare, because this landmark study collected information on service use and standardized the psychometric measures of need for services. However, NSCAW collected little information on policies within child welfare that may serve to improve identification of children and adolescents who need mental health services or on the organization, financing, and supply of mental health services in the study communities. These unsurveyed areas meant that there would be little opportunity to improve services through analysis of regional variation or examination of mental health and child welfare policies related to mental health care. In response, the National Institute of Mental Health (NIMH) funded the Caring for Children in Child Welfare study as a supplemental study to NSCAW. CCCW collected detailed contextual data at the state and local levels on child welfare policies and on the organization and financing of mental health care for children and adolescents involved with the child welfare system.[11] CCCW links this contextual information to the individual-level survey data generated in NSCAW, thereby allowing for the unique opportunity to examine service use for individual children and families within the context of community-level factors. This approach provides much-needed information to agencies and providers planning services on which youths are most in need and what organizational and system designs are best for youths in child welfare.

The CCCW study used the same sampling frame as the NSCAW study, providing data to generate estimates of the number of counties having different policy characteristics and, when linked to NSCAW data, to estimate the number of children affected by different kinds of policies and organizational structures. The CCCW study collected contextual information for the thirty-six states and ninety-seven counties selected by the NSCAW sampling design. Contextual-level information came from three principal sources: semistructured interview data from key informants in relevant agencies at the county or local level, information that has been placed on public websites by state and local agencies or state-level data that has appeared in published or unpublished reports, and contextual indicators available from national secondary data sets such as those available in the Area Resource File.[12] In addition, the CCCW study has used child-level data from the NSCAW study to indicate use of mental health services as well as an array of other child-level variables potentially related to understanding mental health services used in child welfare settings.

The CCCW semistructured interview protocol was developed for telephone administration in two waves of interviewing: wave 1, conducted between September 2000 and June 2001, and wave 2, conducted between February 2003 and March 2004. The final protocol consisted of a set of modules that were used with informants from state, regional, and local agencies to collect information on the policies and systems in place in the public sectors that serve the child welfare system population. Eleven modules were developed for wave 1 and seven modules for wave 2, which examined policies regarding mental health services for children in out-of-home care as well as for those remaining in their homes. Table 8-1 describes the contextual-level domains covered in the data collection process, organized by modules covering the following overall domains: organizational relationships between agencies; organization and financing policies for children and adolescents involved in the child welfare system; screening, assessment, and monitoring policies in the child welfare system; linkages between the system and other agencies; child welfare system

Table 8-1. *Description of Contextual-Level Domains by Wave and Interview Module*

Module name	Targeted agency	Domains
Wave 1		
Overview of county public agency structures	Child welfare	How public agencies are organized and related to state agencies Use of the court-appointed special advocate program
Mental health agency	Mental health	Structure of child services and funding sources Payment mechanisms, reimbursement rates, and managed care Involvement in reform of system of care
Medicaid agency	Medicaid	Structure and administration (of physical and mental health services) Enrollment, payment mechanisms, reimbursement rates, and managed care Programs specific for children in child welfare services
State Child Health Insurance Program (SCHIP)	SCHIP	Structure and administration Enrollment, payment mechanisms, reimbursement rates, and managed care Linkages with child welfare services
Entry screening and standards	Child welfare	Health screening and evaluation on entry into system Comprehensive physical exam on entry Mental health assessment on entry Developmental assessment on entry
Mental health services	Child welfare	Periodic mental health screening and follow-up Access via Medicaid or SCHIP Access for uninsured Child welfare facilitation and coordination of care, use of a multidisciplinary service plan, use of health passport Consent issues Court involvement in mental health services
Developmental services	Child welfare– early intervention programs	Periodic developmental screening and follow-up Access via Medicaid or SCHIP Access for uninsured Child welfare facilitation and coordination of care, use of a multidisciplinary service plan, use of health passport Consent issues Court involvement in developmental services

Module name	Targeted agency	Domains
Mental health agency linkages	Child welfare	Relationship-shared mechanisms, coordination of care, memorandums of understanding Involvement of child welfare in mental health managed care
Medicaid linkages	Child welfare	Relationship-shared mechanisms, coordination of care, memorandums of understanding Involvement of child welfare services in Medicaid managed care Coordination of application process, recertification, continuous eligibility Proportions of children on Medicaid by placement
Training of caregiver and child welfare staff	Child welfare	Required or optional: when, hours, topic Mental health and developmental resources available
Placement information	Child welfare	Initial placement proportions and percentages in in-home and out-of-home care Average placement changes per year Licensing requirements and reimbursement rates by placement type
Wave 2		
Use of child welfare services funds for mental health services	Child welfare	Types of services funded, provider, location, criteria, and reasons for use
Mental health service providers	Child welfare	Identification of primary mental health providers for child welfare services, overall impressions, barriers to care
Child welfare services and local juvenile justice program	Child welfare	Shared mechanisms, coordination of care, memorandums of understanding
Out-of-home placements	Child welfare	Availability, criteria, oversight
Parent training	Child welfare	Types of training available, requirements for in-home, out-of-home, and reunified cases
Medicaid and SSI	Child welfare	Use of managed care, application process
Status offenders and adjudicated delinquent youths	Child welfare	Use of shared supervision with child welfare services, placements, funding

Source: Authors' calculations.
SSI = Supplemental Security Income.

training for caregivers and agency staff (two separate modules); and child welfare system placement policies.

Findings

We present findings related to access to mental health care from two papers using data from the CCCW study. The first paper, by Leslie and her colleagues, used CCCW data at the primary sampling unit level to examine community variation in policies relating to assessment practices in child welfare for mental health and developmental needs of children entering out-of-home care.[13] The second paper by, Michael S. Hurlburt and others, used community-level data from the CCCW study that was then linked to child-level data from the NSCAW study to examine how patterns of specialty mental health service use might vary as a function of the degree of coordination between local child welfare and mental health agencies.[14] These findings are used to draw implications for policy and practice.

Comprehensive Assessments for Children Entering Foster Care

One module of the CCCW interview, entitled "Entry Screening and Services," specifically addressed assessments performed within the first thirty days of entry into foster care. The module consisted of four sections: initial health screenings, comprehensive physical health examinations, mental health assessments, and developmental assessments for children aged five and younger. To differentiate between the initial health screening and the comprehensive physical exam, informants were first asked whether they provide an initial health screening and then were asked to clarify whether the health screening is done in addition to a later, more comprehensive, physical exam or as part of a comprehensive physical exam.

For each domain (physical, mental, and developmental health), a series of six questions was asked:

—Does the county have any written policies in place that require this assessment for any children? If yes, is it for all children or only for specific groups of children entering out-of-home care?

—Does the county have any formal system or program in place to ensure that children receive this assessment? If yes, is it for all children or only for specific subgroups of children entering out-of-home care?

—On average, what percentage of children entering out-of-home care actually receives this assessment?

—What is the primary location where these assessments occur?

—Who is the primary provider of these assessments?

—Does your PSU require any specific measure or tool for this assessment?

A measure or tool was defined to include any standardized questionnaire or directly administered screening or evaluation test that was used to assess physical, mental, or developmental health. The specific tools used and details regarding the tools (for example, screening test versus evaluation) were not obtained during this wave of interviews. In addition, questions were not asked regarding the specific content of the health examination during this wave of interviews.

Using these methods, the contextual study found significant geographic variation in policies relating to assessment practices for mental health and developmental needs of children entering child welfare systems. The study found that 94 percent of the areas assessed all children entering foster care for physical health problems, but only 48 percent had policies for assessing mental health problems. Less than half (43 percent) provided comprehensive physical, mental health, and developmental examinations inclusive of all children entering out-of-home care, and almost none reported using assessment protocols for children involved with child welfare but not placed in out-of-home care.

Impact of Linkage Mechanisms between Child Welfare and Mental Health

The strength of existing ties between child welfare and mental health agencies at the local level (linkages) was assessed through two different interview modules, one focusing on mental health services available to children in child welfare and one focusing on characteristics of the mental health agency in the county. Linkages were defined on the basis of twenty-six concrete indicators of linkage between the two local agencies that had been adapted from the Access program by Joseph Cocozza and others,[15] for example, co-location of child welfare and mental health services, existence of a formal child welfare committee reviewing mental health service use on a case-by-case basis, shared office space, joint service provision at the caseworker level, and joint trainings).

Caregivers responded to questions about children's mental health services in an adapted version of the Child and Adolescent Services Assessment.[16] The current study included information on the use of outpatient specialty mental health services from investigation onset for roughly one year, including clinic-based specialty mental health services such as community mental health clinics, therapeutic nursery, day treatment, and private professionals, such as psychiatrists, psychologists, social workers, and psychiatric nurses.

Using these methods, the linkage study found significant variation in the degree of linkages between child welfare and mental health. The research team also used the NSCAW survey with child welfare participants to examine how patterns of specialty mental health service use might vary as a function of the degree of coordination between local child welfare and mental health agencies. After controlling for the usual predictors of use such as need as measured by the Achenbach Child Behavior Checklist, age, type of placement, and race or ethnicity, the investigators found that increased coordination between child welfare and mental health agencies was associated with a stronger relationship between need and service use and decreased differences in rates of service use between Caucasian and African American children.[17]

Discussion

The two papers using the CCCW and NSCAW studies data add to the rapidly growing body of empirical knowledge about the need for and use of mental health services by children involved with the child welfare system. They also demonstrate how the NSCAW study represents an important opportunity to test whether findings from local area studies are replicated at the national level and the impact of contextual factors on patterns of use. Here we discuss the implications of this body of knowledge for improving access to mental health in child welfare.

Identification and Referral

The high rate of need for mental health services in the foster care population and the full child welfare population (including those who remain in their own homes) indicates that a comprehensive screening protocol is needed. The screening should use standardized measures across multiple domains with clear subsequent linkage to full clinical assessment for children and adolescents screening positive. Children should then be referred to clinical services with specific interventions as appropriate. There is some question as to whether simple screening, which is appropriate when low base rates of a condition prevail in a population, is a useful approach for a population of children with such high base rates. A number of studies of child welfare systems in diverse states suggest a very high base rate for children and adolescents entering foster care, and the NSCAW study extends this finding to the larger population of children and adolescents involved with the full child welfare system. Therefore, a procedure that uses a kind of comprehensive low-level assessment for a wide range of problems in psychosocial functioning and based on standardized measures should be considered as a routine first step in assessing children entering the child welfare population. The findings from these low-level assessments should then be used to trigger full clinical assessments in areas of need using professional personnel. Although assessment protocols for children entering out-of-home care have been implemented in a number of agencies, these protocols are not likely to cover children served by child welfare who are not in out-of-home care. Given the comparable rates of problems in both out-of-home and in-home settings, full coverage for all children involved with the child welfare system should be seriously considered. The findings from CCCW noted previously found that less than half of the child welfare agencies provided comprehensive physical, mental health, and developmental examinations of all children entering out-of-home care, and almost none reported assessment protocols for children involved with child welfare but not placed in out-of-home care.

Recent studies also suggest that screening and assessment protocols need to be comprehensive in scope and specific in a wide range of developmentally appropriate domains in order to facilitate better treatment planning. This policy recommendation implies that broad-based behavioral problem checklists such as the Child Behavior Checklist may not be sufficient for developing the detailed clinical profiles critical for good treatment planning. Examples of a comprehensive assessment strategy for children entering foster care have been published by Mark D. Simms and by Neal Halfon and others.[18] These protocols cover a wide range of domains relevant to psychosocial functioning and constitute an excellent foundation for future work. Nevertheless, there is a need for assessment-referral practice guidelines with wide support from experienced clinicians that can be implemented by most child welfare systems. The development of these guidelines will require extensive collaboration between the child welfare system, the mental health system, and the medical care system.[19]

Overall, what we are suggesting is that a multistage screening to clinical assessment procedure would be most appropriate in assisting the child welfare population, which presents a high rate of complex problems. We also recommend greater use of standardized measures with levels of problem detail that fall somewhere between usual screening measures and full clinical assessment; such measures would make the proposed multistage procedure less costly in terms of efficient use of expensive clinician time for those children and adolescents who exhibit strong need for care at earlier stages of the procedure. The development and implementation of this multistage procedure will require much greater coordination between the child welfare and mental health sectors than is usually observed in community systems of care. Finally, we would observe that the public health impact of this type of coordinated and systematic procedure will be much greater if the high rates of need for care are acknowledged and dealt with in the in-home child welfare population as well as the out-of-home foster care population.

Linkage of Child Welfare and Mental Health Service Systems

The high rate of mental health service use observed for children in foster care suggests that the child welfare system and the mental health system may be more strongly linked than commonly thought. In California, Washington State, and Pennsylvania, there is consistent evidence that the foster care system may serve as an important gateway into the mental health system for children who have been abused or neglected.[20] Data from North Carolina suggest that this gateway may also serve children who are in contact with child welfare who do not enter out-of-home settings, a finding that has been replicated in the NSCAW sample.[21] In fact, a recently published paper by Leslie and colleagues presents evidence from NSCAW that although placement in foster care was associated with the highest rate of mental health service use, greater use of mental health services was observed for families with an open child welfare case and even for families receiving only investigation services without a subsequent child welfare case being opened.[22] Since these two systems share many child and adolescent clients, more explicit collaborative ties directed at improving the efficiency of service delivery need to be forged. The important findings by Hurlburt and others that increased coordination between these two systems is associated with greater use by children at the highest level of need and with decreased racial and ethnic disparities in receipt of mental health care is very promising in suggesting that explicit links, such as those used in the CCCW study to measure coordination, could be programmatically targeted.[23] Research would then be needed to evaluate whether the linkages can be programmatically implemented with outcomes comparable to those found in the nonexperimental observation study reported in this paper.

It would appear that the Medicaid program, as categorically applied to children in foster care, provides a powerful impetus to the provision of mental health services to this specialized population. Medicaid is currently undergoing a major transition to a managed care form of service delivery. We do not know how this shift in the organization and financing of mental health care will affect the mental health treatment of children in foster care. The policy implication is that leaders of the child welfare system and foster care systems need to be proactive in developing managed care contracting within the Medicaid program in collaboration with the managers of public mental health systems.[24]

There is little information available about the impact of exits from foster care on the continuity of mental health care for these high-risk children. Further study is necessary to determine whether children are only receiving mental health services when they are within the foster care system or whether these treatment services continue across the major permanency plans of reunification and adoption as well as exit from foster care at majority. The potential negative impact of developmental problems and behavior problems on exits from foster care would suggest the continued need for mental health services when exits are considered or completed.

Finally, the widespread use of mental health services for this specialized population is not accompanied by systematic monitoring of service outcomes for the children receiving these services. No studies have been published to date that examined either the quality of care being provided through mental health services or the outcomes of those services. We do not know whether the services are effective in ameliorating the mental health problems observed in children involved with the child welfare system or even those entering foster care. There is a clear need for efficient monitoring of developmental, behavioral, social, and adaptive functioning for children in foster care who are receiving mental health services. Systems of accountability need to be developed to determine the course of treatment at the level of the individual foster child.

A Cautionary Note and Promising New Direction

The primary focus of this chapter is access to mental health care for the high-risk population of children and adolescents involved with child welfare. However, improving access to care does not guarantee that the care received will provide the benefits needed and therefore will improve child well-being. In fact, the research studies by Bickman, undertaken in Ohio, on the impact of systems of care (noted in the introduction to this chapter) represent a clear example of change in access that is not associated with better outcomes.[25] John R. Weisz also has presented meta-analyses of outcomes of usual public mental health care that demonstrate a lack of effectiveness of this care.[26] Although Bickman and Weisz in their studies do not address effectiveness of mental health care specifically for children involved with child welfare, most of the care received by the child welfare population is provided by public mental health systems under Medicaid funding, suggesting that great caution must be taken when any predictions are made that greater access will necessarily result in greater benefit.

However, we also point to a promising new direction that does address the effectiveness of care, namely, rethinking the provision of mental health care by service systems outside the child welfare system.[27] A number of studies have shown that children involved in child welfare demonstrate a high rate of externalizing or disruptive behavior problems.[28] The most promising treatment for these behavior problems uses intensive forms of parent training to change parents' response to their child's problems in lieu of working directly with the child in typical therapy sessions. Recently, Philip A. Fisher and Patricia Chamberlain have demonstrated promising outcomes from the use of Multidimensional Treatment Foster Care, and Chamberlain and others have shown promising outcomes with relative and nonrelative foster parents with a modified version of Multidimensional Treatment Foster Care.[29] In related work, Mark Chaffin and others have demonstrated the effectiveness of Parent-Child Interaction Therapy with biological parents who have had their children placed in foster care.[30] This research direction is taking evidence-based mental health interventions directly into child welfare settings and shows great promise for improving child well-being by strengthening the responses of substitute and biological parents to behavior problems of children and adolescents.[31]

Notes

1. Jane Knitzer, *Unclaimed Children: The Failure of Public Responsibility to Children and Adolescents in Need of Mental Health Services* (Washington: Children's Defense Fund, 1982).

2. Beth Stroul and Robert Friedman, *A System of Care for Children and Youth with Severe Emotional Disturbances,* rev. ed. (Washington: Georgetown University, Child Development Center, CASSP Technical Assistance Center, 1986). The core values of the system-of-care philosophy specify that services should be community based, child centered, family focused, and culturally competent. The guiding principles are that services should be comprehensive; individualized to each child and family; provided in the least restrictive, appropriate setting; coordinated both at the system and service delivery levels; involve families and youth as full partners; and emphasize early identification and intervention.

3. Barbara J. Burns and others, "Children's Mental Health Service Use across Service Sectors," *Health Affairs* 14, no. 3 (1995): 147–59.

4. Charles Day and Michael C. Roberts, "Activities of the Child and Adolescent Service System Program for Improving Mental Health Services for Children and Families," *Journal of Clinical Child Psychology* 20 (1991): 340–50.

5. Leonard Bickman, "Implications of a Children's Mental Health Managed Care Demonstration Project," *Journal of Mental Health Administration* 23 (1996): 107–17; Leonard Bickman, "Reinterpreting the Fort Bragg Evaluation Findings: The Message Does Not Change," *Journal of Mental Health Administration* 23 (1996): 137–45; Leonard Bickman and others, *Evaluating Managed Mental Health Care: The Fort Bragg Experiment* (New York: Plenum, 1995); Leonard Bickman and others, "The Stark County Evaluation Project: Baseline Results of a Randomized Experiment," in *Evaluating Mental Health Services,* edited by Cynthia Nixon and Denese Northrup (Thousand Oaks, Calif.: Sage, 1997), pp. 23–58.

6. Barbara J. Burns and others, "Mental Health Need and Access to Mental Health Services by Youths Involved with Child Welfare: A National Survey," *Journal of the American Academy of Child & Adolescent Psychiatry* 43, no. 8 (2004): 960–70.

7. Laurel K. Leslie and others, "Outpatient Mental Health Services for Children in Foster Care: A National Perspective," *Child Abuse & Neglect* 28, no. 6 (2004): 697–712.

8. Beth Stroul and Robert Friedman, *A System of Care for Children and Youth with Severe Emotional Disturbances.*

9. Institute of Medicine, *Crossing the Quality Chasm: A New Health System for the 21st Century* (Washington: National Academy Press, 2001).

10. Fred Wulczyn and others, *Beyond Common Sense: Child Welfare, Child Well-Being, and the Evidence for Policy Reform* (Piscataway, N.J.: Aldine Transaction, 2005), pp. 7ff.

11. Laurel K. Leslie and others, "Comprehensive Assessments for Children Entering Foster Care: A National Perspective," *Pediatrics* 112, no. 1 (2003): 134–42.

12. The Area Resource File, a national county-level health resource information database, is maintained by Quality Resource Systems, Inc. (www.arfsys.com).

13. Laurel K. Leslie and others, "Comprehensive Assessments for Children Entering Foster Care."

14. Michael S. Hurlburt and others, "Contextual Predictors of Mental Health Service Use among Children Open to Child Welfare," *Archives of General Psychiatry* 61, no. 12 (December 2004): 1184–296.

15. Joseph J. Cocozza and others, "Successful Systems Integration Strategies: The Access Program for Persons Who Are Homeless and Mentally Ill," *Administration Policy in Mental Health* 27 (2000): 395–407.

16. Barbara H. Ascher and others, "The Child and Adolescent Service Assessment (CASA): Description and Psychometrics," *Journal of Emotional and Behavioral Disorders* 4, no. 1 (1996): 12–20.

17. Thomas M. Achenbach, *Integrative Guide for the 1991 CBCL/4-18, YSR, and TRF Profiles* (Burlington: University of Vermont, Department of Psychiatry, 1991).

18. Mark D. Simms, "The Foster Care Clinic: A Community Program to Identify Treatment Needs of Children in Foster Care," *Journal of Developmental and Behavioral Pediatrics* 10 (1989): 121–28; Neal Halfon and others, "Health Status of Children in Foster Care: The Experience of the Center for the Vulnerable Child," *Archives of Pediatric and Adolescent Medicine* 149 (April 1955): 386–92.

19. Jane Knitzer and Susan Yelton, "Collaborations between Child Welfare and Mental Health: Both Systems Must Exploit the Program Possibilities," *Public Welfare* 48 (1990): 24–33.

20. See Elizabeth M. Z. Farmer and others, "Use of Mental Health Services by Youth in Contact with Social Services," *Social Services Review* 75 (2001): 605–24; Neal Halfon and others, "Children in Foster Care in California: An Examination of Medicaid Reimbursed Health Services Utilization," *Pediatrics* 89 (June 1992a): 1230–237; Neal Halfon and others, "Mental Health Service Utilization by Children in Foster Care in California," *Pediatrics* 89 (June 1992b): 1238–244; Jeffrey S. Harman and others, "Mental Health Care Utilization and Expenditures by Children in Foster Care," *Archives of Pediatric and Adolescent Medicine* 154, no. 11 (2000): 1114–117; John Landsverk and others, "Psychological Impact of Child Maltreatment: Final Report to the National Center on Child Abuse and Neglect" (San Diego, Calif.: Child and Family Research Group, 1996); John L. Takayama and others, "Children in Foster Care in the State of Washington: Health Care Utilization and Expenditures," *Journal of the American Medical Association* 271 (June 1994): 1850–855.

21. See Elizabeth M. Z. Farmer and others, "Use of Mental Health Services by Youth in Contact with Social Services."

22. Laurel K. Leslie and others, "Entry into Foster Care: A Gateway to Mental Health Services?" *Psychiatric Services* 56 (2005): 981–87.

23. Michael S. Hurlburt and others, "Contextual Predictors of Mental Health Service Use."

24. See Ramesh Raghavan and Arleen Leibowitz, "Medicaid and Mental Health Care for Children in the Child Welfare System" (chapter 7, this volume).

25. See Leonard Bickman, "Implications of a Children's Mental Health Managed Care Demonstration Project"; Leonard Bickman, "Reinterpreting the Fort Bragg Evaluation Findings"; Leonard Bickman and others, *Evaluating Managed Mental Health Care;* Leonard Bickman and others, "Stark County Evaluation Project."

26. John R. Weisz and others, "Effects of Psychotherapy with Children and Adolescents Revisited: A Meta-Analysis of Treatment Outcome Studies," *Psychological Bulletin* 117 (May 1995): 450–68.

27. See discussion in Fred Wulczyn and others, *Beyond Common Sense,* chapter 6.

28. See June Madsen Clausen and others, "Mental Health Problems of Children in Foster Care," *Journal of Child and Family Studies* 7, no. 3 (September 1998): 283–96; John Landsverk and others, "Mental Health Services for Children Reported to Child Protective Services," in *APSAC Handbook on Child Maltreatment,* 2d ed., edited by John E. B. Myers and others (Thousand Oaks, Calif.: Sage, 2002), pp. 487–507; Daniel Pilowsky, "Psychopathology among Children Placed in Family Foster Care," *Psychiatric Services* 46, no. 9 (September 1995): 906–10; Mark D. Simms and Neal Halfon, "The Health Care Needs of Children in Foster Care: A Research Agenda," *Child Welfare* 73, no. 5 (September-October 1994): 505–24.

29. Patricia Chamberlain, "The Oregon Multidimensional Treatment Foster Care Model: Features, Outcomes, and Progress in Dissemination," *Cognitive and Behavioral Practice* 10 (Fall 2003): 303–12; Philip A. Fisher and Patricia Chamberlain, "Multidimensional Treatment Foster Care: A Program for Intensive Parenting, Family Support, and Skill Building," *Journal of Emotional and Behavioral Disorders* 8, no. 3 (Fall 2000): 155–64; Patricia Chamberlain and others, "Enhanced Services and Stipends for Foster Parents: Effects on Retention Rates and Outcomes for Children," *Child Welfare* 71 (September-October 1992): 387–401; Patricia Chamberlain and others, "Who Disrupts from Placement in Foster and Kinship Care?" *Child Abuse & Neglect* 30, no. 4 (April 2006): 409–24.

30. Mark Chaffin and others, "Parent-Child Interaction Therapy with Physically Abusive Parents: Efficacy for Reducing Future Abuse Reports," *Journal of Consulting and Clinical Psychology* 72, no. 3 (June 2004): 500–10.

31. See Raghavan and Leibowitz, chapter 7 of this volume.

9

Predictors of Reunification

JUDITH WILDFIRE, RICHARD P. BARTH,
AND REBECCA L. GREEN

The quest for permanency begins the day a child enters out-of-home placement. Many children who enter out-of-home placement will ultimately
be reunified with their biological families. Yet there is no clear understanding of
the reasons why some children return home while others remain in out-of-home
placement for extended periods of time or enter into other living arrangements
such as adoption, independent living, or relative guardianships. This paper
examines two questions relating to reunification. First, what are the characteristics of children who are reunified with their biological families? Second, how do
activities of child welfare agencies and actions of permanent caregivers influence
the rate of reunification?

Reunification is, on the whole, the most likely end result of any given foster
care placement. Although there are subgroups of children for whom an alternative form of permanency such as adoption is quite likely (for example, children
younger than six-months-old who are placed out-of-home), reunification is still
more likely for nearly every age group.[1] In a 1990 cohort from ten states, reunification was the most common reason for leaving foster care during the first
three years after placement. The median duration of care for reunified cases is
less than one year, whereas the median duration is close to thirty-five months for
children who are adopted. Although recent child welfare reforms are showing
strong evidence of a narrowing of the difference in the length of stays between
adopted children and those who are reunified, there can be little doubt from the

155

national data collected as part of the Adoption and Foster Care Analysis and Reporting System (AFCARS) or from state data sources that reunification is the predominant reason for leaving foster care during the early years.[2]

Administrative data collected by child welfare agencies to document case activity are often the basis for examining the achievement of permanency, including reunification, for children in foster care.[3] These studies usually include the age of the child, race and ethnicity of the child, child's gender, type of most serious maltreatment, and initial type of placement. Yet these studies often lack meaningful data about salient child and parental behaviors and family circumstances. Because the National Survey of Child and Adolescent Well-Being (NSCAW) has many additional possible predictors, reunification can be studied for a nationally representative sample of children using a larger array of child characteristics than are available to most studies done to date. For this paper, these additional predictors include behavior problems measured by the Child Behavior Checklist (CBCL), family risk factors, previous or current substance abuse by the permanent caregiver, and history of involvement with the child welfare system. This study is also able to consider case activity such as parental participation in developing the case plan, youth placement in the youth's own neighborhood, and family receipt of parenting support services. Like many previous studies of reunification, adoption, or independent living, this study examines only predictors of one exit pathway, reunification.[4]

Previous efforts to understand the dynamics of reunification have examined a wide array of factors, some of which have been found to be correlated with reunification. A child's age and race are found routinely to be related to reunification. Very young children are the least likely to return home, while adolescents return home more quickly.[5] Recent research suggests that age and placement outcomes are related in ways that can involve very small age spans. So, the likelihood of reunification for children younger than one year of age who are placed into foster care is only about 35 percent, whereas the reunification rate for children aged one to five is more than 50 percent.[6] Moreover, children placed into foster care when they are younger than age one are almost equally likely to be adopted as to be reunified.[7] This low likelihood of reunification is almost certainly influenced by the factors that cause infants to enter care, such as abandonment and prenatal drug exposure. Some, but probably a relatively small percentage, of these cases are also likely to be expedited for adoption because they meet state criteria for cases that do not require reunification efforts.[8] Reunification of young children may result in especially risky developmental circumstances when it fails, making reunification a less attractive option when few postreunification services exist.[9] These significant factors that contribute to the likelihood that children under the age of one will not be reunified, combined with the greater attractiveness of young children to adoptive families, result in higher adoption rates for this group.[10]

Many studies have found that children of color are less likely to return home than other children.[11] More in-depth analyses have found that race sometimes interacts with other variables to produce racial effects on reunification. In a study by Wells and Guo, there was no difference in the reunification rate by race for children older than thirteen years of age; in a separate study by Goerge, Black children living in an urban setting were slower to return home than were White children in the same city, but this racial difference was not observed in other parts of the state.[12] Finally, studies using administrative data have shown that as more factors that are correlated with race are included in the analyses, the effects of race, though sometimes mediated, continue to be associated with reunification rates.[13]

Other child characteristics found to be related to reunification in addition to age and race include child behavioral problems and prenatal drug exposure. A study conducted in San Diego County found that children with behavioral problems were less likely to return home than were children without problems.[14] A study of infants and toddlers in six California counties found that children exposed to drugs and alcohol prenatally were less likely to return home.[15]

In addition to these studies that showed the effects of child characteristics on reunification rates, some reunification studies have found that parental and family characteristics influence the rate of reunification. Children from drug-affected families had slower reunification rates.[16] Since parents receiving mental health services often require more time before they are considered capable of caring for their children than courts allow for reunification, one study identified parents requiring mental health care as being at a disadvantage in reunification efforts.[17] Finally, familial economic status had an impact on reunification in some studies. "Reasons of poverty" were related to reunification in a study by Eamon and Kopels that examined court cases, while Kortenkamp, Geen, and Stagner found that parents who were employed at the time when a child was placed out-of-home were more likely to reunify with the child.[18]

Although child and family characteristics are often found to be related to reunification, studies that examine the impact of agency practice and parental interactions with the agency may offer the most promise for understanding how to increase reunification rates for children. Researchers have routinely examined the relationship between type of out-of-home placement and reunification. In some studies, children in kinship homes had longer times to reunification, but shorter times in other studies.[19] And in yet another study, Wells and Guo found no difference in reunification rates between kinship care and nonkinship care in Cleveland.[20]

Some studies have shown that family-centered child welfare practice, parental visitation, and parental involvement in case activities increase the likelihood of reunification.[21] Although scientific evidence does not yet exist for many promising practices, child welfare workers are implementing practices such as neighborhood-based foster care, collaboration between foster parents and birth parents, and team decisionmaking with the hope that these will result in faster reunifications.[22]

Federal law seeks to shorten the amount of time it takes to achieve permanency for children in out-of-home placement. The law requires states to initiate the termination of parental rights for children who have been in foster care for fifteen of the past twenty-two months, unless the agency can demonstrate that termination is not in the best interests of the child. This time frame, however, may not account for the complexity of the interactions that have to be considered before a decision is made (such as court continuations, the time required to achieve and maintain sobriety, the length of time needed for mental health services, and so on).

Previous studies have analyzed the relationship of child characteristics, family risk factors, and agency practices to reunification, often focusing on only one group of factors. Although this paper also examines reunification, it includes in the same models multiple factors concerning the child, family, and agency, and it can assess the relationship of each to reunification while controlling for the others.

Methods

Of the 5,501 children in the NSCAW sample, 1,568 children entered out-of-home placement at least once during the eighteen months following entry into the sample. By the end of the eighteen-month period, 463 of these children had returned to their own home, 120 had left out-of-home placement to live with a relative, 3 were adopted, and 982 remained in placement. Our analyses examine the rate of reunification for study children following the first episode of out-of-home placement, with reunification defined as "returning to own home."[23]

We examine three categories of factors potentially related to reunification: child-specific characteristics, familial risk factors, and actions of the agency or parent following a report of abuse or neglect. Child-specific factors include race and ethnicity, gender, an overall score on a mental health rating scale (for children older than two years), type of abuse, and self-reported delinquent activity for youths between eleven- and fifteen-years-old. Familial risk factors, which are reported by the child welfare worker, include active substance abuse, recent arrest, history of domestic violence, history of contact with the child welfare system, and whether the family had difficulty paying basic living expenses (which is a proxy for poverty). In addition to these single indicator variables, a cumulative score of risk is included that aggregates all family risk factors into one risk score. All identified risk items are summed so that families are assigned into risk categories based upon tertiles (low, medium, high). Agency or parent actions, reported by the child welfare worker and by older youths include type of initial placement, participation of the permanent caregiver in developing the case plan, family member adherence to the case plan, and receipt of parenting services by the family member. Youths older than eleven years were asked about moving to a new neighborhood and the frequency of contact with their mother after placement.

The analyses begin by providing bivariate descriptive information on the characteristics of children who entered out-of-home care and then compare children who were reunited with their families or placed with a relative with children who remain in out-of-home placement. Since the number of children who were subsequently placed with a relative is small, it was not possible to fit multivariate models with the variables of interest. Thus the examination of secondary placement into relative care ends here. Summary information is presented on the amount of time children spend in out-of-home placement before returning home. We then make a statistical estimate of the probability of reunification by eighteen months for children by age and race. Models that estimate the relative rate of reunification within eighteen months for children with different characteristics and risk factors complete the analyses.

We employ statistical models to test the relationship between characteristics and actions of the child, family, and agency and the relative rate of reunification. These models calculate a relative risk ratio for each variable entered into the model. The risk ratio estimates the relative rate of reunification for children with different characteristics. For example, a relative risk ratio equal to 2.0 for Hispanic children, when compared with that of White children (the reference group in the model), means that Hispanic children are twice as likely to be reunified by the eighteen-month mark. Conversely, a relative risk ratio of less than 1 for Black children signifies that they are less likely to be reunified than White children. The inclusion of other variables in the model results in a relative risk ratio that controls for the relationship of other characteristics of the child and family to reunification.

Before multivariate analyses were conducted, we determined the correlation between family risk factors and subsequent agency and parental actions. A significant correlation indicated the need to include a specific familial risk factor in models that examined the relationship between actions of the agency and parent and reunification.

Since children of different ages have different experiences in out-of-home placement, the models are age specific. There are five age strata: birth to six months, seven months to two years, three to five years, six to ten years, and older than ten years. Models that include only child-specific characteristics compose the first phase of modeling. To determine whether familial risk factors increased the explanatory power of the model, the next phase of modeling adds familial risk factors to the age-specific basic models. All individual familial risk factors found to be significantly correlated with reunification are added to the basic model. To this second model we then add, one at a time, each agency and parent action plus any additional correlated familial risk factors. After individually testing all agency and parent actions, we fit a combined model that includes all agency and parent actions that achieved a specified level of significance ($p <$ 0.10) in the individual models. For some models it is necessary to collapse categorical variables into fewer groups to achieve stable estimates.

Results

Of 1,565 children (three children were adopted so they were subsequently dropped from the analyses) who entered out-of-home placement at any time during the first eighteen months of the study, 30 percent were reunified by the time the eighteen-month follow-up interview was completed. Table 9-1 presents descriptive statistics for these children placed in out-of-home care, by total number of children as well as by reunification status at eighteen months. Approximately one-quarter (24 percent) of the children placed in out-of-home care were two years old or younger at baseline, which was the same percentage for the group aged eleven or older. One-fifth were between three and five years of age; approximately one-third (32 percent) were between six and ten years of age. The sample has a slightly higher proportion of females (53 percent) and White children (41 percent). Slightly over one-third (36 percent) were Black; 17 percent were Hispanic.

Just less than half (47 percent) of the children were initially placed in foster homes or therapeutic foster homes; approximately one-quarter (24 percent) were placed with a relative or friend; 29 percent were initially placed in group homes or in other out-of-home arrangements.[24] For three-fifths (60 percent) of children placed in out-of-home care, neglect (failure to provide or failure to supervise) was reported as their primary type of maltreatment. About one-quarter (23 percent) were physically abused; 7 percent were sexually abused. The mental health score indicates that behavior problems were at a borderline or clinical level at baseline for almost half (45 percent) of the children placed in out-of-home care.

According to the baseline risk assessment, 29 percent and 21 percent of the permanent primary caregivers of these children were active drug or alcohol abusers, respectively. About one-third (32 percent) of the caregivers had a recent history of arrest. Almost half (47 percent) had trouble paying for basic necessities. The overall cumulative risk score that combines multiple familial risk factors is considered high for approximately half (48 percent) of the cases and medium for another 30 percent. Families in approximately half (49 percent) the cases had previous child welfare experience.

By the time of the eighteen-month interview, only about one-third (36 percent) of permanent caregivers, usually parents, had completed most or all of the

Table 9-1. *Characteristics of Children Placed in Out-of-Home Care and Their Parents, by Placement Status at Eighteen-Month Interview*[a]

Characteristic	Total (N = 1,565) percent	Still in care (n = 982) percent	Reunified (n = 463) percent	Left care to live with relative (n = 120) percent
Child age at baseline				
Younger than 7 months	8	9	7	7
7 months–2 years	16	14	19	29
3–5 years	20	23	13	14
6–10 years	32	32	34	19
11–15 years	24	23	27	32
Child gender				
Male	47	43	54	59
Female	53	57	46	41
Child race and ethnicity				
Non-Hispanic Black	36	40	26	44
Non-Hispanic White	41	40	48	26
Hispanic	17	15	18	28
Other	6	5	8	2
Initial placement type				
Relative or friend	24	28	17	23
Foster home or therapeutic foster home	47	43	57	40
Group home or other	29	29	26	36
Maltreatment type				
Physical abuse	23	18	30	45
Sexual abuse	7	7	6	5
Failure to provide	23	28	14	17
Failure to supervise	37	35	43	27
Other	10	12	7	6
CBCL at baseline				
Normal	56	55	52	81
Borderline	6	5	7	2
Clinical	39	40	41	17
Parent risk factors				
Active drug abuse	29	31	24	41
Active alcohol abuse	21	22	17	31
Recent history of arrests	32	33	31	36
Trouble paying for basic necessities	47	48	41	65
Family cumulative risk				
Low	21	22	22	9
Medium	30	30	32	36
High	48	48	45	55
Previous experience with child welfare system	49	47	57	28

(continued)

Table 9-1 *(continued)*

Characteristic	Total (N = 1,565) percent	Still in care (n = 982) percent	Reunified (n = 463) percent	Left care to live with relative (n = 120) percent
Parent completed case plan goals[b]				
None or some	64	73	45	51
Most or all	36	27	55	49
Parenting support services dose (mean)[c]	31	25	44	33
Parent participated in developing case plan	67	62	75	88
Youth (aged 11 or older) was placed in same neighborhood	16	16	15	16
Frequency of contact between mother and youth (aged 11 or older)				
Never	34	48	9	10
One to two times a month or less	17	18	14	22
One time a week or more	49	34	79	68
Self-reported delinquency (mean)[de]	22	12	44	33

Source: Authors' calculations.

CBCL = Child Behavior Checklist.

a. Percentages and standard errors (not shown) are weighted. *N*s are unweighted and may vary by characteristic.

b. Significant difference between children who are still in placement and those who have been reunified ($p < 0.01$).

c. Significant difference between children who are still in placement and those who have been reunified ($p < 0.05$).

d. Significant difference between children who are still in placement and those who have left care to live with a relative ($p < 0.001$).

e. Significant difference between children who have been reunified and those who have left care to live with a relative ($p < 0.05$).

goals outlined in their case plan. Permanent caregivers of children who have been reunified, however, were more than twice as likely to have completed most or all of their goals as caregivers of children still in placement (55 percent and 27 percent, respectively). Permanent caregivers of children who have been reunified also received a significantly higher level of parenting support services than caregivers of children still in placement.

Only 16 percent of youths aged eleven and older reported being placed in the same neighborhood as the home from which they were removed. Reports of contact with their mother varied widely for the older youths, as about one-third (34 percent) reported no contact, while about half (49 percent) indicated visiting with their mother at least once a week.

The estimates presented in table 9-2 show the rate of reunification with the child's caregiver within eighteen months after out-of-home placement by age and race of the child. The rate of reunification differs by age and race, ranging

Table 9-2. *Cumulative Probability of Child's Reunification with Family within Eighteen Months of Out-of-Home Placement, by Child Age and Ethnic Group*[a]

	Ethnic group			
Age at baseline	Black	White	Other	Total
Younger than 7 months	0.16	0.30	0.31	0.25
7 months–2 years	0.40	0.38	0.51	0.44
3–5 years	0.41	0.25	0.23	0.27
6–10 years	0.29	0.42	0.55	0.40
11–15 years	0.20	0.58	0.45	0.40
Total	0.27	0.41	0.43	0.37

Source: Authors' calculations.
a. All analyses were done with weighted data.

from a low of 0.16 for Black infants to a high of 0.58 for White youths aged eleven to fifteen. As a group, Black children had the lowest reunification rates. Later multivariate models that include additional variables provide a more in-depth look at the relationship of age and race to these reunification rates.

The results of models presented in table 9-3 reveal both similarities and differences across the age groups when looking at the relationship between characteristics of the child, family, and agency and reunification. Child characteristics were significantly related to reunification for all age groups except children aged seven months to two years. Conversely, familial risk factors were related to reunification for only one age group, six- to ten-year-olds. At least one action by the agency or parent for each age group increased the rate of reunification.

Infants who experienced neglect left placement care at a significantly slower rate than physically abused infants. For infants whose parents received parenting support services and who were in compliance with most or all components of the case plan, the rate of reunification was greater than that for those whose parents were not in compliance. In addition, the rate of reunification for Black infants was less than half of the White infant reunification rate.

For young children between the ages of seven months and two years, the only factor related to the rate of reunification was compliance with the case plan. The rate of reunification for children whose parents were in compliance with the case plan was almost five times greater than that of children with parents complying with some or none of the plan.

Gender, abuse type, and case plan compliance were significantly related to reunification for three- to five-year-old children. The reunification rate of male children was more than four times greater than that of female children. Children experiencing sexual abuse and "other" abuse, which included emotional or educational abuse or exploitation, were about 80 percent less likely to be reunified with their parents during this time period than those who were physically abused.

Table 9-3. Significant Results from Multivariate Analyses of Reunification Rate, by Child's Age at Baseline

Significant variables	Relative risk ratio
Birth–6 months[a]	
Race (reference is non-Hispanic White)*	
Black	0.42**
Abuse type (reference is physical abuse)***	
Failure to provide or supervise	0.24***
Parenting support (reference is none)	6.74***
Compliance with case plan (reference is compliance with none or some of the goals)	5.4****
7 months–2 years[b]	
Male	1.78*
Compliance with case plan (reference is compliance with none or some of the goals)	4.47****
3–5 years[c]	
Male	4.21**
Abuse type (reference is physical abuse)**	
Sexual abuse or other	0.13***
Compliance with case plan (reference is compliance with some or none of the goals)	6.03**
6–10 years	
Male	2.2**
Borderline or clinical CBCL score (reference is normal)	0.27***
Active substance use by permanent caregiver	0.53**
Initial nonkinship placement (reference is initial placement with kin)	4.53**
Older than 10 years[d]	
Race (reference is non-Hispanic White)***	
Black	0.14***
Other	0.13***
Placed in own neighborhood (reference is placed in new neighborhood)	2.0*
Frequency of seeing mother (reference is never)**	
Less than one time per week	3.33**
One time per week or more	4.76**

Source: Authors' calculations.

CBL = Child Behavior Checklist.

* $0.05 < p \leq 0.10$; ** $0.01 < p \leq 0.05$; *** $0.001 < p \leq 0.01$; **** $p \leq 0.001$.

a. Other variables in the final model for children younger than seven months old included child's gender, parent having trouble paying basic expenses, and parental substance use.

b. Other variables in the final model for children between the ages of seven months and two years included child's race, parental substance use, parent having trouble paying basic expenses, level of cumulative risk for family, and initial placement with kin.

c. Other variables in the final model for children between the ages of three and five years included child's race and CBCL (Child Behavior Checklist) score.

d. Other variables in the model for children older than ten years included child's gender, CBCL score, self-reported delinquency score, initial placement with kin, and parent compliance with case plan.

Parental compliance with the case plan increased the rate of reunification by about six times.

For six- to ten-year-olds, males reunified at twice the rate as females, and children initially placed in a nonkinship setting were five times more likely to reunify than children initially placed with kin. Children with a borderline or clinical mental health score or whose caregivers were active substance users returned home at significantly lower rates.

Black youths older than 10 years, as well as youths of other race and ethnicity groups, had significantly lower reunification rates than White youths. The one other factor that appeared influential for youths of this age group was the frequency of visits with their mother. Youths who saw their mother returned home more quickly than did those who never visited with her. In addition, youths placed in their own neighborhood tended to have a greater reunification rate ($0.05 < p < 0.10$).

Discussion

Although consistently calculated national reunification rates are not available, the reunification estimate from eleven states represented in the Multistate Foster Care Data Archive averaged 43 percent, ranging from 28 percent of children who initially entered placement between 1988 and 1995 in Alabama to 62 percent of the 1988 through 1995 entry group in Wisconsin.[25] The 30 percent reunification rate reported in this study is lower than expected and may be the result of multiple factors including the nature of the sample and declining trends in the number of children entering out-of-home placement. This sample included no children older than age fifteen and few older than age fourteen, which reduces the number of adolescents who have more rapid reunification rates. The sample included children who were initially entering out-of-home placement as well as children reentering placement. The sample was also selected from the group of children referred to child welfare agencies in late 1999 and 2000. During these years, child welfare agencies across the country were experiencing reductions in the numbers of children entering out-of-home placement.[26] As the number of children entering placement declined, perhaps partially because child welfare agencies were able to serve children and families with less significant needs in their own homes, child welfare agencies may have experienced an increase in the length of stay because children entering placement were likely to have had more significant needs.[27] A substantial change may be required to the way reunification is handled to accelerate the rate of reunification under these circumstances.

These analyses are further constrained by the limited follow-up time available for the children who entered out-of-home placement. At most only eighteen months are available in which to observe whether children are reunified with family members. We cannot say what happens after eighteen months, which ultimately might change some of the results.

The predictors of reunification differ markedly by age (table 9-4). Some of the relationships observed in these analyses have not been studied before, and the information about these relationships is potentially consequential. In particular, at least one agency or parent action is positively related to reunification for all age groups. For the youngest children, parental participation in parenting support services increases the relative rate of reunification sevenfold, suggesting that there are available mechanisms for addressing some of the parent and child factors that are impeding the achievement of permanency. Although we do not see this same relationship for other age groups, subsequent research seeking to understand this dynamic may offer insights into types of parenting services that benefit parents and speed reunification. Analyses by federal and local agencies that treat reunification as if it had common rates or dynamics, regardless of the age of the children, are likely to offer little useful information.

For all children younger than age six, parental compliance with the case plan increases the rate of reunification significantly. Whereas child welfare workers suggest that family compliance with case plans is an important element that is considered when making reunification decisions, this study is one of the first to examine compliance while controlling for child characteristics and parental risk factors. Although the results offer promise to child welfare clients seeking to reunite with their children, they also show that there are some cases in which parental compliance with the case plan has not resulted in reunification by eighteen months. Reunification may ultimately occur—and quite lengthy reunification periods have been found in other studies—but these apparently successful cases are still slower to close than what is required by statutory time frames.[28] It is appropriate to ask whether all parents who are in compliance with the case plan should be expected to reunify with their children within eighteen months. Further investigation to understand why compliant parents are not reunited is needed.

The reunification rates of Blacks and other minority children differ by age. After controlling for child characteristics, family risk factors, and agency and parent actions, the racial disparity in reunification disappears for children between seven months and ten years of age. However, since these analyses target reunification specifically, it would be premature to assume that the overall racial disparity in length of stay disappears as well for these children. For infants and older youths of color, the rate of reunification continues to be significantly smaller compared with the rate for White children, even when controlling for risk factors, child behavior, and agency and parent actions.

However, there is some promise for reunification efforts for older youth. Youths older than ten who have some contact with their mother reunify more often than those who never have contact. Child welfare practitioners consider visitation to be an important component of reunification efforts.[29] We still do not

Table 9-4. *Summary of Factors Related to Reunification, by Child Age at Baseline*[a]

	Age at baseline				
Factors	Younger than 7 months	7 months– 2 years	3–5 years	6–10 years	11 or older
Child characteristics					
Gender		•	•	•	
Race	•				•
CBCL score				•	
Delinquency score					
Abuse type	•		•		
Family risk factors					
Recent arrest					
Domestic violence					
Substance abuse				•	
Trouble paying basic expenses					
Previous child welfare involvement					
Cumulative risk			•	•	
Agency or parent actions					
Parenting services	•				
Parental participation in developing case plan					
Initial kin placement				•	
Compliance with case plan	•	•	•		
Placed in same neighborhood					•
Frequency seeing mother					•

Source: Authors' calculations.
CBCL = Child Behavior Checklist.
a. Not all variables are included in all age group models. See table 9-3 for a summary of variables in age-specific models.

know, however, how much this relationship rests on the predisposition of families that are visiting to also make the changes needed to achieve reunification. If this is the case, then the actions of child welfare workers to encourage visits may influence the behavior of parents to achieve case plan goals. Rigorous tests of methods to increase visits among those families who have a propensity not to visit should be undertaken to better understand the role of visitation in reunification.

Child welfare agencies are not often able to provide concerted efforts to facilitate visiting among families with or without a propensity to visit. Thus the achievement of visits may depend in good measure on the ability of families to arrange visits in a reasonably convenient way. This may explain the tendency toward higher reunification rates for children who live in foster homes in the same neighborhood as their biological family. In essence, reunification may require three conditions: a propensity to visit, permission to visit (perhaps also captured, in part, by a rating by child welfare workers that the family is compliant), and proximity of the child to facilitate the logistics of the visit. If these three stars must be aligned before reunification can occur, then the low rates of reunification observed in this study are not surprising. The good news is that the location of foster care placements and the facilitation of visits are largely within the agency's control.

Federal policy emphasizes permanency, with reunification being the primary path to permanency. Although reunification has been studied for nearly fifty years, few prior studies have been able to include as much information about the children, caregivers, and services as reported here. The large sample size also has major advantages because analyses could be stratified by age, which allowed the study to build on several decades of findings that have found that age is a significant contributor to permanency and that reunification rates are very different for children of different ages. Our study has generated much more detailed information than what is available in models that fail to separate children by age. It is clear from these analyses that factors affecting reunification vary considerably by age of child, as well as by other family characteristics, suggesting that future research and child welfare policy and practice would be remiss to return to the "one size fits all" model of child welfare.

Statistical Note

All of our analyses used weighted data and were implemented using SUDAAN software. We present Kaplan Meier life table estimates in table 9-2 and results from Cox Proportional Hazards Models for our multivariate analyses in table 9-3.

Notes

1. Fred Wulczyn, "Closing the Gap: Are Changing Exit Patterns Reducing the Time African American Children Spend in Foster Care Relative to Caucasian Children?" *Children and Youth Services Review* 25, nos. 5-6 (May 2003): 431–62.

2 . For information on length of stay of reunified and adopted children, see Richard P. Barth, Fred H. Wulczyn, and Tom Crea, "Adoption from Foster Care since the Adoption and Safe Families Act," *Journal of Law and Social Policy* (forthcoming). For state data of reunification after exit from foster care, see Fred Wulczyn, "Closing the Gap."

3. See Andrew Grogan-Kaylor, "The Effect of Initial Placement into Kinship Foster Care on Reunification from Foster Care: A Bivariate Probit Analysis," *Journal of Social Service Research* 27 (November 2001): 1–32; Kathleen Wells and Shenyang Guo, "Reunification and Reentry of Foster Children," *Children and Youth Services Review* 21, no. 4 (April 1999): 273–94; Mark E. Courtney, "Factors Associated with the Reunification of Foster Children with Their Families," *Social Service Review* 68, no. 1 (March 1994): 81–108; Robert M. Goerge, "The Reunification Process," *Social Service Review* 64, no. 3 (1990): 422–45.

4. For examples of reunification, see Robert M. Goerge, "The Reunification Process"; Cathryn C. Potter and Susan Klein-Rothschild, "Getting Home on Time: Predicting Timely Permanence for Young Children," *Child Welfare* 81, no. 2 (March-April 2002): 123–50. For

examples of adoption, see Richard P. Barth, Mark E. Courtney, and Marianne Berry, "Timing Is Everything—An Analysis of the Time to Adoption and Legalization," *Social Work Research* 18, no. 3 (September 1994): 139–48; Brenda D. Smith, "After Parental Rights Are Terminated: Factors Associated with Exiting Foster Care," *Children and Youth Services Review* 25, no. 12 (December 2003): 965–85. For examples of independent living, see Mark E. Courtney and Richard P. Barth, "Pathways of Older Adolescents out of Foster Care: Implications for Independent Living Services," *Social Work* 41, no. 1 (January 1996): 75–83.

5. Robert M. Goerge, "The Reunification Process"; Fred Wulczyn, "Closing the Gap."

6. Fred Wulczyn, "Closing the Gap."

7. Fred Wulczyn and others, *Beyond Common Sense: Child Welfare, Child Well-Being, and the Evidence for Child Welfare Policy Reform* (New York: Aldine Transaction, 2005).

8. Laura Frame, Jill Duerr Berrick, and Melissa Lim Brodowski, "Understanding Reentry to Out-of-Home Care for Reunified Infants," *Child Welfare* 79, no. 4 (July-August 2000): 339–69.

9. Ibid.

10. Devon Brooks, Sigrid James, and Richard P. Barth, "Preferred Characteristics of Children in Need of Adoption: Is There a Demand for Available Foster Children?" *Social Service Review* 76, no. 4 (December 2002): 575–602.

11. Fred Wulczyn, "Family Reunification," *Future of Children* 14, no. 1 (Winter 2004): 95–113; Annie Woodley Brown and Barbara Bailey-Etta, "An Out-of-Home Care System in Crisis: Implications for African American Children in the Child Welfare System," *Child Welfare* 76, no. 1 (January-February 1997): 65–83; Richard P. Barth and others, *From Child Abuse to Permanency Planning: Child Welfare Services Pathways and Placements* (New York: Aldine de Gruyter, 1994); Yuhwa Eva Lu and others, "Race, Ethnicity and Case Outcomes in Child Protective Services," *Child Youth Services Review* 26, no. 5 (May 2004): 447–61; Paul Delfabbro, James Barber, and Lesley Cooper, "Predictors of Short-Term Reunification in South Australian Substitute Care," *Child Welfare* 82, no. 1 (January-February 2003): 27–51.

12. Kathleen Wells and Shenyang Guo, "Reunification and Reentry of Foster Children;" Robert M. Goerge, "The Reunification Process."

13. Mark E. Courtney and Yin-Ling Irene Wong, "Comparing the Timing of Exits from Substitute Care," *Children and Youth Services Review* 18, nos. 4-5 (1996): 307–34; Barbara Needell, Alan M. Brookhart, and Seon Lee, "Black Children and Child Welfare Services in California," *Children and Youth Services Review* 25, nos. 5-6 (May-June 2003): 393–408.

14. John Landsverk and others, "Impact of Child Psychosocial Functioning on Reunification from Out-of-Home Placement," *Children and Youth Services Review* 18, nos. 4-5 (1996): 447–62.

15. Laura Frame, "Maltreatment Reports and Placement Outcomes for Infants and Toddlers in Out-of-Home Care," *Infant Mental Health Journal* 23, no. 5 (September 2002): 517–40.

16. U.S. Department of Health and Human Services, *National Study of Protective, Preventive, and Reunification Services Delivered to Children and Their Families* (Washington: DHHS, Administration for Children and Families, Administration on Children, Youth and Families, 1994); Mary Keegan Eamon, *The Effect of Economic Resources on Reunification of Illinois Children in Substitute Care* (Urbana: University of Illinois at Urbana-Champaign, School of Social Work, Children and Family Research Center, 2002).

17. Christina Risley-Curtiss and others, "Identifying and Reducing Barriers to Reunification for Seriously Mentally Ill Patients Involved in Child Welfare," *Families in Society* 85, no. 1 (January-March 2004): 107–18.

18. Mary Keegan Eamon and Sandra Kopels, "'For Reasons of Poverty': Court Challenges to Child Welfare Practices and Mandated Programs," *Children and Youth Services Review* 26, no. 9 (September 2004): 821–36; Katherine Kortenkamp, Rob Geen, and Matthew Stagner,

"The Role of Welfare and Work in Predicting Foster Care Reunification Rates for Children of Welfare Recipients," *Children and Youth Services Review* 26, no. 6 (June 2004): 577–90.

19. For studies demonstrating that children in kinship care have a longer time to reunification, see Robert M. Goerge, "The Reunification Process"; Richard P. Barth, Mark E. Courtney, and Marianne Berry, "Timing Is Everything." For a discussion of kinship care shortening the length of time to reunification, see Research Triangle Institute and Jordan Institute for Families, "Evaluation of Family to Family" (Research Triangle Park, N.C.: RTI Health and Social Policy Division, and Chapel Hill: University of North Carolina, School of Social Work, 1998).

20. Kathleen Wells and Shenyang Guo, "Reunification and Reentry of Foster Children."

21. For family-centered child welfare practice, see Cathleen A. Lewandowski and Lois Pierce, "Does Family-Centered Out-of-Home Care Work? Comparison of a Family-Centered Approach and Traditional Care," *Social Work Research* 28, no. 3 (September 2004): 143–51. For parental visitation, see Inger P. Davis and others, "Parental Visiting and Foster Care Reunification," *Children and Youth Services Review* 18, nos. 4-5 (1996): 363–82; Sonya J. Leathers, "Parental Visiting and Family Reunification: Could Inclusive Practice Make a Difference?" *Child Welfare* 81, no. 3 (July-August 2002): 595–616; Shannon Dougherty, "Promising Practices in Reunification," report prepared for the National Resource Center for Foster Care and Permanency Planning (New York: Hunter College School of Social Work, 2004). For parental involvement in case activities, see Sonya J. Leathers, "Parental Visiting and Family Reunification."

22. Shannon Dougherty, "Promising Practices in Reunification"; Annie E. Casey Foundation, "Implementing the Values and Strategies of Family to Family" (Baltimore, Md.: Annie E. Casey Foundation, n.d.).

23. A child was identified as experiencing out-of-home placement if the caseworker, using the case record, indicated that the child was placed away from the permanent caregiver and that the child welfare agency had placement authority or legal custody for the child.

24. We have no certain way to distinguish whether foster care is designed to be treatment or therapeutic foster care, so we have combined the two types of foster care.

25. Fred Wulczyn, Kristen Brunner Hislop, and Robert M. Goerge, "An Update from the Multistate Foster Care Data Archive: Foster Care Dynamics 1983–1998" (Chapin Hall Center for Children at the University of Chicago, 2000).

26. U.S. Department of Health and Human Services, "Foster Care FY1999–FY2003 Entries, Exits, and Numbers of Children in Care on the Last Day of Each Federal Fiscal Year" (Washington: DHHS, Administration for Children and Families, Administration on Children, Youth and Families, Children's Bureau, April 2005).

27. Charles L. Usher, Judy B. Wildfire, and Deborah A Gibbs, "Measuring Performance in Child Welfare: Secondary Effects of Success," *Child Welfare* 78, no. 1 (January-February 1999): 31–51; Charles L. Usher and others, "Evaluation of the Title IV-E Waiver Demonstration in North Carolina" (Chapel Hill, N.C.: Jordan Institute for Families, the University of North Carolina, School of Social Work, 2002).

28. See, for example, Charles L. Usher and Judy B. Wildfire, "Evidence-Based Practice in Community-Based Child Welfare Systems," *Child Welfare* 82, no. 5 (September-October 2003): 597–614.

29. Inger P. Davis and others, "Parental Visiting and Foster Care Reunification."

10

Placement Stability and Early Behavioral Outcomes among Children in Out-of-Home Care

DAVID M. RUBIN, AMANDA L. R. O'REILLY,
LAUREN HAFNER, XIANQUN LUAN,
AND A. RUSSELL LOCALIO

More than half a million children in the United States currently reside in foster care. Nearly half of these children have been there for more than eighteen months, and many children have been in care for much longer.[1] A major concern for children placed in foster care is that frequent placement moves threaten a child's well-being and ability to form successful long-term relationships. Attachment theory suggests that the more quickly a child finds stability in an out-of-home setting, the better able that child will be to overcome early attachment failures that are associated with child maltreatment.[2] Attachment theory helps explain, from a practical perspective, why disruptions in the first year of foster care are highly correlated with poor long-term outcomes.[3] Simply stated, "The cycle of multiple placements contributes to an increase in overall behavior pathology (including school difficulties) and fundamentally undermines attempts to provide a consistent environment wherein attachment to caregivers can be nurtured."[4]

This work has been supported by a K23 mentored career development award from the National Institutes of Child Health and Development (grant no. 1K23HD045748-01A1). The authors wish to thank Dr. John Landsverk of San Diego State University for his ongoing assistance; Katy Dowd of the Research Triangle Institute for her advice in identifying the sample of children used in this study; Dr. Anne Kazak and Dr. Chris Feudtner at the Children's Hospital of Philadelphia; and Dr. Trevor Hadley at the Center for Mental Health Policy and Services Research at the University of Pennsylvania, for feedback and support on study design, data analysis, and manuscript preparation.

Although the association of placement stability with child well-being is rooted in attachment theory, outcome studies of children in out-of-home care have not adequately disentangled the relationship. A few studies to date have revealed increased rates of mental health problems, homelessness, and incarceration among children who experienced multiple placement changes while in out-of-home care, but these studies have been limited in their capacity to shape decisionmaking for children currently moving within the system.[5] Study findings concerning the health and well-being of all children in foster care have been painted in broad strokes, and for the most part have been limited in defining how the stability of a child's placement history might independently influence long-term outcomes. Neglect of the child's placement history has also been a major limitation of studies of more intermediate outcomes describing—often through cross-sectional snapshots of behavioral or educational functioning— the functioning of children currently in care. Although these investigations have demonstrated that 40 to 80 percent of children in foster care have significant behavioral or emotional problems and are likely to languish in foster care and experience frequent placement moves, they were not able to discern whether placement instability and obstacles to permanency were more the result of a child's attributes at entry into care, a contributor to subsequent outcomes, or both.[6]

The current study attempts to disentangle the relationship between placement stability and child well-being by considering the association of placement stability during the first eighteen months in foster care with behavioral outcomes at eighteen and thirty-six months among a longitudinal, nationally representative cohort of foster care children in the National Survey of Child and Adolescent Well-Being (NSCAW). Expanding on a novel method of categorizing placement stability from a prior study of foster care children in San Diego, the study authors hypothesized that children who achieved early stability in foster care would have better behavioral outcomes than children who achieved late stability or remained unstable throughout the study.[7]

Methods

The population for this study was drawn from NSCAW's nationally weighted sample of 5,501 children. A description of this population can be seen in figure 10-1. The study population was restricted to children who were residing at home during the initial investigation for maltreatment and who were subsequently placed into out-of-home care shortly after the investigation, which led to their inclusion in the NSCAW study. Restricting the population to this time period of entry into out-of-home care maximized the likelihood that the out-of-home placement was related to the initial investigation that resulted in the child's being included in the survey. It also provided a consistent starting point

Figure 10-1. *Study Population Criteria from NSCAW for Children Entering Out-of-Home Care*[a]

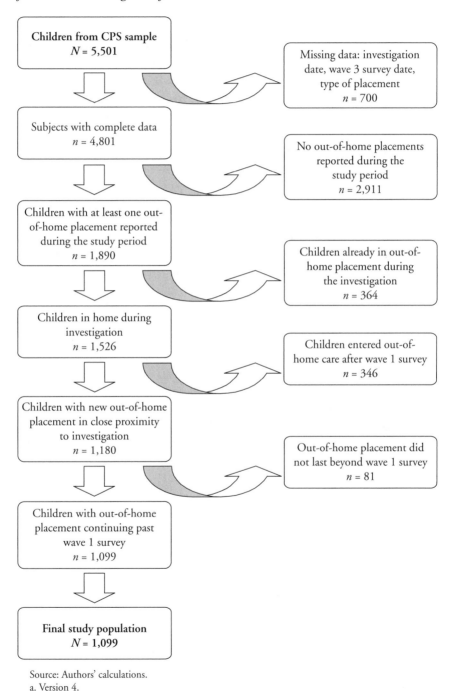

Source: Authors' calculations.
a. Version 4.

for the children's entry into care, such that placement and permanency experiences of these youths could be tracked for the duration of the study. Subjects with missing data were also excluded from the sample, which ultimately yielded a cohort of 1,099 children zero to fifteen years of age.

Information collected to describe the children included demographics, baseline health, and type of abuse reported. Demographic variables included age (younger than two years, two to ten years, older than ten years), sex, race (White, Black, other), and ethnicity (Hispanic, yes or no). Health status at baseline was assessed from the NSCAW caregiver report and included information on the child's baseline health status (excellent, very good, good, and fair or poor), history of chronic health problems, and baseline well-being (as measured by the child's behavioral problems). Finally, the type of maltreatment reported for investigation was categorized into broad categories that included physical abuse, sexual abuse, and neglect or abandonment.

Data are described for the entire cohort using frequencies for categorical variables and means and standard deviations for continuous variables. Because of the stratified, clustered design elements in the NSCAW data, weighted frequencies are reported to generalize the findings to a nationally representative group of children entering out-of-home care.

Placement Stability

Sigrid James and her colleagues developed a method of categorizing placement stability in response to the concern that a simple enumeration of placements would fail to fully capture if and when a child stabilized in a foster care placement after the first eighteen months in continuous out-of-home care.[8] They identified four categories of placement stability:

—"early stability": children achieved a stable placement until the end of the eighteen-month follow-up within forty-five days of placement.

—"late stability": a long-lasting placement was achieved, but beyond the forty-fifth day of placement.

—"variable stability": a long-lasting placement of at least nine months was achieved, but the child had moved again by eighteen months.

—"unstable": the child failed to achieve any placement of at least nine months' duration.

James demonstrated a strong relationship between these placement stability categories and both behavioral functioning and various sociodemographic attributes known to influence future placement trajectories for children in foster care.[9]

However, a significant limitation of the James criteria for placement stability was the study's inclusion only of children who remained in continuous foster care over the eighteen-month follow-up period. In an effort to increase the generalizability of the placement stability variable, and because reunification is a key intermediate outcome in child welfare policy and practice, children for whom a reunification was attempted (both successfully and unsuccessfully) during the first eighteen months of follow-up were grouped into a new category called "reunified." We compared children in this category with children in continuous foster care who remained categorized according to the James criteria. Finally, because of the small sample size in the "variable stability" and "unstable" groups within the NSCAW data, and because preliminary analysis showed these groups to be similar in process and behavioral outcomes, the two groups were combined into a single "unstable" category. The final categories for placement stability for this analysis thus were "reunified," "early stability," "late stability," and "unstable."

Outcome Measures

Outcome measures were divided into permanency outcomes that were obtained for all children in the cohort and well-being outcomes that could only be measured uniformly on an older subsample of the population. Permanency outcomes included assessments at eighteen and thirty-six months for whether children had reunified to home, continued to remain in foster care, or achieved adoption. Additional data were collected on whether children who were reunified subsequently returned to foster care before the end of the study. Other variables included total number of placements during the thirty-six-month study period, time spent in a restrictive setting (group home, residential treatment facility, or inpatient care), and additional placements between eighteen and thirty-six months not captured in the placement stability variable (dichotomized as no further movement versus continuing movement).

The Child Behavior Checklist (CBCL) was used to assess the behavioral functioning of a subsample of older children after eighteen and thirty-six months in foster care.[10] The CBCL was administered for children two years of age and older at baseline and again at eighteen and thirty-six months. Because a sizable proportion of children in our cohort were less than two years of age at baseline and a baseline CBCL measure could not be obtained, analyses that considered CBCL outcome scores were restricted to include only the 601 children two years of age or greater for whom data collection on the CBCL measure was complete. To further investigate the well-being outcomes among children in this cohort, subjects were stratified by normal versus abnormal baseline CBCL scores. Placement stability characteristics of each of these groups and the CBCL scores at eighteen and thirty-six months are reported given these placement trajectories.

Children with missing CBCL scores at either eighteen or thirty-six months were included in this analysis because all analyses were weighted for the sampling strategy, nonresponse, and loss due to follow-up.

Results

The characteristics of the 1,099 children who entered out-of-home care between the date of investigation and the baseline data collection are shown in table 10-1. Data were stratified by age, given expected age-related differences in characteristics between groups. A little more than a third (34 percent) of the children were younger than two years old, 42 percent were between two and ten years, and the remaining 24 percent were older than ten years. Fifty percent of the population was White, 36 percent were Black, and 14 percent were of another racial group. Fourteen percent of the population had Hispanic ethnicity and 54 percent were female. Older children were more likely than younger children to be non-Hispanic White and to have experienced sexual abuse.

The majority of all children were reported to be in good to excellent health (87 percent), but for 27 percent a chronic health problem was reported at baseline. The youngest children were more likely to have chronic health problems than the oldest children (38 percent versus 17 percent) and were also more likely than the two- to ten-year-olds to have fair or poor baseline health status (17 percent versus 9 percent). Of the children eligible for baseline CBCL testing, nearly half (49 percent) were listed as having abnormal levels of behavioral functioning.

Permanency Outcomes

The mean number of placements per child by eighteen months was 2.9, with a range of one to thirteen placements. By thirty-six months, the mean number of placements per child averaged 3.2 and ranged from one to eighteen placements. After three years in the study, 19 percent of children experienced more than four placements in foster care. Children of ten years of age and older were significantly more likely to experience more than four placement changes (34 percent) compared to younger children (15 percent) and were also much more likely to spend time in a restrictive setting (38 percent versus 6 percent).

After eighteen months of follow-up, 33 percent of children had attempted reunification, 34 percent achieved early stability, 12 percent achieved late stability, and 21 percent were unstable. Older children were significantly more likely than younger children to have difficulties attaining stability, with 31 percent of older children classified as unstable compared to only 17 percent of children under age two. In contrast, the youngest children were much more likely to achieve early stability, 40 percent compared with 22 percent of children older than ten years (see table 10-1).

Placement stability over the first eighteen months was significantly related to all permanency outcomes, demonstrating that placement stability over the first eighteen months is highly predictive of future stability and permanency. By the

Table 10-1. *Characteristics of Children Entering Out-of-Home Care in the National Survey of Child and Adolescent Well-Being*[a]

Characteristic	Age		
	Younger than two years (34 percent)	*Two to ten years (42 percent)*	*Older than ten years (24 percent)*
Child demographics			
Sex			
Female (53.6)	51.6	53.3	57.1
Male (46.4)	48.4	46.7	42.9
Race			
White (49.9)	42.8	55.3	50.3
Black (35.7)	40.9	29.5	39.3
Other (14.4)	16.4	15.2	10.4
*Ethnicity**			
Hispanic (13.7)	19.1	11.9	9.4
Other (86.3)	80.9	88.1	90.6
Child health			
Baseline CBCL score[b]			
Normal (51.3)	…	54.4	45.5
Borderline or clinical (48.7)	…	45.6	54.5
*Chronic health problems**			
Yes (26.6)	38.0	22.6	16.9
No (73.4)	62.1	77.4	83.1
*Baseline health**			
Excellent (36.5)	40.5	34.5	34.5
Very good (30.3)	18.9	38.7	31.6
Good (20.4)	23.3	17.7	21.2
Fair or poor (12.8)	17.4	9.2	12.7
*Type of abuse**			
Neglect or abandonment (34.7)	30.9	38.2	33.7
Physical (45.2)	54.0	43.9	35.2
Sexual (7.0)	2.2	7.0	13.9
Other (13.0)	12.9	10.9	17.2
*Placement stability**			
Reunified (33.5)	29.2	37.3	32.0
Early (33.9)	40.3	35.6	21.8
Late (12.2)	13.2	10.2	14.1
Unstable (20.5)	17.3	16.9	31.2

Source: Author's calculations.

*$p < 0.05$.

a. Data are reported with nationally weighted percentages; percentages of the population are totaled among children for each characteristic and presented in parentheses; proportions are then stratified by age. Percentages may not total 100 because of rounding. $N = 1,099$.

b. CBCL = Child Behavior Checklist (children younger than age two are not covered by the CBCL).

Table 10-2. *Permanency Outcomes for Children in NSCAW,*
by Placement Stability at Eighteen Months [a]

	Placement stability			
Permanency outcome	Reunified (31.4 percent)	Early stability (32.6 percent)	Late stability (15.5 percent)	Unstable (20.6 percent)
*Continued movement after eighteen months**				
Yes (19.6)	23.3	21.0	11.7	44.0
No (80.4)	36.1	35.9	12.7	15.3
*Aggregate placements by thirty-six months**				
Two or fewer (42.5)	20.8	63.2	11.9	4.0
Three or four (39.0)	45.5	12.2	15.6	26.7
More than four (18.5)	37.2	3.9	7.3	51.6
*Spent time in restrictive facility**				
Yes (13.8)	33.6	5.8	15.6	45.0
No (86.2)	33.2	37.3	11.9	17.6
*Final status at thirty-six months**				
Adopted (19.8)	14.3	49.8	16.3	19.6
Successfully reunited (26.7)	80.4	4.9	2.8	12.0
Unsuccessful reunification (7.3)	92.6	0.7	< 0.1	6.7
Continuously in placement (46.2)	0.0	49.5	19.3	31.1

Source: Author's calculations.

NSCAW = National Survey of Child and Adolescent Well-Being.

*$p < 0.0001$.

a. Data are reported with nationally weighted percentages; percentages of the population are totaled among children for each characteristic and presented in parentheses; proportions are then stratified by placement stability. Percentages may not total 100 because of rounding. $N = 1,099$.

end of the thirty-six-month follow-up period, 46 percent of children continuously remained in out-of-home care, compared with 67 percent at eighteen months, and 20 percent of children had additional placements between eighteen and thirty-six months (see table 10-2). A total of 54 percent of children had attempted to transition out of the foster care system through adoption or reunification by the end of the study. Adoptions were few at eighteen months (5 percent), but rose to 20 percent by thirty-six months, with children who achieved stability much more likely to be adopted; 50 percent of early stabilizers were adopted, compared to just 20 percent of unstable children. The youngest children were the most likely to be adopted, 29 percent as compared to 1.3 percent of children ages older than ten years.

Over the course of the study, 34 percent of the sample had attempted reunification, but reunification was unsuccessful for over one quarter of these children, and they eventually returned to foster care. Most children who successfully reunified did so by eighteen months; 25 percent were successfully reunified by this time, a portion that rose to only 27 percent by thirty-six months. Nearly half of the children reunifying after eighteen months had unstable placement histories; 4 to 6 percent of children who stabilized in the first eighteen months were later reunified. Only 22 percent of younger children were successfully reunified by the completion of the study, as compared to 32 percent of the older children.

Well-Being Outcomes

Figure 10-2 reports the behavioral outcomes of a subgroup of 601 children over two years of age who had CBCL measurements at baseline, eighteen, and thirty-six months. Children were first separated by their baseline CBCL scores so that a stratified analysis of the association between placement stability with eighteen- and thirty-six-month CBCL outcomes could be conducted. At baseline, 49 percent of children were in the borderline or abnormal range of CBCL scores, and there were significant differences in the placement stability of children with different CBCL categories. Although there were no significant differences in the proportion of children who attempted reunification (34 percent among children scoring normally, 38 percent among children scoring abnormally), 12 percent of children who scored normally at baseline failed in reunification, compared to 17 percent among those with abnormal baseline scores. There were also significant differences in stability measures; 36 percent of children scoring normally achieved early placement stability compared with only 25 percent of the children who scored poorly.

The association of the placement stability variable with eighteen- and thirty-six-month CBCL outcomes demonstrated the importance of stratifying the children by their baseline CBCL scores. Among the children scoring normally at baseline there was a significant association between placement stability and both eighteen- and thirty-six-month outcomes. In particular, 85 percent of early stabilizers in continuous out-of-home care were scoring normally by thirty-six months, compared with 70 percent of the reunified children and only 60 percent of children who never achieved stability. By contrast, placement stability did not seem to affect the children who began their out-of-home care with poor CBCL scores; outcomes were uniformly poor across all categories of placement stability, with only 40 percent of children scoring normally on their CBCL by thirty-six months.

Discussion

This paper is the first to report the impact of placement stability on behavioral outcomes for a nationally representative sample of children entering out-of-home care. We found that 85 percent of children who did not have behavioral problems at baseline and then achieved early stability in foster care continued to

Figure 10-2.   *Child Behavioral Checklist Outcome Scores for Children Older than Two Years of Age at Eighteen Months and Thirty-Six Months, Stratified by Baseline CBCL Categories*[a]

Wave 1 baseline CBCL	Placement stability	18-month CBCL	36-month CBCL
	Reunified 34 (103)	G 59 (53)[b] / B 41 (31)	G 70 (60)[c] / B 30 (24)
Good 51 (298)	Early stability 36 (99)	G 79 (69)[b] / B 21 (22)	G 85 (66)[c] / B 15 (20)
	Late stability 11 (34)	G 80 (23)[b] / B 20 (8)	G 77 (23)[c] / B 23 (7)
	Unstable 19 (62)	G 54 (33)[b] / B 46 (26)	G 60 (30)[c] / B 40 (25)
	Reunified 38 (106)	G 43 (41) / B 57 (54)	G 41 (40) / B 59 (53)
Bad 49 (303)	Early stability 25 (72)	G 35 (18) / B 65 (49)	G 38 (24) / B 62 (41)
	Late stability 13 (46)	G 49 (18) / B 51 (26)	G 21 (16) / B 79 (26)
	Unstable 24 (79)	G 28 (18) / B 72 (54)	G 40 (29) / B 60 (41)

Source: Authors' calculations.

a. The figure reports weighted frequencies (percentages) with actual cell counts in parentheses. The baseline CBCL scores are further stratified by category of placement stability achieved by eighteen months. CBCL scores are dichotomized as "good" (G, that is, normal range of standardized score) and "bad" (B, that is, borderline [bln] or clinical [cln] range of standardized score).

b. Denotes significant design-based p value = 0.04 (uncorrected chi-square p value = 0.002) for comparison of eighteen-month CBCL scores between placement stability groups among children with baseline normal CBCL scores.

c. Denotes nearly significant design-based p value = 0.09 (uncorrected chi-square p value = 0.01) for comparison of thirty-six-month CBCL scores between placement stability groups among children with baseline normal CBCL scores.

display normal behavior at thirty-six months. Their outcomes were better even than children in reunified settings, where only 70 percent of the children were scoring normally on the CBCL at thirty-six months.

We believe these findings have particular relevance in understanding the needs and pathways for children entering out-of-home care and provide a possible benchmark for measuring systemic improvements. Our method of categorizing placement stability is not without limitations, but these limitations do not diminish the capacity for studying child welfare practice and outcomes. We sought to capture both quantitative and qualitative aspects of the placement experience by distinguishing between children who were attempting reunification and children who were continuing in out-of-home care. We recognize, though, that we could not simplify all relevant aspects of a child's placement, including the restrictiveness of a child's setting and certain types of placements (such as kinship care) that could not be accounted for within our categories. Expanding the number of categories to incorporate these attributes risked over-elaboration and the potential loss of interpretable policy implications.

Criticism could be directed at our decision to include unsuccessful attempts at reunification in the reunified group as opposed to categorizing them separately. An argument could be made to include unsuccessfully reunified children in the "late stability" or "unstable" categories, since they returned to out-of-home care. From the perspective of the child welfare system, however, these children represent attempted reunifications, and so their inclusion with other children who are reunifying is reasonable. In any event, even if those children were excluded from this analysis, it would not appreciably change the CBCL outcome results, as children in continuous out-of-home care who stabilize early continue to have better outcomes than their reunified peers. However, the bias introduced by this assumption was in the stability categories themselves. We found that 24 percent of children scoring poorly on the CBCL at baseline were unstable in out-of-home care, and 19 percent of children scoring normally had unstable placement histories. Had we included the unsuccessfully reunified children within our placement categories, this difference would have been magnified; 33 percent of the children with poor CBCL scores at baseline would have been categorized as unstable compared to the 22 percent of the children with normal CBCL scores at baseline.

Criticism of our methods has also been directed at our decision to estimate placement stability solely over the first eighteen months of the study, when we could have chosen stability over the entire thirty-six-month follow-up as the primary predictor variable. Although this latter type of analysis can be helpful, and although we continue to explore more sophisticated longitudinal methods that can handle time-dependent variables between outcomes assessments, we preferred to report the eighteen-month stability variable because of its relevance to practice since passage of the federal Adoption and Safe Families Act (ASFA) in 1997. Indeed, with federal policy calling for case reviews within a year after a child's entry into care, the eighteen-month time period roughly coincides with the permanency decisions that are (or should be) made for children across the nation. Further, most of our reunifications had occurred by eighteen months, thereby supporting our decision to estimate stability at that time. It is critical that placement stability measurements meet the performance expectations of child welfare systems in order to be carry the most weight in practice and policy.

An intriguing finding from this analysis is that among children whose behavioral functioning at baseline was normal, the children who achieved early stability in continuous out-of-home foster care were doing better after thirty-six months than children who attempted reunification. For many years, reunification and family preservation were touted as a preferred outcome for children in out-of-home care, despite concerns about high rates of recurrence of abuse and neglect, as well as about reentry to out-of-home care.[11] Traditionally, there has been a tension between reunification and adoption in child welfare policy and practice.[12] Since the passage of the Adoption and Safe Families Act in 1997, there has been a steady increase in adoptions, while the overall rate of reunifications has continued to decrease.[13] The data we present are likely to add to this debate around family preservation, although we would exercise caution in interpreting early stability in out-of-home care as superior to reunification for several reasons. First and foremost, our analysis cannot consider the level of services provided to biological families, particularly before and after reunification, and whether the intensity of those services might have influenced outcomes for children returning home.[14] In this regard, we should highlight that 70 percent of reunified children who had normal baseline CBCL scores were doing well in follow-up (at least by the report of their biological caregivers). Understanding the attributes of these children will be important in clarifying the experiences after out-of-home care that promote resiliency in children who return home.

The poor long-term outcomes among children who scored poorly on the CBCL at baseline were revealed. Children in this subgroup were much less likely to achieve early stability, but even when they did so, outcomes were poor across the board, with only 40 percent of children having normal CBCL outcomes at thirty-six months. It would appear that for this subgroup, interventions that simply promote placement stability might not be enough to improve outcomes. We cannot, however, determine whether placement stability may have prevented children from getting worse, particularly because these children were already scoring very high on the CBCL at baseline. Furthermore, we were unable to examine service use among the children, yet such an examination would be important to document whether children with demonstrated need were receiving services. Prior research has consistently demonstrated that children in foster care are significant users of outpatient mental health services, but other studies have questioned the quality of screening provided to children by community providers and the consistency with which child welfare units promote screening and referral for children under their supervision.[15] Even less is known about the quality of services that children receive and about whether those services are meeting minimum standards to improve outcomes.[16] Our results provide a benchmark by which to measure system improvement for children entering out-of-home care in the future. However, these findings underscore the difficulty of improving outcomes for children who are at the highest risk at baseline, and they emphasize the importance of careful studies of the quality of services children are receiving. Providing real help for these children may require more collaborative and novel approaches than have been attempted to date.[17]

Placement stability not only impacts children directly but also impacts other systems that affect children in out-of-home care, especially the health care system, which has faced difficulties in providing timely services to children entering care and particularly to those who are drifting within the system. A 1995 report by the U.S. General Accounting Office (now the Government Accountability Office) estimated that 12 percent of children entering foster care did not receive basic preventative health care and 34 percent failed to receive required immunizations. Nearly 50 percent of the children had health care needs for which they did not receive services.[18] As a result of the inability to meet the routine health care needs of children with placement instability, these children are also much more likely to seek routine care in emergency departments, hampering efforts to develop a coordinated strategy to improve their health.[19] Finally, for those who ask whether a child welfare system can influence placement decisions to promote stability, we would draw attention to a recent study that reported that 70 percent of placement moves are administrative in nature and unrelated to the behavior or health of the child.[20] This study illuminates a critical need to improve placement stability through child welfare practice and policy.

Although we did not comprehensively adjust for the multitude of factors that can influence well-being at baseline, the stratified descriptive data, inclusive of the child's baseline behavior, still offer a powerful demonstration of how placement trajectories may influence the health and well-being of children in out-of-home care. Although our findings cannot unequivocally demonstrate that interventions to promote placement stability at the system-level—such as recruitment of foster parents, respite services to foster parents, improved early treatment plans for children, and adoption subsidies—will influence outcomes, our findings strongly suggest that the interventions will.

Finally, we considered only one measure of well-being (the CBCL) and were unable to study the outcomes of younger children, for whom we have not yet developed a strategy to measure their baseline well-being. Replicating our findings using other measures of well-being, advancing more sophisticated models to adjust for a multitude of child attributes, and broadening our ability to study younger children will clearly be necessary to more precisely assess the impact of placement stability on child well-being. Despite these critiques, we believe that our results have important implications for policy and practice. Our data show that particularly among children who were scoring normally on the CBCL at baseline, early stabilization in out-of-home care can promote their long-term well-being.

Statistical Note

This analysis required the use of sampling weights that adjusted for the design elements in the NSCAW data collection as well as for nonresponse. Because of the great variability of the design weights (range 1 to 6908), we truncated the design weights above the 95th percentile. Separate analyses (not provided) revealed that truncating at the 95th percentile had minimal effect on point estimates for unadjusted associations but reduced the variance of estimates by a factor of 2. Additional truncating did not reduce variance substantially to warrant further adjustment of the weights for analyses. This method facilitated dramatic improvements in the precision of estimates without increases in variance.

With established reliability and validity, the CBCL has been used in many studies of children in foster care. During the time of this study, there were separate versions for children between four and eighteen years of age and between two and three years of age. The four- to eighteen-year-olds' CBCL includes 113 questions about behavioral problems, which overlap with the 99 questions on the two- to three-year-olds' CBCL. Individual items are rated using a three-point Likert scale in which the caregiver is asked about the frequency of a behavioral problem, and answers may be "not or never true," "somewhat or sometimes true," and "very or often true." The scores on individual items are then summed in a total-behavioral-problems scale, eight narrowband scales (for instance, withdrawn, anxious or depressed, social problems, aggressive behavior), and two broadband scales for internalizing (withdrawn, somatic complaints, anxious or depressed) and externalizing behavior (delinquent, aggressive behavior).

To account for the heterogeneity in behavior by age, CBCL narrow-band and broad-band scores are normed by age to produce T scores with cut points that delineate children who are in a normal ($T < 60$), borderline ($T = 60$ to 63), or clinical range ($T > 63$) for referral for treatment. Ultimately, the primary dependent variable developed from the eighteen- (wave 3) and thirty-six-month (wave 4) CBCL scores included the continuous raw scores and a second categorical variable derived from the normed categories of the summed CBCL scores and dichotomized as normal behavior versus borderline or clinically important abnormal behavior.

Notes

1. U.S. Department of Health and Human Services, Administration for Children and Families, Administration on Children, Youth and Families, Children's Bureau, "Adoption and Foster Care Analysis and Reporting System," (Washington: DHHS, 1995) (www.acf.hhs. gov/programs/cb/stats_research/afcars/tar/report10.pdf).

2. John Bowlby, *A Secure Base: Parent-Child Attachment and Healthy Human Development* (New York: Basic Books, 1988).

3. Richard P. Barth and others, *From Child Abuse to Permanency Planning: Child Welfare Services Pathways and Placements* (New York: Aldine de Gruyter, 1994); Mark D. Simms and others, "Health Care Needs of Children in the Foster Care System," *Pediatrics* 106 (2000): 909–18; R. R. Newton and others, "Children and Youth in Foster Care: Disentangling the Relationship between Problem Behaviors and Number of Placements," *Child Abuse & Neglect* 24, no. 10 (2004): 1363–74; Daniel Webster and others, "Placement Stability for Children in Out-of-Home Care: A Longitudinal Analysis," *Child Welfare* 79, no. 5 (2000): 614–32; Sigrid James and others, "Placement Movement in Out-of-Home Care: Patterns and Predictors," *Children and Youth Services Review* 26, no. 2 (2004): 185–206; Charles L. Usher and others, "Placement Patterns in Foster Care," *Social Service Review* 73 (1999): 22–36; Richard P. Barth and Melissa Jonson-Reid, "Outcomes after Child Welfare Services: Implications for the Design of Performance Measures," *Children and Youth Services Review* 22, nos. 9-10 (2000): 763–87.

4. Eric W. Trupin and others, "Children on Child Protective Service Caseloads: Prevalence and Nature of Serious Emotional Disturbance," *Child Abuse & Neglect* 17, no. 3 (1993): 345–55.

5. **On mental health problems:** Peter J. Pecora and others, *Improving Family Foster Care: Findings from the Northwest Foster Care Alumni Study* (Seattle: Casey Family Programs, 2005); Heather N. Taussig, "Children Who Return Home from Foster Care: A Six-Year Prospective Study of Behavioral Health Outcomes in Adolescence," *Pediatrics* 108, no. 1 (2001): E10. **On homelessness:** Heather N. Taussig, "Children Who Return Home from Foster Care." **On incarceration:** Richard P. Barth and Melissa Jonson-Reid, "Outcomes after Child Welfare Services"; Melissa Jonson-Reid and Richard P. Barth, "From Maltreatment to Juvenile Incarceration: Uncovering the Role of Child Welfare Services," *Child Abuse & Neglect* 24, no. 4 (2000): 505–20.

6. Mark D. Simms and others, "Health Care Needs of Children in the Foster Care System"; Eric W. Trupin and others, "Children on Child Protective Service Caseloads"; Mark D. Simms, "The Foster Care Clinic: A Community Program to Identify Treatment Needs of Children in Foster Care," *Journal of Developmental and Behavioral Pediatrics* 10, no. 3 (1989): 121–28; Alvin A. Rosenfeld and others, "Foster Care: An Update," *Journal of the American Academy of Child and Adolescent Psychiatry* 36, no. 4 (1997): 448–57; Neal Halfon and others, "Health Status of Children in Foster Care: The Experience of the Center for Vulnerable Children," *Archives of Pediatrics and Adolescent Medicine* 149, no. 4 (1995): 386–92; Robin Chernoff and others, "Assessing the Health Status of Children Entering Foster Care," *Pediatrics* 93, no. 4 (1994): 594–601; John A. Landsverk and others, *Mental Health Services for Children Reported to Child Protective Services,* vol. 2 (Thousand Oaks, Calif.: Sage, 2002); June M. Clausen and others, "Mental Health Problems of Children in Foster Care," *Journal of Child and Family Studies* 7, no. 3 (1998): 283–96.

7. Sigrid James, John A. Landsverk, and Donald J. Slymen, "Placement Movement in Out-of-Home Care: Patterns and Predictors," *Children and Youth Services Review* 26, no. 2 (February 2004): 185–206.

8. Sigrid James, "Why Do Foster Care Placements Disrupt? An Investigation of Reasons for Placement Change in Foster Care," *Social Service Review* 78 (2004): 601–27.

9. Sigrid James and others, "Placement Movement in Out-of-Home Care."

10. Thomas M. Achenbach, *Manual for the Child Behavioral Checklist/4-18 and 1991 Profile* (Burlington: University of Vermont, Department of Psychiatry, 1991).

11. Anthony N. Maluccio and others, "Family Reunification of Children in Out-of-Home Care: Research Perspectives," *Children and Youth Services Review* 18 (1996): 287–305; Anthony N. Maluccio and others, "Protecting Children by Preserving Their Families," *Children and Youth Services Review* 16 (1994): 295–307; Elaine Farmer, "Family Reunification

with High Risk Children: Lessons from Research," *Children and Youth Services Review* 18 (1996): 403–24; Toni Terling, "The Efficacy of Family Reunification Practices: Reentry Rates and Correlates for Abused and Neglected Children Reunited with Their Families," *Child Abuse & Neglect* 23 (1999): 1359–370.

12. Lucy Berliner, "Is Family Preservation in the Best Interest of Children?" *Journal of Interpersonal Violence* 8 (1993): 556–57; Richard J. Gelles, "Family Reunification/Family Preservation: Are Children Really Being Protected?" *Journal of Interpersonal Violence* 8 (1993): 557–62.

13. Fred H. Wulczyn and others, *Adoption Dynamics: The Impact of the Adoption and Safe Families Act* (University of Chicago, Chapin Hall Center for Children, 2004) (http://aspe. hhs.gov/hsp/fostercare-issues02/dynamics2/).

14. Edith Fein and Anthony N. Maluccio, "Permanency Planning: Another Remedy in Jeopardy?" *Social Services Review* 66 (1992): 335–48; Richard P. Barth and Marianne Berry, "Implications of Research on the Welfare of Children under Permanency Planning," in *Child Welfare Research Review,* edited by Richard P. Barth and others, vol. 1 (New York: Columbia University Press, 1994); Richard P. Barth, "Family Reunification," in *Child Welfare Research Review,* edited by Richard P. Barth and others, pp. 219–28.

15. **On the use of outpatient mental health services:** John A. Landsverk and others, *Mental Health Services for Children Reported to Child Protective Services,* vol. 2; Neal Halfon and others, "Mental Health Service Utilization by Children in Foster Care in California," *Pediatrics* 89 (1992): 1238–244; David M. Rubin and others, "Placement Stability and Mental Health Costs for Children in Foster Care," *Pediatrics* 113, no. 5 (2004): 1336–41; John Landsverk and others, "Impact of Child Psychosocial Functioning on Reunification from Out-of-Home Placement," *Children and Youth Services Review* 18 (1996): 447–62; Ann F. Garland and others, "Type of Maltreatment as a Predictor of Mental Health Service Use for Children in Foster Care," *Child Abuse and Neglect* 20, no. 8 (August 1996): 675–88; Charles Glisson, "The Effects of Services Coordination Teams on Outcomes for Children in State Custody," *Administration in Social Work* 18, no. 4 (1994): 1–23; Jeffrey S. Harman and others, "Mental Health Care Utilization and Expenditures by Children in Foster Care," *Archives of Pediatrics and Adolescent Medicine* 154, no. 11 (2000): 1114–117. **On screenings:** Sarah M. Horwitz and others, "Specialized Assessments for Children in Foster Care," *Pediatrics* 106, part 1 (2000): 59–66. **On referrals:** Laurel K. Leslie and others, "Comprehensive Assessments for Children Entering Foster Care: A National Perspective, *Pediatrics* 112, no. 1 (2003): 134–42.

16. John A. Landsverk and others, *Mental Health Services for Children Reported to Child Protective Services,* vol. 2; Sigrid James and others, "Predictors of Outpatient Mental Health Service Use: The Role of Foster Care Placement Change," *Health Services Research* 6, no. 3 (2004): 127–41.

17. Jan McCarthy, *Meeting the Health Care Needs of Children in the Foster Care System* (Georgetown University, 2002).

18. U.S. General Accounting Office, *Foster Care: Health Needs of Many Young Children Are Unknown and Unmet,* GAO publication no. GAO/HEHS-950114 (Washington: GAO, 1995).

19. David M. Rubin and others, "Placement Changes and Emergency Department Visits in the First Year of Foster Care," *Pediatrics* 114, no. 3 (2004): e354–e360.

20. Sigrid James, "Why Do Foster Care Placements Disrupt?"

11

Kinship Care and Nonkinship Foster Care: Informing the New Debate

RICHARD P. BARTH, SHENYANG GUO,
REBECCA L. GREEN, AND JULIE S. McCRAE

The century-old debate about the ability of out-of-home care to meet child welfare goals and objectives has evolved into a debate about two predominant forms of care: kinship care versus foster care.[1] Parties to the debate weigh the ability of each type of care to meet the three recognized goals of child protective services: safety, permanency, and well-being.[2] The debate includes the extent to which children in kinship and nonkinship care receive necessary services, although there is general agreement that kin are less likely to enroll children in additional services.[3]

The preference for placing children with extended family members is deeply rooted. First, relatives offer the opportunity for having a broad and lasting (beyond age eighteen) source of support. Indeed, many kinship cases are never opened formally by public child welfare agencies, or the cases are closed when children go to live with relatives who care for them without the support or supervision of formal child welfare services. Second, placement with relatives makes it more likely that children will be placed with their siblings, a factor of care that is enjoying rising practice and policy support.[4] Third, by most accounts children prefer to live with relatives, a preference that may reduce stress for children removed from their homes.[5] Consequently, the general preference

The authors thank the Annie E. Casey Foundation for its support of this work, and Patricia Kohl, Laura Chintapalli, and the NSCAW Research Group for their contributions.

for placing children with relatives would be likely to persist, even if developmental outcomes for children living with relatives were significantly worse than for children living in nonkinship foster care.

Nonetheless, understanding whether kinship and nonkinship homes are different and how these differences relate to child outcomes is important for at least three reasons. First, some decisions about placement are more marginal because the relatives may be distant by geography or lineage. Second, child welfare and allied service providers can benefit from having some general information that can help them anticipate the parenting and disciplinary tendencies of kinship and nonkinship caregivers. Last, foster parent training could be enhanced by such information. In the event that we can demonstrate that foster caregivers or kinship caregivers provide a uniformly better or worse result with regard to safety from reabuse and developmental outcomes, the information could be used to improve outcomes.

Children's safety is the most important goal of child welfare services and, especially, of child placement. Previous analyses of data from the National Survey of Child and Adolescent Well-Being (NSCAW) found that when reports of children in out-of-home care are examined by placement type at baseline, children in kinship care are less likely than children in foster care to have had an additional child abuse report by eighteen months (9.7 percent versus 25.6 percent).[6] Most of these reports were not substantiated—about 3 percent of children in kinship care at baseline had a substantiated report of maltreatment compared to 10.6 percent of children living in foster care. These rates are small and the differences become much smaller when we examine maltreatment by the caregiver and in the home, rather than maltreatment by other perpetrators in other settings. These comparisons are also limited because they are based on the child's initial placement and the child may have transitioned into a different placement over the course of eighteen months.

Selection of different types of children into kinship and nonkinship care also complicates the interpretation of safety in out-of-home care. Mary I. Benedict and her colleagues identified substantial preplacement differences between children in kinship care and nonkinship care.[7] They concluded that children in kinship care appear less likely to experience subsequent maltreatment while in care, even though their analysis did not correct for the differences between children who enter foster care and those who enter kinship care.

Child welfare researchers have generally found that children in kinship foster care experience fewer moves than children in nonkinship care. A study from the early 1990s in Illinois showed that kin placements are more stable than nonkin placements but that the advantage diminishes with lengthier durations of care.[8] Results of more recent research in Illinois indicate a greater potential for legal permanency with kin than earlier literature had suggested, but the results imply that placement disruptions with kinship care may also mount over a relatively long period of time.[9] A more recent goal of child welfare programs that has now been widely accepted is promotion of child well-being. Very few studies of children in kinship care have followed them to adulthood to determine their functioning. The few studies that have done so have indicated that it does not appear that nonkinship care is associated with greater problems in functioning for young adults, basing their results on unstandardized measures of the subjects' education, employment, physical and mental health, risk-taking behaviors, and stresses and supports in their lives. This appears to be the case, despite the evidence that the children in nonkinship care had more problems, including greater exposure to child maltreatment during foster care, than children in kinship care.[10]

A follow-up analysis of a San Diego long-term foster care sample by Heather N. Taussig and Robert B. Clyman found that children raised in out-of-home care who spent more time in kinship care had more problems in functioning than children raised with more time in nonkinship care.[11] In this study, youths who spent more time in kinship care had worse outcomes, in terms of delinquency, sexual behaviors, substance abuse, total risk behaviors, tickets and arrests, and grades, after adjusting for age, gender, and initial level of behavior problems.

The quality of kinship care has become particularly germane because kin placements have become the model placement type in many states.[12] When the quality of care falls below an acceptable level, safety concerns are signaled. In addition, the ascendance of well-being among the goals of child welfare services means that the quality of parenting and the home environment become more critical because they predict child well-being.[13]

Few studies that use direct measures of the foster caregiving environment have been conducted, and most were deeply flawed by accidental sampling and high attrition.[14] A recent critique of the kinship and nonkinship foster care literature identified four critical methodological issues: longitudinal research designs are best, standardized measures are preferred, selection bias should be minimized, and measures of the quality of the environment are needed.[15]

The relationships that children have with their out-of-home caregivers and the overall quality of the caregiving environment have been of long-standing concern to scholars of child welfare.[16] The intention of having children in the most family-like setting arises from the assumption that this setting will provide the most emotionally responsive, individualized caregiving. A related possibility is that because kinship foster care is a more family-like setting than nonkinship foster care, and has been shown to be somewhat more comfortable and satisfying, children in kinship foster care could well have better outcomes.[17] Our study tests these presumptions.

Highly punitive parenting may be particularly disturbing for maltreated children.[18] Alan J. Litrownik and his colleagues examined the punitiveness of caregiving environments for 254 children who had been removed from their homes prior to age four and were in long-term placements.[19] Nonkinship foster parents self-reported about half the rate of use of physical punishment as did kinship foster parents, although both were significantly lower than self-reports by adopted parents or biological parents. Rates of "psychological violence" did not differ for kin and nonkin foster parents. In a related analysis, Megan Tripp De Robertis and Alan Litrownik found that kinship foster parents were far more likely than nonkinship foster parents to report using harsh discipline with eight-year-old children in their care.[20] Further evidence from a sample of kinship foster care providers in Baltimore suggests that kin may have more problematic parenting attitudes than foster parents, although the difference disappears when controlling for caregivers' ages, suggesting the existence of some generational differences in beliefs about parenting.[21] Even when controlling for age, kinship care providers reported that they have fewer economic and social resources and poorer health than reported by traditional foster parents. These findings of poorer health for kin are supported by a previous study based on the NSCAW.[22]

The National Survey of Child and Adolescent Well-Being of children sub-study of children one year in foster care produced other findings germane to this discussion.[23] Findings show that ratings of the quality of the home environment are generally lower for foster family care families (kinship care and nonkinship care combined) than they are for a random sample of families in the National Longitudinal Survey of Youth.[24] Further, NSCAW analyses found that kinship and nonkinship caregivers were statistically indistinguishable on scores derived from a measure of the home environment. This result is inconsistent with claims that kin have fewer resources and riskier physical environments.[25] Some differences were apparent by age group and subscale. Caregivers with foster children younger than three years of age demonstrated more emotional support and higher total scores than kinship care homes with children younger than three years of age. Echoing previous findings, caregivers ages thirty-five to forty-four caring for children younger than three years old were found to provide more favorable environments than caregivers over fifty-four years old.[26] The difference between these findings and earlier studies may signal a general convergence, over time, in the quality of care for kinship and nonkinship caregivers.

The NSCAW One Year in Foster Care substudy also assessed the level of punitiveness in the homes in which children resided, using questions from the observational section of a home-rating scale. Examples included whether the mother or guardian shouted, expressed hostility, or slapped or spanked the child during the home visit. For children three to five years old, kin and nonkin care-givers' score on the home-rating scale were statistically indistinguishable on punitiveness: about one-third of each showed some punitiveness. Nor did kin and nonkin differ in punitiveness without emotional support—a particularly undesirable style of parenting.[27] This study also confirmed that households with an annual income of more than $50,000 received significantly higher (that is, more positive) overall scores than households with income below $25,000; the same was true of home environments in which the caregiver held an academic degree categorized as "other" (such as a certificate of technical skills) as compared to households where the caregiver held no academic degree.

In the NSCAW one-year-in-foster-care substudy analysis, kinship and nonkinship foster caregivers are of similar ages, although the age range for kin is greater. Still, 20 percent of kinship and 11 percent of nonkinship foster parents were sixty years old or older. Caregivers in nonkin foster homes are somewhat more likely to be married (73 percent) than those in the kinship group (55 percent) ($p < 0.09$). Children in kinship foster care are more likely to live with caregivers without a high school education and who are older than caregivers of children in nonkin foster homes or children in general.[28] Generally, both kinship and nonkinship foster parents have limited educational achievement, with 55 percent of kinship caregivers and 58 percent of nonkinship caregivers having a high school education or less.

Methods

This study addresses a fundamental assumption of child welfare services, namely, that the environment in which an abused or neglected child resides after child welfare intervention will be safe and developmentally appropriate, and examines how well kin and non-kin can meet these and related standards. The literature review indicates the importance of retesting previous findings because they were local, may be dated, and did not correct for differential selection of children into kin and non-kin care.

Sample

This study uses data from the NSCAW core samples. Initially involving 5,501 children, this number is reduced to approximately 1,075 when children who had initial kinship and nonkinship foster care placements at baseline are identified. This number is reduced to 567 by the time of the follow-up at eighteen months. Only those children are included who have remained in foster care or kinship care, respectively, for at least 75 percent of the time, roughly one year. Although the children (one per family) were the sampling unit, the caregivers also represent a national probability sample of foster and kinship caregivers caring for children in out-of-home care for one year.

Developmental Measures

Multiple measures were used to capture child well-being. Each measure is relevant to a unique age range, so that the sample for each analysis is slightly different.

—Child Behavior Checklist (CBCL). The CBCL was used to measure children's level of emotional and behavioral problems at baseline and at eighteen months. This study used the total, internalizing, and externalizing scores of the CBCL.

—Social Skills Rating System (SSRS). Social skills were measured by caregiver reports for children aged three and older, using the SSRS with standardized scores based on a mean of 100 and a standard deviation of 15.[29] Social skills were categorized as low (< 85), average (85 to 115), or high (> 115).

—Mini-Battery of Achievement (MBA). Academic achievement was measured for children aged 6 and older using the Mini-Battery of Achievement (MBA).[30] Reading and math scores were generated (mean = 100 and standard deviation = 15).

—Kaufman Brief Intelligence Test (K-BIT). The K-BIT was used as an additional measure of cognitive performance for children aged four and older.[31]

—Vineland Adaptive Behavior Scales (VABS). Adaptive behavior of children from birth to ten years was measured using the VABS Screener, a standardized measure designed to assess a child's competence and independence ("adaptive behavior") in the daily living environment. The daily living skills scale measures self-help skills and the ability to complete activities of daily living in the natural environment.

—Trauma Symptom Checklist for Children (TSC-C 1996). The TSC-C was developed to evaluate children's responses to unspecified traumatic events.[32] The Posttraumatic Stress Scale (PTS) of the TSC-C was used in this study and was administered to children ages seven and older.

—An additional variable, called the proportion of clinical scores, was created to assess the proportion of scores on the standardized measures for each case considered to be at a "clinical" level.[33] If specific cutoff points were not available for a measure, a strict criterion of two standard deviations beyond the mean was used. This variable is meant to provide an indication of the overall severity of children's developmental issues.

Environmental and Parenting Measures

Child welfare workers, parents, and youths provided information used in the analyses that follow.

Types of alleged maltreatment. Using a modified Maltreatment Classification Scale, child welfare workers identified the types of maltreatment alleged in the report that led to the child's inclusion in the study.[34] Categories of maltreatment in this study include physical abuse, sexual abuse, physical neglect, supervisory neglect, and "other." When more than one type was reported, workers identified the most serious type.

Prior child welfare services. Workers indicated whether the child had a prior history of involvement with child welfare services, not including investigations.

Cumulative family risk assessment. Workers identified risk factors during the time of the investigation, for example, caregiver drug or alcohol abuse, cognitive impairment, and domestic violence. A summary score was created that sums all identified risk items and assigns families into three categories: low, medium, high.

Home Observation Measure of the Environment–Short Form (HOME-SF). The HOME-SF measures the quality and quantity of stimulation and support in the home environment of children from birth to ten years.[35] Items assess the mother's behaviors toward the child and aspects of the physical environment (such as safe play environment), with higher scores indicating a more developmentally advantageous environment.

Conflict Tactics Scale Parent to Child Version (CTSPC). Youths aged eleven and older reported violence at the hands of their caregivers using the CTSPC. Parenting tactics were categorized as harsh, severe, or very severe. The authors created a cumulative score that weighted acts considered severe (hit with fist or kicked) or very severe (beat up, burned, or scalded) at two or three times the value of "harsh" acts. Severity and frequency of the acts were also used to create the scales.

Short Form Health Survey (SF-12). This instrument provides estimates of the physical and mental health status of caregivers.[36] The measure was used with out-of-home caregivers and was the only direct measure of their health and well-being.

Analysis Approach

The goal of this study is to determine differences in developmental outcomes for children in kinship and nonkinship care during the first eighteen months of care. This goal is not easily accomplished because of preexisting differences between children who enter kinship care and those who enter nonkinship care.[37] In one of the few studies to explicitly test the influence of selection effects on service outcomes, Andrew Grogan-Kaylor found that many characteristics of children and their families were related to the type of foster care setting in which children were placed, including children's age and race, caregiver's health status, welfare eligibility of the family from which children were removed, and the reason the children were removed.[38] Further, some of the effects of placement in kinship care on reunification rates are attributable to this differential selection.[39] Because there are no studies of random assignment of children into kinship and nonkinship care (if kin are available to care for children and meet agency standards, children are likely to be placed with them), analysis of the effects of kinship and foster care placement requires adjustments for these preexisting differences. A strategy called propensity-score matching (PSM) is used to mitigate the effects of these preexisting differences. In propensity-score matching, the subjects are resampled according to a single score that captures their similarity to each other. The intention is to obtain a matched resampled group whose members are all about equally likely to have been given a certain "treatment" or not.[40] In this case, the "treatment" is being in kinship care, so members of the nonkinship care sample are given a score, using logistic regression, that captures the likelihood that they could also have been placed into kinship care. Those with a score most like the children who actually were in kin care are then retained in the study so that the groups are relatively equal in background characteristics.

Results

The findings describe the child and caregiver characteristics and examine their relationship to developmental outcomes.

Child and Caregiver Demographics

Tables 11-1 and 11-2 present bivariate statistics on child and caregiver characteristics, respectively, for children and their kin or nonkin caregivers. The first two columns in table 11-1 present figures for all children, and the last two columns apply to a subgroup of children and their counterparts selected using propensity-score matching.[41] With regard to the overall prematched sample of children, a significantly higher proportion of children in kinship care were female (0.75) than in nonkinship care (0.54).

A significantly higher proportion of children in nonkinship care than in kinship care were classified as needing special education services (0.23 versus 0.06). Social skills, as measured by the Social Skills Rating System, and daily living skills, as measured by the Vineland Adaptive Behavior Scales Screener, were both significantly higher for children in kinship care than in nonkinship care. Similarly, the proportion of clinical scores was significantly higher for children living in nonkinship care (0.3) than for those living in kinship care (0.2).

None of these differences between children in nonkinship and kinship care appeared in groups generated by propensity-score matching, indicating that the selection effects are mitigated. Several differences not present in the overall sample later emerged in the matched group. A significantly higher proportion of matched children living with nonkinship caregivers had three or more out-of-home placements between baseline and eighteen months (0.39 and 0.22, respectively). In addition, in the matched analysis children living with nonkinship caregivers had a significantly higher mean MBA mathematics score (99.6 versus 85.4), as well as a significantly higher mean score on the Trauma Symptom Checklist (56.1 versus 50.0), than children living with kinship caregivers.

Table 11-2 shows that kin and nonkin caregivers differed significantly in the overall sample on age (kin were older) and caregiver education (kin were less educated). Differences in self-reported caregiver mental health and the number of children were not significant at baseline but were marginally significant ($p < 0.05$) after matching.

Table 11-1. *Child Characteristics and Tests for Differences between Nonkinship and Kinship Caregivers*[a]

	Full sample		Matched sample	
Characteristic	Nonkinship caregivers (n = 398)	Kinship caregivers (n = 169)	Nonkinship caregivers (n = 93)	Kinship caregivers (n = 93)
Background characteristics (percent)				
Gender[b]				
Male	46	25	44	41
Female	54	75	56	59
Race or ethnicity				
Non-Hispanic Black	38	35	43	38
Non-Hispanic White	40	46	27	35
Hispanic	15	15	20	22
Other	8	4	10	5
Maltreatment type				
Physical abuse	22	21	19	15
Sexual abuse	11	1	4	4
Neglect				
Failure to provide	24	35	35	41
Failure to supervise	33	37	38	35
Other	10	6	5	5
Child has IEP (baseline)[b]	23	6	8	8
Lives with siblings (baseline)	33	59	47	51
Number of out-of-home placements (baseline to eighteen months)[c]				
One or two	57	72	61	78
Three or more[c]	43	28	39	22
Age and scores at baseline (means)				
Age	5.5	5.2	2.5	2.1
CBCL, externalizing	58.8	54.5	55.8	58.5
CBCL, internalizing	57.8	51.7	57.8	56.1
CBCL, total	60.8	54.4	58.3	59.7
SSRS[b]	83.9	101.4	86.6	90.0
VABS[b]	91.6	111.7	98.8	99.8
MBA, reading	101.8	113.7	98.1	95.4
MBA, mathematics[c]	98.6	102.1	99.6	85.4
K-BIT	93.4	102.9	90.5	90.3
Trauma Symptom Checklist[c]	53.6	50.2	56.1	50.0
Proportion of clinical scores at baseline[b]	0.3	0.2	0.2	0.2

Source: Author's calculations.

CBLC = Child Behavior Checklist; IEP = individual education plan; K-BIT = Kaufman Brief Intelligence Test; MBA = Mini-Battery of Achievement; SSRS = Social Skills Rating System; VABS = Vineland Adaptive Behavior Scale Screener.

a. Prematched statistics are weighted; postmatched statistics are unweighted. For the developmental scores, the "matched" analysis was done using the matched group corresponding to the particular score with *n*s as follows: CBCL (*n* = 57/57), SSRS (*n* = 55/55), MBA (*n* = 37/37), K-BIT (*n* = 41/41), Trauma (*n* = 25/25).

b. Full sample differences (χ^2/*t*-tests), $p < 0.05$.

c. Matched sample differences (χ^2/*t*-tests), $p < 0.05$.

Table 11-2. *Caregiver Characteristics and Tests for Differences between Nonkinship and Kinship Caregivers*[a]

percent unless otherwise noted

	Full sample		Matched sample	
Characteristic	Nonkinship caregivers (n = 398)	Kinship caregivers (n = 169)	Nonkinship caregivers (n = 93)	Kinship caregivers (n = 93)
Age (baseline)[b]				
Younger than 35	16	12	27	18
35–44	34	17	30	28
45–54	28	33	22	40
55 and older	22	38	21	14
Race or ethnicity				
Non-Hispanic Black	28	29	39	33
Non-Hispanic White	49	55	44	45
Hispanic	18	11	16	16
Other	5	4	1	5
Urbanicity[c]				
Urban	82	97	96	95
Nonurban	18	3	4	5
Below poverty level	20	24	27	24
Foster caregiver education[c]				
Less than high school	8	25	16	21
High school degree	50	23	43	43
More than high school	42	52	41	36
Parental active drug abuse (baseline)	39	62	59	62
Parental prior CPS history	61	47	48	52
Number of children in household (baseline)[b]				
One or two	43	61	33	53
Three or more	57	39	67	47
Foster Caregiver Short Form–Health Survey scores (baseline)				
Physical health	49.6	50.3	51.1	48.8
Mental health[b]	54.4	54.6	54.6	51.9
HOME-SF score (baseline)	1.5	1.6	1.5	1.6
Harsh or severe parenting score (baseline)[c,d]	40.0	48.2	60.4	40.0

Source: Authors' calculations, based on NSCAW.

CPS = child protective services; HOME-SF = Home Observation Measure of the Environment–Short Form.

a. Prematched statistics are weighted; postmatched statistics are unweighted; all *n*s are unweighted and may vary by characteristic.

b. Postmatched sample differences (χ^2/*t*-tests), $p < 0.05$.

c. Prematched sample differences (χ^2/*t*-tests), $p < 0.05$.

d. Because of comparable age ranges, the "matched" analysis for harsh or severe parenting score was done using the CBCL (Child Behavior Checklist) matched group (*n* = 57/57).

*Comparison of Developmental Measures for Children
in Kinship and Nonkinship Care*

After constructing the most similar groups possible, we tested for differences in changes of developmental measures over eighteen months, as shown in table 11-3.[42] Results show that, on the Vineland Adaptive Behavior Scales Screener, the entire sample of kinship care ($N = 109$) and nonkinship care ($N = 233$) children had declines of about 10 points, with a difference between their changes of 1.3 points. The adjusted mean difference estimate was negligible.

The amount of change in the Social Skills Rating System was also statistically indistinguishable for children in kinship and nonkinship care. Scores for children in kinship care declined slightly (0.25) and those for children in nonkinship care increased (1.40), but the overall difference was not significant. The change in the externalizing Child Behavior Checklist score was more positive for children in kinship care in the test of unadjusted mean difference. The scores of children in kinship care improved by about 2 points, whereas those of children in nonkinship care got about 2.5 points worse ($p < 0.05$). This result was also found in the OLS adjusted analysis of mean differences. The findings appear quite robust.

For the internalizing Child Behavior Checklist score, the findings were also in the direction of greater improvement for the children in kinship care, although children in both forms of care made gains. None of the analyses pointed to large differences between the gains for children in kin and nonkin care.

Analyses of Possible Mechanisms for Developmental Change

Only three of the measures—the Vineland Adaptive Behavior Scales Screener, the Social Skills Rating System, and the Child Behavior Checklist—had enough matched cases to allow for additional multivariate analyses regarding contributors to change in development (see table 11-4). In these analyses we included kinship care as a variable but also included four or five other predictors of development that were not used to create the propensity scores. One of these predictors was the propensity score itself, maintained in this model to try to provide additional control for selection. The child's age at baseline was included because of its important role in explaining developmental outcomes in our previous work.[43] Also included were the number of placements a child had experienced between baseline and eighteen months and the number of children in the home at baseline. The findings indicate that the contributors to development vary by measure and sample.

The Home Observation Measure of the Environment–Short Form contributed to change on the Vineland Adaptive Behavior Scales Screener: the

Table 11-3. *Changes in Developmental Scores between Baseline and Eighteen Months for Children in Kin and Nonkin Care, Using Unadjusted and Adjusted Mean Differences*

Score	Unadjusted mean difference			Adjusted mean difference estimated by OLS
	Kin care	Nonkin care	Difference	
Self-care skills (VABS)[a]	–9.45	–10.75	1.30	–0.15
Social skills (SSRS)[b]	–0.25	1.40	–1.65	–2.30
Problem behaviors (CBCL), externalizing[c]	–2.04	2.34	–4.38*	–3.99*
Problem behaviors (CBCL), internalizing[c]	–2.95	–0.44	–2.48	–1.59
Problem behaviors (CBCL), total[c]	–2.84	0.83	–3.66*	–3.10
School achievement (MBA), math[d]	5.21	–2.86	8.07	6.17
School achievement (MBA), reading[d]	2.30	2.26	0.04	–2.38
Intelligence (K-BIT)[e]	3.21	3.86	–0.66	–2.17
Trauma symptoms (PTS)[f]	–2.71	–6.14	3.43	2.70

Source: NSCAW data analysis.

CBCL = Child Behavior Checklist; K-BIT = Kaufman Brief Intelligence Test; MBA = Mini-Battery of Achievement; OLS = ordinary least squares; PTS-TSC-C = Posttraumatic Stress Test of the Trauma Symptom Checklist for Children; SSRS = Social Skills Rating System; VABS = Vineland Adaptive Behavior Scale Screener.

*$p < 0.05$.

a. $N = 109$ children in kin care and 233 in nonkin care.

b. $N = 67$ (kin care) and 144 (nonkin care).

c. $N = 73$ (kin care) and 154 (nonkin care).

d. $N = 47$ (kin care) and 99 (nonkin care).

e. $N = 53$ (kin care) and 116 (nonkin care).

f. $N = 34$ (kin care) and 72 (nonkin care).

higher (better) the HOME-SF total score, the greater the improvement on the VABS. Children's age at baseline was also a significant predictor for the VABS, with the older children having significantly greater changes in score ($p < 0.001$). The number of placements (one or two versus three or more) did not contribute significantly to the Vineland. The number of children in the home was a significant factor yielding the result that the more children in the home, the greater the improvement in the Vineland ($p < 0.05$).

The number of placements and kinship care have a substantial influence on the Child Behavior Checklist scores. Kinship care results in more positive changes in externalizing ($p < 0.01$) and total ($p < 0.05$) scores. A higher number of placements also has a positive relationship to change—a somewhat counterintuitive finding; children who have three or more placements have a greater reduction in internalizing ($p < 0.01$) and total ($p < 0.05$) scores than those with fewer placements. It is possible that the effects of placement changes on behavior are not as pronounced when those placements may occur in order to place

Table 11-4. *Regression Models Explaining Changes in Development in Matched Sample*

| | Change in VABS (n = 186) | Change in SSRS (n = 110) | Change in CBCL (n = 14) | | |
| | | | External-izing | Internal-izing | Total |
Measure					
Kinship care[a]	2.71	−1.93	−5.86**	−2.26	−4.49*
Propensity score	−1.98	−10.44	0.65	0.98	−0.99
Child age at baseline	5.12***	0.24	−0.19	0.01	−0.28
Three or more placements[b]	−5.00	1.55	−3.96	−6.41**	−5.15*
Three or more children in home[c]	8.65*	1.85	−2.13	3.12	−0.09
HOME-SF, total score	17.46*	n.a.	n.a.	n.a.	n.a.

Source: NSCAW data analysis.

n.a. Not available.

CBCL = Child Behavior Checklist; HOME-SF = Home Observation of the Environment–Short Form; SSRS = Social Skills Rating System; VABS = Vineland Adaptive Behavior Scales Screener.

*$p < 0.05$, **$p < 0.01$, ***$p < 0.001$.

a. The reference group for the kinship care analysis is foster care.

b. The reference group for three or more placements is the group with one or two placements.

c. The reference group for three or more children in the home is the group with one or two children in the home.

children with relatives. None of these predictors helped to explain changes in the Social Skills Rating System score.

Results of Parenting Style and Safety Analyses

Two additional analyses were conducted regarding caregiver punitiveness and low responsiveness among children aged five and younger, and violence at the hands of caregivers, as reported by children aged eleven and older. The first analysis compared the weighted proportions of caregivers with "low" and "high" punitiveness, responsiveness, and the combination of high punitiveness with low responsiveness, using the Home Observation Measure of the Environment–Short Form. Low responsiveness was defined as being approximately in the lower 50 percent of scores on responsiveness. Punitiveness was defined as having a score of 1 or more on the punitiveness scale.

About one-fifth of the children were rated as experiencing both low responsiveness and high punitiveness at both baseline and eighteen months (0.21 and 0.17, respectively). Proportions for this combination measure are similar when broken down by children living with nonkinship and those with kinship caregivers at each assessment point.

Children's reports of harsh or severe parenting at the hands of caregivers were compared at baseline and eighteen months, using the Conflict Tactics Scale–Parent to Child Version. Results show that overall, children living with nonkinship caregivers and kinship caregivers are not significantly different in their exposure to harsh and severe parenting. Interpretation of the baseline data is complicated by the likelihood that the child is reporting on the parenting he or she experienced prior to placement. The eighteen-month data are less likely to be similarly influenced because most of the children had been in care for most of the eighteen months. Although the sample is small (N = 138), the rate of harsh or severe parenting by kin at eighteen months (26.8) is a concern, yet not significantly different than that reported by children of nonkinship caregivers at eighteen months (9.3).

Discussion

The results of this analysis clearly confirm the results of prior studies: children in kinship and nonkinship care are significantly different from each other at the time of placement. Differences between children in kinship and nonkinship care that are measured following placement may simply reflect these preexisting differences. These findings reaffirm the importance of developing ways to deal with the greater level of problems among children in nonkinship care, when comparing the two groups of children. We found that there was little evidence of developmental or behavioral advantages for either group, although the children in kinship care did appear to experience greater reductions in externalizing and total problem behaviors.

These findings are important because the primary child welfare service provided to most abused and neglected children is the direct care they receive from substitute caregivers. Even when children have behavior problems, educational problems, and a need for mental health services, they do not routinely get them.[44] It follows that developmental progress for children in foster care must often be generated through the foster care environment itself.[45] Yet foster care environments have been shown in prior NSCAW research to be less positive than the environments provided by average families in national surveys.[46] In this study, lower home environment scores are associated with less gain on the Vineland Adaptive Behavior Scales Screener. Although we lack a definitive standard for assessing caregiver responsiveness and punitiveness, as many as one in five caregivers can be considered from the home environment observation to be punitive and to have low responsiveness to the children.

There is modest evidence that home environments can be enriched through parent training interventions, although the overall effects are limited and are smaller in lower-income families.[47] Thus even though some short-term interventions may help both foster and kinship foster families to have a more stimulating home environment, these interventions are unlikely to bring low-scoring families up to a level at which their care is rehabilitative. New methods need to be developed to enhance the quality of foster families.

It is important to understand the likely impact on children of living with caregivers who are older, less educated, and of lower income than families in the general population. Any general notion that foster parents are predominantly middle class is untrue. That 25 percent of kinship caregivers have less than a high school education and only 42 percent of nonkinship foster parents have educational attainment beyond high school indicates that the growing concerns about the educational underachievement of foster children may require substantial educational support in their homes, which are not, otherwise, educationally enriched. The general finding of little difference in gains for children in kinship and nonkinship foster care, on any developmental measure aside from the CBCL, was not predicted from prior research. Although the sample sizes for some of the comparisons are modest, they are large enough to make apparent a medium-size difference between the groups. The consistent results from the many approaches to analyzing change, only some of which are reported here, offer assurances that the findings do not depend on the methods used. A possible explanation for the findings is that likely developmental advantages of having nonkinship foster parents with higher education and incomes and greater years of experience as foster parents are, apparently, counterbalanced by some elements of the caregiving environments of the kinship foster parents. Although kinship caregivers did not show a higher level of emotional responsiveness than nonkinship caregivers, there may be other influences that stem from their family relationships with the children in their care. In both settings there was a reduction in youth-reported trauma across the eighteen months. Changes in educational achievement were quite small—less than half a standard deviation—and there was no difference between the groups.

The sizable proportion of children living in foster care with three or more other children is striking and not previously reported. Most of these large households have a stay-at-home foster parent, and the regression analysis indicates that these larger homes are not associated with worse developmental change. Still, the way that parenting occurs in these homes requires more understanding. When a young child with a variety of developmental vulnerabilities lives with three or more other children, each of whom may also have special problems, one is entitled to raise questions about the level of individual attention the child will receive. Prior analyses indicated that infants are more likely than older children to be placed in out-of-home settings with more children, perhaps an ominous developmental circumstance.[48]

Sizable challenges are faced by caregivers involved in the care of maltreated children, whether the caregivers are their biological parents, relatives, or someone else. Numerous prior studies have clarified the substantial educational and behavioral difficulties experienced by the children in this population; our national findings are confirmatory.[49] Few training resources are available to help these well-intentioned families achieve their objectives.[50]

The public goal for services to children in out-of-home care should clearly be to improve the quality of both kinship and nonkinship care. A vision for excellence in foster care is needed. One place to begin is to examine the reasons why such a large proportion of kinship and nonkinship homes, more than one in five, is below the poverty level. Reimbursing foster parents more for the care they provide would improve the resource base in existing homes. This could very well increase the likelihood that foster children get the kinds of developmental experiences that other nonpoor children receive. Increasing foster care payments will require a change in the perspective of the role of foster parents. Cost is also a factor, although this is not an insurmountable barrier, because many states spend far more money on group care than on foster care and are often willing to increase the rate of expenditures for group homes and to expand the use of treatment foster care (which has more services and is more costly than foster care). More centrally, there is a clash of values and concerns about fairness. These constraints on arriving at an acceptable rate of reimbursement derive in part from a concern about not paying foster parents substantially more to care for children than biological families receive from welfare to care for their own children. There is also a concern that if government reimburses foster parents a substantial amount, grifters rather than altruistic foster parents might be attracted to serve.

Another approach to improving the developmental benefits of out-of-home care is better linkages of care to services. Linking every foster home to a resource center, which serves as an informal source of support such as a local religious or civic organization, or a resource person (such as a contact family) might be a component of a vision for foster care that would support families and improve child development. Ensuring that all foster parents receive consistent, powerful, supportive, in-home training would be another appropriate component of the vision. Pilot work is under way in several jurisdictions to see that foster parents and kinship foster parents get the kind of support that has been provided to treatment foster parents.[51] This approach may be the most expeditious and feasible way to bring compensatory resources to high-risk children in low-resource homes. Still, foster families should not have to reduce their own standard of living and that of their other children in order to look after children who are the responsibility of the state. The possibility of such a virtual reverse subsidy occurring should be reduced by increasing the resources available to foster and kinship parents—perhaps by broadening the types of educational, tutorial, recreational, and holiday expenditures that are reimbursable.

Child welfare researchers have not seriously studied whether they can raise the quality of parenting in foster care. Perhaps too much attention has been paid to the differences between kinship and nonkinship foster care with regard to licensing and reimbursement issues and not enough to the quality of care. Further research is needed to determine what it takes to improve these caregiving environments. The required strategies are likely to require examining the adequacy of the foster care reimbursement rate, training, and support.

Key elements in the improvement of the well-being of foster children appear to be getting overlooked. The recruitment, training, and support of foster parents have made few gains in recent decades. The initiation of longer foster parent training programs have been viewed as progress by some, but there is almost no empirical basis for suggesting that these programs provide any benefit for children.[52] These foster care orientation groups are largely designed to help increase foster parents' knowledge of child welfare services and to decide what role they want to have in the foster care and adoption continuum of care. Yet there are models of foster care that appear to result in better recruitment, training, and retention of foster parents who are effective with children. Project KEEP at Children's Hospital in San Diego shows that using the techniques employed in treatment foster care with kinship and foster families increases parenting skills and reduces behavioral problems and placement disruptions. These techniques include support groups, family therapy, and parent daily reports, which help the families to identify problems before they become overwhelming. The positive outcomes are especially likely when the number of children placed in a home is small. Casey Family Programs, a foster care agency in Seattle, has developed guidelines for their foster parents and kinship foster parents to help close the achievement gap.[53] The approach includes setting high expectations for children, establishing and practicing structured study routines in the home, limiting after-school jobs, discussing schoolwork and events, staying involved with youths at the secondary level, and monitoring peer and out-of-school activities. In a few communities, educational assistance is provided to kin to support the children in their care and improve their own literacy and numeracy.[54]

Notes

1. Martin Wolins and Irving Piliavin, *Institution and Foster Family: A Century of Debate* (New York: Child Welfare League of America, 1964).

2. **On safety:** Mary I. Benedict and others, "Adult Functioning of Children Who Lived in Kin Versus Nonrelative Family Foster Homes," *Child Welfare* 75 (September–October 1996): 529–49. **On permanency:** Mark F. Testa, "Kinship Care and Permanency," *Journal of Social Service Research* 28 (December 2001): 25–43. **On well-being:** Heather N. Taussig and Robert B. Clyman, *Kinship Care and Foster Care: Differential Outcomes Following Six Years in Care* (Denver, Colo.: International Congress on Child Abuse and Neglect, 2002).

3. Jill Duerr Berrick and others, "A Comparison of Kinship Foster Homes and Foster Family Homes: Implications for Kinship Foster Care as Family Preservation," *Children and Youth Services Review* 16 (1994): 33–64; Sara C. Carpenter and others, "Are Children in Kinship Care Getting the Mental Health Services They Need?" *Pediatric Research* 55 (April 2004): 228A.

4. Aron Shlonsky and others, "The Other Kin: Setting the Course for Research, Policy, and Practice with Siblings in Foster Care," *Children and Youth Services Review* 27 (July 2005): 697–716.

5. Mimi V. Chapman and others, "Children's Voices: The Perceptions of Children in Foster Care," *American Journal of Orthopsychiatry* 74 (July 2004): 345–52.

6. U.S. Department of Health and Human Services, Administration for Children and Families, *National Survey of Child and Adolescent Well-Being: Children Involved with the Child Welfare System (Wave 1)* (Washington: GPO, 2004).

7. Mary I. Benedict and others, "The Reported Health and Functioning of Children Maltreated while in Family Foster Care," *Child Abuse & Neglect* 20 (July 1996): 561–71.

8. Mark F. Testa, "Kinship Care and Permanency."

9. Ibid.

10. Mary I. Benedict and others, "The Reported Health and Functioning of Children Maltreated while in Family Foster Care"; Mary I. Benedict and others, "Adult Functioning of Children Who Lived in Kin Versus Nonrelative Family Foster Homes."

11. Heather N. Taussig and Robert B. Clyman, *Kinship Care and Foster Care.*

12. Rob Geen and Jill Duerr Berrick, "Kinship Care: An Evolving Service Delivery Option," *Children and Youth Services Review* 24 (January-February 2002): 1–14.

13. Robert Bradley and others, "The Home Environments of Children in the United States, Part II: Relations with Behavioral Development through Age Thirteen," *Child Development* 72 (November 2001): 1868–886.

14. For example, see Jill Duerr Berrick and others, "Comparison of Kinship Foster Homes"; Maureen C. Smith, "An Exploratory Study of Foster Mother and Caseworker Attitudes about Sibling Placement," *Child Welfare* 74 (July–August 1996): 357–76.

15. Gary S. Cuddeback, "Kinship and Family Foster Care: A Methodological Substantive Synthesis of Research," *Children and Youth Services Review* 26 (July 2004): 623–39.

16. Henry S. Maas and Richard E. Engler, Jr., *Children in Need of Parents* (New York: Columbia University Press, 1959); Michael S. Wald, "Thinking about Public Policy toward Abuse and Neglect of Children: A Review of 'Before the Best Interests of the Child,'" *Michigan Law Review* 78 (March 1980): 645–93.

17. Mimi V. Chapman and others, "Children's Voices."

18. Gayla Margolin and Elana B. Gordis, "The Effects of Family and Community Violence on Children," *Annual Review of Psychology* 51 (February 2000): 445–79.

19. Alan J. Litrownik and others, "Long-Term Follow-up of Young Children Placed in Foster Care: Subsequent Placements and Exposure to Family Violence," *Journal of Family Violence* 18 (February 2003): 19–28.

20. Megan Tripp De Robertis and Alan J. Litrownik, "The Experience of Foster Care: Relationship between Foster Parent Disciplinary Approaches and Aggression in a Sample of Young Foster Children," *Child Maltreatment* 9 (February 2004): 92–102.

21. Brenda Jones Harden and others, "Kith and Kin Care: Parental Attitudes and Resources of Foster and Relative Caregivers," *Children and Youth Services Review* 26 (July 2004): 657–71.

22. Richard P. Barth and others, "Characteristics of Out-of-Home Caregiving Environments Provided under Child Welfare Services," *Child Welfare* (in press).

23. Richard P. Barth and others, "Characteristics of Out-of-Home Caregiving Environments Provided under Child Welfare Services"; U.S. Department of Health and Human Services, Administration for Children and Families, *National Survey of Child and Adolescent Well-Being: Children Living for One Year in Foster Care* (Washington: DHHS, 2003).

24. Center for Human Resource Research, "National Longitudinal Survey of Youth/1979 Cohort," selected tables (Ohio State University) (www.chrr.ohio-state.edu/nls-info/nlscya/childya_userguide.html [June 2002]).

25. For example, see Richard P. Barth, "Abusive and Neglecting Parents and the Care of Their Children," in *Public Policy for the Evolving American Family*, edited by Steven Sugarman and others (Oxford University Press, 1998), pp. 217–35.

26. Brenda Jones Harden and others, "Kith and Kin Care."

27. See Miriam R. Linver and others, "Family Processes as Pathways from Income to Young Children's Development," *Developmental Psychology* 38 (September 2002): 719–34.

28. Richard P. Barth and others, "Characteristics of Out-of-Home Caregiving Environments Provided under Child Welfare Services."

29. Frank M. Gresham and Stephen N. Elliot, *Social Skills Rating System Manual* (Circle Pines, Minn.: American Guidance Service, 1990).

30. Richard W. Woodcock and others, *Mini-Battery of Achievement* (Itasca, Ill.: Riverside Publishing, 1994).

31. Virginia Delaney-Black and others, "Violence Exposure, Trauma, and IQ and/or Reading Deficits among Urban Children," *Archives of Pediatrics and Adolescent Medicine* 156 (March 2002): 280–85.

32. John Briere, *Trauma Symptom Checklist for Children: Professional Manual* (Odessa, Fla.: Psychological Assessment Resources, Inc., 1996).

33. Clinical-level measures may include Social Skills Rating System, Bayley Infant Neurodevelopmental Screener, Kaufman Brief Intelligence Test, Child Behavior Checklist, Children's Depression Inventory, Vineland Adaptive Behavior Scale Screener, Preschool Language Scale–3, Mini-Battery of Achievement, Battelle Developmental Inventory, Youth Self-Report (YSR), and Teacher Report Form (TRF), depending on the ages of the children. Although there are three measures from the CBCL suite, only school-age youths had the Teacher Report Form, and only youths older than eleven had the Youth Self-Report.

34. Jody T. Manly and others, "The Impact of Subtype, Frequency, Chronicity, and Severity of Child Maltreatment on Social Competence and Behavior Problems," *Development and Psychopathology* 6 (Winter 1994): 121–43.

35. Robert Bradley, "The HOME Inventory: Review and Reflections," *Advances in Child Development and Behavior* 25 (1994): 241–87.

36. John E. Ware and others, *SF-12: How to Score the SF-12 Physical and Mental Health Summary Scales,* 3d ed. (Lincoln, R.I.: Quality Metric, Inc., 1998).

37. Gary S. Cuddeback, "Kinship and Family Foster Care."

38. Andrew Grogan-Kaylor, "Who Goes into Kinship Care? The Relationship of Child and Family Characteristics to Placement into Kinship Foster Care," *Social Work Research* 24 (September 2000): 132–41; Andrew Grogan-Kaylor, "The Effect of Initial Placement into Kinship Foster Care on Reunification from Foster Care: A Bivariate Probit Analysis," *Journal of Social Service Research* 27 (November 2001): 1–31.

39. Andrew Grogan-Kaylor, "Who Goes into Kinship Care?"

40. For a discussion of the method with a NSCAW sample, see Shenyang Guo, Richard P. Barth, and Claire Gibbons, "Propensity Score Matching Strategies for Evaluating Substance Abuse Services for Child Welfare Clients," *Children and Youth Services Review* 28, no. 4 (2006): 357–83.

41. The matched groups were slightly different depending on the measure used because of missing data. The matched group represented in the table is the group included in the Vineland analysis (except where otherwise indicated), presented to illustrate an example of the more parallel statistics of the matched group. Statistics for the matched groups selected for the CBCL and SSRS analyses would likely vary somewhat but could be expected to exhibit a similar pattern.

42. Two additional analyses using the matched sample were conducted (adjusted mean differences and *t*-tests). Details about the procedure and results are available from the authors.

43. For example, see Richard P. Barth and others, "Characteristics of Out-of-Home Caregiving"; Barbara J. Burns and others, "Mental Health Need and Access to Mental Health Services by Youth Involved with Child Welfare: A National Survey," *Journal of the American Academy of Child and Adolescent Psychiatry* 43 (August 2004): 960–70; Fred Wulczyn and others, *Beyond Common Sense: Child Welfare, Child Well-Being, and the Evidence for Policy Reform* (New York: Aldine Transaction, 2005).

44. Barbara J. Burns and others, "Mental Health Need and Access to Mental Health Services by Youth Involved with Child Welfare."

45. U.S. DHHS, Administration for Children and Families, *National Survey of Child and Adolescent Well-Being*.

46. Richard P. Barth and others, "Characteristics of Out-of-Home Caregiving."

47. Marian Bakermans-Kranenburg and others, "Those Who Have, Receive: The Matthew Effect in Early Childhood Intervention in the Home Environment," *Review of Educational Research* 75 (Spring 2005): 1–26.

48. U.S. Department of Health and Human Services, *National Survey on Adolescent and Child Well-Being*; Richard P. Barth and others, "Characteristics of Out-Of-Home Caregiving."

49. See, for example, John Landsverk and others, "Mental Health Services for Children Reported to Child Protection Services," in *The APSAC Handbook on Child Maltreatment,* 2nd ed., edited by John E. B. Myers and others (Thousand Oaks, Calif.: Sage, 2002).

50. Michael Hurlburt and others, "National Variation in Efforts to Train Child Welfare Workers and Foster Caregivers on Children's Mental Health and Development," *Journal of Social Service Research* (in press).

51. Patricia Chamberlain and others, "Who Disrupts from Placement in Foster and Kinship Care?" *Child Abuse & Neglect* (in press).

52. Richard Puddy and Yo Jackson, "The Development of Parenting Skills in Foster Parent Training," *Children and Youth Services Review* 25 (2003): 987–1013.

53. National Human Services Assembly, "Parental Involvement in Education," Family Strengthening Policy Center, Policy Brief 3 (October 2004) (www.nassembly.org/fspc/practice/documents/ParentalInvolvementBrief2.pdf).

54. Marianne Takas, *Relatives Raising Children: A Guide to Finding Help and Hope* (New York: Brookdale Foundation, 2000).

12

Child Maltreatment Recurrence among Children Remaining In-Home: Predictors of Re-Reports

PATRICIA L. KOHL AND RICHARD P. BARTH

T he fundamental mission of child welfare services is to protect the safety of children.[1] To assess success in protecting children, evaluators generally rely on indicators constructed from reabuse reports collected by child welfare service agencies.[2] It is no secret that official reports offer limited information. Maltreatment has to be reported before it is included in official counts, and when it is reported, detailed data about child and family characteristics are not routinely collected. To develop a deeper understanding of maltreatment recurrence, such deficiencies have to be addressed.[3] The aim of this chapter is to expand current knowledge about the relationship between child welfare involvement, case characteristics, and new maltreatment reports and to draw implications for practice from the enhanced knowledge base. Child welfare involvement is defined here as receipt of a maltreatment report or the opening of an investigation by child protective services, regardless of the outcome or of whether in-home or out-of-home services were provided following the investigation.

Available evidence from state studies of maltreatment reports indicates that new maltreatment reports are received for many children following child welfare

The conclusions are the authors' own and do not necessarily represent those of the Administration for Children and Families of the U.S. Department of Health and Human Services. The authors thank the University of North Carolina at Chapel Hill and the National Survey of Child and Adolescent Well-Being research group for contributions to this work, with special thanks to Shenyang Guo, Julie McCrae, Rebecca Green, and Claire Gibbons.

involvement. In a study of 189,375 maltreated children in Florida, researchers found that 26 percent had a substantiated re-report over the two years following their index maltreatment investigation.[4] A Washington state study determined that of 120,000 initial reports to child protective services, 29 percent were followed by a re-report within two years of the initial report and 11 percent by a substantiated re-report.[5] Data from Oklahoma and Pennsylvania indicated that 25 percent of families had a re-report over four years (although the authors did not report substantiation rates for those re-reports).[6] Findings from these two states revealed that, over time, the re-report rate was similar regardless of whether the prior maltreatment had been substantiated. Another multistate study, this one using National Child Abuse and Neglect Data System (NCANDS) data from ten states, found that 20 percent of confirmed (substantiated or indicated) cases had a confirmed re-report within the next year.[7]

Even broader national data now inform the discussion of recurrent abuse. Findings from forty-four states reporting to NCANDS indicated that 8.4 percent of children had another substantiated or indicated report of maltreatment within six months.[8] Of all children in the National Survey of Child and Adolescent Well-Being (NSCAW), regardless of whether they remained in-home or were placed in out-of-home care, 22 percent (ages zero through sixteen) had at least one re-report and 5 percent had a substantiated re-report within eighteen months of the close of the index child maltreatment investigation.[9] The findings of all these studies clearly indicate that about a quarter of children had a re-report (either substantiated or unsubstantiated) and most within two years. However, there was more variation in the findings on substantiated re-reports than in the findings on any other re-reports. The reported range for substantiated re-reports was from 5 percent to 26 percent of children.

Comparisons across studies are complicated by variations in the definitions of recurrent maltreatment and in time to follow-up. Despite the differences, recurrent maltreatment affects a substantial number of children. According to national data, 906,000 children were found to be victims of maltreatment in 2003.[10] More than 225,000 of those children may be victims of recurrent maltreatment. However, given that some children may enter the recurrence pool multiple times, 225,000 is likely to be an overestimation of the actual number of children.

Predictors of Recurrent Maltreatment

Although maltreated children frequently are reabused despite child welfare intervention, the case characteristics that explain recurrence are unclear. Our review of research on case characteristics (that is, child, caregiver, family, environmental, maltreatment, and service characteristics) predicting recurrent maltreatment provides an overview of the current state of knowledge and offers evidence to support the set of variables to predict recurrence that we included in our analyses. Child demographics are considered first.

Children's gender and race and ethnicity are not clearly related to re-reporting of maltreatment. Differences in the rates of report for males and females have been found by some scholars but not by most others.[11] The same inconsistency holds true for race/ethnicity, with some studies revealing a significant difference but others finding no association.[12]

An association between recurrent maltreatment and age frequently is reported, most commonly for the youngest children. One analysis found that while 30 percent of children under the age of four years had a new report, only 24 percent of children between the ages of twelve and fifteen did.[13] Studies in both Colorado and Washington also found that younger children were at greater risk for recurrent maltreatment.[14] Studies of recurrent maltreatment with samples limited to infants also reveal high levels of re-reports for the youngest children. Analyzing data from NCANDS, Palusci and colleagues found that 21 percent of children younger than age of one at the time of their first confirmed maltreatment report had another confirmed report by the age of three.[15] In California, 42 percent of infants had re-reports within three years of the first report.[16] However, drawing conclusions about the relationship between age and recurrent maltreatment is complicated by the statistical methodology. These studies do not account for the independent contribution of age when accounting for other case characteristics. Our study expands the current knowledge base by analyzing the relationship between age and recurrent maltreatment within the context of other case characteristics.

Characteristics of previous child welfare involvement also are related to recurrent maltreatment. Any prior child welfare involvement, unspecified postinvestigative services, and out-of-home placement at the time of the initial investigation followed by reunification have each been found to be associated with re-reports.[17] Furthermore, the length of time before a re-report became incrementally shorter for each additional prior referral to child welfare services.[18] Substantiation of the index maltreatment report also may be important, but the literature on this question is ambiguous.[19] Finally, the identified maltreatment type of the initial report has been shown to be related to recurrent maltreatment, with higher rates of recurrence typically associated with neglect.[20]

In addition, certain caregiver and environmental characteristics may predict re-reports. Evidence suggests that domestic violence, substance abuse by the caregiver, the caregiver's own childhood history of abuse and neglect, and the caregiver's emotional problems are all associated with re-reports.[21] Wolock and colleagues found poverty, as measured by receipt of welfare, to be a significant predictor of a re-report.[22] In a Missouri study, researchers found that higher neighborhood income was associated with a reduced risk of recurrent maltreatment.[23]

Child Welfare Services and Recurrent Maltreatment

A key goal of child welfare services is to increase the safety of children by reducing maltreatment. Yet many families involved with child welfare services—even those having a substantiated report of maltreatment—do not receive services following the maltreatment investigation. Among 646 families investigated for child maltreatment in California, 83 percent received no further services at the end of the intake process.[24] Even after maltreatment was substantiated, more than two-thirds (67 percent) of the cases were closed with no additional services provided. In NSCAW, 49 percent of families with a substantiated maltreatment report whose child remained in home did not receive child welfare services following the index investigation.[25]

An additional concern is that even when services are provided, they may be ineffective. Evidence that recurrent maltreatment was frequent among families who received child welfare services emerged as early as the 1970s, and many subsequent investigations have reinforced it.[26] Although Diane DePanfilis and Susan J. Zuravin considered recurrent maltreatment while families were receiving child welfare services and found that families that actively participated in services were less likely to have re-reports, other research suggests that the association between services and recurrent maltreatment runs in the opposite direction.[27] That is, services are associated with an increased likelihood of recurrent maltreatment. Because families with the highest risk of recurrent maltreatment are more likely than families with lower risk to receive services, the high-risk families are also less likely to benefit from services. Because of this selection bias, the results of the studies discussed here should be interpreted with caution.

Child Behavior and Safety

Child behavior problems have been largely ignored in the study of child abuse reports. Children's behavior problems may certainly result from child maltreatment;[28] they may also place children more at risk by eliciting extreme acts of physical punishment and adding to the overall level of stress within the family.[29] In the same way, child behavior problems may increase the risk of recurrent maltreatment. This study therefore offers an estimate of the relationship between children's behavior problems and the recurrence of maltreatment.

The Study

This study expands the current knowledge base by using the NSCAW national probability sample of children investigated for maltreatment and focusing on recurrent maltreatment among children who remained in home following the index maltreatment investigation. Children placed in out-of-home care are likely to have different recurrent maltreatment experiences and therefore were excluded from the study.

The aim of the study was to examine reports of maltreatment between the index maltreatment investigation and the eighteen-month follow-up interview ("re-reports"). The specific research questions were

—What proportion of children had one or more re-reports?

—What proportion of children had substantiated re-reports?

—What is the likelihood that in-home or out-of-home services were provided following re-reports?

—What family and case characteristics were associated with re-reports?

The subset of NSCAW used for this study consisted of children remaining in-home following the index maltreatment investigation and their families (*N* = 3,143).

Outcome Measures

Re-report. In our study, a re-report was defined as a new maltreatment allegation reported to a child welfare agency between the index investigation (that is, the investigation that led to inclusion of a child in the NSCAW study) and the eighteen-month follow-up interview, regardless of the disposition of a case following any subsequent investigation. Information about re-reports was obtained from the child welfare worker at twelve months and eighteen months but only if the case was currently open for in-home services or had been opened at some point between interviews. The worker was asked whether there had been any reports of abuse or neglect involving the child since the index investigation. If so, the worker indicated whether the investigation of the re-report was completed. Families were considered to have a re-report only if the investigation had been completed. If information on a re-report was missing because the case did not meet requirements for conducting an interview (that is, there was no new involvement with child welfare services), the re-report variable was coded as "no re-report." Reports that came only one day after the index report were considered to be about the same maltreatment incident and were not counted as a re-report. After each affirmative response about investigated re-reports, workers were asked about additional re-reports. The number of re-reports identified at twelve months and at eighteen months were added together to obtain the total number of re-reports. A measure of multiple re-reports was developed from the total number of re-reports and categorized into "no re-reports," "one re-report," "two re-reports," "three re-reports," and "four or more re-reports."

Substantiation. Once it was ascertained that a re-report had occurred, child welfare workers were asked to identify the case by the following terms: substantiated, indicated, neither substantiated nor indicated, high risk, medium risk, and low risk. Substantiation was the disposition when the allegation of maltreatment was supported by state law or state policy; indication was the determination when there was reason to suspect maltreatment but it could not be substantiated under state law. Indicated cases were coded as "unsubstantiated." In addition, a few states in NSCAW opt for a completely different coding system; they use high, medium, or low risk as their case determination following investigation. Those codes were included in the current analyses by recoding "high risk" to "substantiated" and "medium" and "low risk" to "unsubstantiated." We believe that this approach results in a conservative count of substantiated re-reports.

Services following re-reports. For each new report, the child welfare worker was asked about services provided following the re-report. Possible responses were

—child welfare agency involvement with the child's family ended (that is, the case was closed to services)

—the child was left in-home and the case was opened to child welfare services

—the child was placed in out-of-home care.

Families with multiple re-reports may have had different outcomes after each investigation. Therefore, cases were coded as "closed" only if they were closed following all investigations that may have occurred. If, after any investigation, the child went into out-of-home care, the case was coded as "out-of-home care."

Other Measures

Most serious maltreatment type. Child welfare workers first indicated all maltreatment types included in the report from ten possible categories: physical abuse, sexual abuse, emotional abuse, neglect (failure to provide), neglect (failure to supervise), abandonment, moral/legal maltreatment, educational maltreatment, exploitation, and other. Next, they designated the most serious maltreatment type. These ten categories were collapsed into five categories: physical abuse, sexual abuse, neglect (failure to provide), neglect (failure to supervise), and other.

Child service setting. There were two service categories for families whose children remained in-home following the index maltreatment investigation: closed to services (that is, no child welfare services provided) and receipt of in-home child welfare services.

Child welfare worker risk assessment. Child welfare workers identified family risks using a checklist of twenty-two potential risks. Seven of the risk items were used for this study: prior report of child maltreatment, prior receipt of child welfare services, active domestic violence, caregiver alcohol abuse, caregiver drug abuse, caregiver history of childhood maltreatment, and financial difficulties. Prior maltreatment reports and prior receipt of child welfare services referred to experiences that occurred before the index investigation. Active domestic violence was an indication that violence between adult intimate partners was present at the time of the investigation. Caregiver alcohol abuse and caregiver drug abuse were combined into a single item: substance abuse by the primary caregiver. Caregiver history of childhood maltreatment was scored if the caregiver had a known history of childhood abuse or neglect. Finally, financial difficulties were assessed with the question, "At the time of the investigation, did the family have trouble paying for basic necessities such as food, shelter, clothing, electricity, or heat?"

Domestic violence. Information about domestic violence also was assessed through a caregiver's self-report of victimization. The physical violence subscale of the Conflict Tactics Scale was used to assess caregivers' experiences of physical violence by an intimate partner.[30] Because of the sensitive nature of the questions, the scale was administered to caregivers through audio computer-assisted self-interview technology. Caregivers reported on experiences of domestic violence within the twelve months preceding each interview.

Child behavior. The Child Behavior Checklist total problem behavior score was used to measure children's behavior problems.[31] Caregivers reported on their children's behavior at both baseline and eighteen months. To account for changes in behavior over the study period, the Child Behavior Checklist score was included in multivariate analyses.

Urbanicity. The definition of urbanicity of the primary sampling unit, usually a county, was consistent with the U.S. Census Bureau definition. A county was considered urban if more than 50 percent of its population lived in an urban area.

Poverty. Financial status at baseline and eighteen months was determined using the federally defined poverty level. This measure was calculated according to procedures followed by the U.S. Census Bureau, which includes both the family's income level and the number of adults and children in the household.[32] The poverty measure was used as a continuous variable in the analyses. Values below 1.0 indicated that the family's income was below the poverty level (for example, 0.70 = 70 percent of the poverty level) and values above 1.0 indicated that the family's income was above the poverty level (for example, 1.50 = 150 percent of the poverty level). To account for changes in a family's poverty status from baseline to eighteen months, the change in poverty level was used in the multivariate models.

Parenting support services. A variable was created to capture total parenting support services received by a family. Included in the definition of support services were parenting training, respite care, parent aide, family counseling, assistance in cleaning and repairing the home, and home management skills training. The primary source of information was the caregiver report, which was supplemented with the child welfare worker's report when caregiver information was missing or unavailable. The total number of units of parenting support services received was divided by the average number of days in a month (30.475) so that parenting support service units would represent months of parenting support services received.

Results

Nearly a quarter (23.0 percent) of all children who remained in-home at the time of the initial investigation had at least one re-report over the study period (table 12-1). Provision of child welfare services following investigation and urbanicity of the area were associated with re-reports. Nearly a third (32.4 percent) of children in families that received in-home child welfare services following the initial investigation had at least one re-report; that figure was significantly higher than the 19.6 percent of children with re-reports in families that did not receive such services. Interpretation of this finding must be done with caution, however, because of the potential bias associated with the selection of the highest-risk families into services. Significantly more children living in urban areas had at least one new report (25.1 percent) than children living in nonurban areas (16.9 percent). Child age, gender, race and ethnicity, and maltreatment were not associated with the probability of a re-report.

While 23 percent of children had at least one re-report, the range in number of re-reports extended from one to ten over eighteen months (table 12-2). Among all children remaining in home following the initial investigation, 13 percent had one re-report, 6.8 percent had two re-reports, 1.6 percent had three re-reports, and 1.6 percent had more re-reports. From another perspective, of children with at least one re-report, more than half had one re-report (56.6 percent), while 30 percent had two re-reports, 7 percent had three re-reports, and another 7 percent had four or more re-reports over the eighteen-month study period (figures not in table). Significantly more children in families that received child welfare services had multiple re-reports than children in families that did not.

Although there were not significant differences across age groups for a single re-report, there were significant differences in multiple re-reports across age groups (table 12-2). Multiple re-reports were more likely among three- to five-year-olds. Among that age group, 9.6 percent had two new reports, whereas among zero- to two-year-olds, only 4.7 percent had two reports. Among youths eleven years of age and older, the percentage was 5.3 percent. More three- to five-year-olds had at least four re-reports (2.8 percent) than any other age group. While overall, 1.6 percent of children had three re-reports, 4.2 percent of zero- to two-year-olds did.

Overall, 38.4 percent of children with at least one re-report had a substantiated re-report. There was no statistically significant relationship between the number of re-reports and the substantiation rate.

In-home or out-of-home services or both were provided to some children or their families following the re-report investigation. The outcome of the investigation was case closure for 52.5 percent of the children who had at least one re-report, while 18.2 percent of the children were placed in out-of-home care and the families of 29.3 percent were provided in-home child welfare services. A

Table 12-1. *Official Report of New Maltreatment Allegations by Case Characteristics*[a]

Characteristic	Re-report (percent)
*In-home setting***	
No child welfare services	19.6
Child welfare services	32.4
Child age (baseline)	
0–2	22.7
3–5	26.7
6–10	24.0
11 and older	18.0
Child gender	
Male	23.3
Female	22.7
Child race and ethnicity[b]	
Non-Hispanic Black	26.2
Non-Hispanic White	19.6
Hispanic	26.1
Other	23.9
Most serious maltreatment type[c]	
Physical abuse	19.6
Sexual abuse	20.8
Neglect (failure to provide)	27.1
Neglect (failure to supervise)	24.5
Other	26.1
*Urbanicity status**	
Urban	25.1
Nonurban	16.9
Total	23.0

Source: Authors' calculations.

*$p < 0.05$, **$p < 0.01$, chi-square test.

a. Unweighted $N = 3,143$, except where noted. All analyses done with weighted data.

b. Unweighted $N = 3,140$.

c. Unweighted $N = 2,802$.

comparison of substantiated and unsubstantiated re-reports reveals that service provision was more likely following substantiated re-reports. Significantly fewer cases were closed (28.7 percent) following a substantiated re-report, and significantly more families received in-home (35.6 percent) and out-of-home (35.7 percent) services when the re-report was substantiated. In contrast, when the re-report was unsubstantiated, 67.3 percent of cases were closed, only 25.3 percent of families received in-home services, and 7.3 percent had a child placed into out-of-home care. Because the relationship between substantiation and subsequent services included multiple reports—that is, some of these substantiations

Table 12-2. *Percentage of Children in Selected Age Categories
and in Two Child Service Settings*[a]

| Characteristic | Number of re-reports | | | | |
	0	*1*	*2*	*3*	*4 or more*
*Age (baseline)**					
0–2	77.3	12.8	4.7	4.2	1.0
3–5	73.3	13.3	9.6	1.0	2.8
6–10	76.0	14.3	7.2	0.7	1.8
11 and older	82.0	10.9	5.3	1.5	0.4
*Child service setting***					
No CPS	80.4	11.4	6.2	1.2	0.8
CPS	67.6	17.4	8.7	2.6	3.7
Total	77.0	13.0	6.8	1.6	1.6

Source: Authors' calculations.
CPS = child protective services.
*$p < 0.05$, **$p < 0.01$, chi-square test.
a. Unweighted $N = 3,143$. Analysis done with weighted data.

were not on the first report—the relationships to service opening could also be affected by the number of re-reports that occurred, not just whether they were substantiated.

Figure 12-1 depicts the flow of families' experiences with child welfare services, taking into account the number of re-reports, whether at least one of the re-reports was substantiated, and whether services were subsequently provided. While substantiation rates were similar across each of the multiple re-report categories, differences across groups became more evident when services provided following a substantiated re-report were considered. The proportion of cases closed without services became smaller with each increase in the number of re-reports. For instance, 36.3 percent of cases were closed with one re-report, but only 2.9 percent remained closed throughout the entire study period when there were four or more re-reports.

Even though the vast majority (91.6 percent) of all the children in the NSCAW study remained in-home for the entire eighteen months, the remainder (8.4 percent) spent at least a small proportion of time in out-of-home care (not shown in figure). A higher number of re-reports increased the likelihood of placement. A higher proportion (43.5 percent) of children for whom there were four or more re-reports, at least one of which was substantiated, spent time in out-of-home care than did children with only one re-report (which was substantiated) (35.3 percent). The association between the number of re-reports and service status (that is, case closed, in-home services, or out-of-home care) was significant for children with one, three and, four re-reports.

Figure 12-1. *Pathway through Child Welfare Services for Children with Multiple Re-Reports*

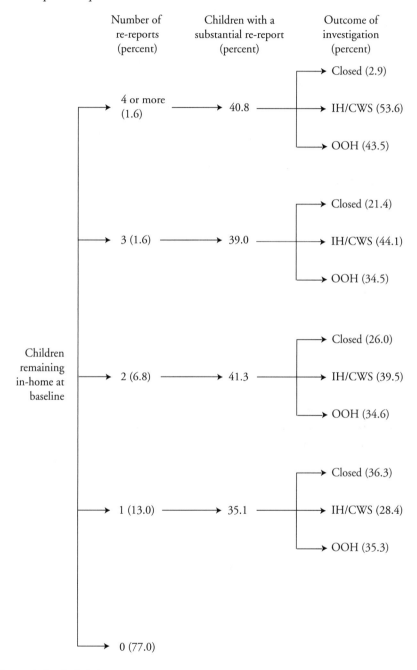

Source: Authors' calculations.
CWS = child welfare services; IH = in-home placement; OOH = out-of-home placement.

Multivariate analyses were conducted to investigate the relationship between recurrent maltreatment and case characteristics. We examined predictors of re-report (regardless of the case disposition) over the study period.[33] Reports of maltreatment prior to the index investigation, domestic violence, caregiver history of abuse and neglect, urbanicity, the child's Child Behavior Checklist score, and receipt of parenting support services were significantly associated with re-report when we controlled for other variables in the model (table 12-3). Children who had reports prior to the index investigation were more than twice as likely to have a re-report as children who had no previous maltreatment reports (that is, those children for whom the investigation leading to inclusion in NSCAW was their first maltreatment report). Self-report of recent domestic violence victimization of the caregiver at baseline also was associated with re-reports. The likelihood of re-report increased 1 percent for each one-unit increase in the frequency of domestic violence reported by the caregiver on the Conflict Tactics Scale. Furthermore, if the caregiver had a childhood history of abuse and neglect, re-report was twice as likely as it was with caregivers who did not have such a history. Children with behavior problems were significantly more likely to have a re-report. For every 1 point increase in their standardized score on the Child Behavior Checklist, they were 3 percent more likely to have a re-report.

Service receipt also predicted re-reports. Families receiving more parenting support services were more likely to be re-reported. For every additional month of services received, they were 19 percent more likely to have a re-report. Families in nonurban areas were about half as likely to have a re-report as those in urban areas. Finally, a re-report was 1.5 times more likely for families whose cases were opened to child welfare services following the index maltreatment investigation than for families not receiving services. This finding, however, must be interpreted in light of the fact that selection into services was not random. Families at most risk of re-involvement were likely to have a greater propensity to receive services.

Discussion

Knowledge of estimates and correlates of re-reports can aid child welfare workers in identifying families at the highest risk of child welfare re-involvement. When considering the independent effects of multiple case characteristics, workers should note that factors such as domestic violence, child's behavior problems, and receipt of parenting support services are associated with an increased likelihood of re-report. Furthermore, study results revealed that a substantial proportion of families in NSCAW had one or more new maltreatment allegations between baseline and eighteen months. As the number of re-reports increased, so did the likelihood that the case would be open to child welfare services.

Table 12-3. *Predictors of at Least One Re-Report*[a]

| | At least one re-report | |
Predictors	F *statistic*	Odds ratio
Model minus	4.28 (24)****	. . .
In-home child service setting	2.808*	. . .
No CWS (reference group)		
CWS	. . .	1.52
Child age	1.59	—
0–2	. . .	0.69
3–5	. . .	0.58
6–10 (reference group)		
11 and older	. . .	0.47
Child gender	0.91	. . .
Female (reference group)		
Male	. . .	0.78
Child race and ethnicity	1.98	. . .
Non-Hispanic Black	. . .	1.60
Non-Hispanic White (reference group)		
Hispanic	. . .	1.77
Other	. . .	1.10
CBCL score	11.52***	1.03
Prior reports of maltreatment[b]	7.28***	2.30
Prior CWS	0.97	0.79
Most serious maltreatment type	0.32	. . .
Physical abuse (reference group)		
Sexual abuse	. . .	0.95
Neglect (failure to provide)	. . .	1.29
Neglect (failure to supervise)	. . .	1.06
Other	. . .	0.82
Substantiated index report	1.92	0.69
Number of re-reports	n.a.	n.a.
Caregiver reported domestic violence	4.95*	1.01
Caregiver mental health problem	1.32	0.68
Caregiver substance abuse problem	0.73	1.36
Caregiver history of abuse and neglect	5.39**	1.90
Financial difficulties	2.96*	1.63
Poverty	0.43	0.92
Urbanicity status	5.29**	. . .
Urban (reference group)		
Nonurban	. . .	0.56
Receipt of parenting support services	11.28***	1.19

Source: Authors' calculations.
*$p < 0.10$, **$p < 0.05$, ***$p < 0.01$, ****$p < 0.001$, Cox Snell Psuedo $R^2 = 0.13$.
n.a. not available; . . . not applicable.
CBCL = Child Behavior Checklist; CWS = child welfare services.
a. Unweighted $N = 1,587$. Analysis done with weighted data.
b. Absence of risk is reference group for dichotomous variables.

Nearly a quarter (23 percent) of children in NSCAW who remained in-home following the index maltreatment investigation had at least one re-report, a rate similar to that in findings from studies with longer study periods.[34] In another finding consistent with other research, around half of the children with re-reports had only one re-report, whereas a substantial number of children had multiple re-reports over eighteen months.[35] That nearly 4 percent of children had three or more re-reports is remarkable in view of the relatively short study period. This finding is especially troubling in light of recent research indicating that a higher frequency of re-reports is associated with poorer child development outcomes.[36]

An examination of the relationship between age and re-report shows that younger children are at most risk of multiple re-reports. Children between the ages of three and five years seem to be at the highest risk, especially for multiple re-reports. This age group is also least likely to enter out-of-home care following the index maltreatment investigation, which implies that child welfare workers assessed preschool children to be safe to remain in the home.[37] Although we do not have a measure of the seriousness of the reabuse, 33 percent of the re-reports on three- to five-year-olds were substantiated. Substantial and sustained risks to preschoolers seem to be overlooked. Children between zero and two years of age, the most vulnerable of children, are also at considerable risk for recurrent maltreatment. This is a particular concern because of their developmental vulnerability; abuse can result in lasting cognitive and neurobiological change.[38]

Adolescents appear to be at less risk of re-report and multiple re-reports. Adolescents are likely to spend more time away from home, thereby reducing the opportunity for abuse to occur. In addition, some agencies are reluctant to accept reports on adolescents. The evidence of substantially different rates of reabuse for adolescents reinforces the importance of understanding the context in which adolescents receive services. This population stands apart from other age groups in many ways that remain largely unstudied.

Despite the important distinctions in the relationships between age and re-report, further examination relying on statistical techniques that consider the simultaneous contribution of multiple case characteristics reveals that age does not make a significant, unique contribution to re-report when the analysis controls for other family and case characteristics. That finding suggests that such characteristics as reports prior to the index investigation, child behavior, domestic violence, and urbanicity are more important than age.

Emphasizing the importance of substantiated re-reports as an indicator of recurrent maltreatment, the Child and Family Service Reviews (CFSR) national standard states that fewer than 6.1 percent of children should have another substantiated or indicated report within six months of the index report.[39] In all, about 8.7 percent of all children in the study had a substantiated re-report, a rate higher than the CFSR standard.

Such a high reabuse rate raises concerns about the role of services in reducing re-reports. Our findings do not point to a reduction in reabuse for children who receive services. This finding is not new.[40] Our analyses offer additional information about this relationship because we are able to examine receipt of child welfare services at three points: prior to the index investigation, following the index investigation, and following re-reports. Receipt of child welfare services following the index investigation increases the likelihood of a re-report. That relationship holds true when considering the relationship solely between re-reports and receipt of child welfare services as well as when accounting for other case characteristics. Variability in how families are selected into services, however, may influence the outcomes. That is, families assessed as having the greatest risk of recurrent maltreatment are subsequently selected into child welfare services and are, because of their inherently greater problems, more likely to have a re-report, despite service provision. Another possible explanation for the relationship includes greater "surveillance" of service recipients. Re-reports may occur because, through continued involvement with families, professionals are more likely to become aware of any ongoing maltreatment.

Child welfare services, as currently provided, are not reducing maltreatment reports in the lives of some children. However, we presume that a re-report in an open child welfare case is often preventative in nature and may result from reabuse that is less severe and less lasting and that therefore the harm to children is substantially mitigated. Unfortunately, we do not have a measure of the severity of maltreatment for subsequent reports, so that possibility cannot be addressed with NSCAW data. These findings must be interpreted with caution because selection bias is a serious problem in evaluating the effectiveness of services on child safety. While the process of selection into child welfare services is sometimes guided by explicit protocols, more often it is unobservable and difficult to identify. The resulting selection biases prevent researchers from efficiently estimating the true effects of service use. One possible reason for selection bias is that more seriously affected families often use the most services and may sustain the poorest outcomes because of their greater pre-service problems. Without services, families at the highest risk of recurrent maltreatment may have even poorer outcomes.

Some family characteristics, such as victimization of the caregiver, are associated with re-report. A re-report is nearly twice as likely when the caregiver has a childhood history of abuse and neglect. Recent domestic violence reported at baseline also increases the likelihood of a re-report. Despite the growth of information about the overlap between domestic violence and child abuse, child welfare workers often fail to identify domestic violence during maltreatment investigations.[41] Programmatic efforts must continue to be developed to improve the discovery of and response to domestic violence to ensure the safety of both children and their caregivers.

Especially critical is the need to address risks to children arising from domestic violence, which affects at least a third of families investigated for child maltreatment and has ripple effects that last and increase the odds of recurrence.[42] Recurrence may be partially explained by the low rate of placement of children into foster care from families affected by domestic violence, which underscores the need for child welfare workers to remain involved with those families.[43] Furthermore, although protocols to improve coordination of domestic violence and child welfare services are under development, evidence-based interventions are urgently needed.

Substance abuse has been found to be associated with re-reports, but the results are mixed.[44] When children removed from home after the NSCAW index investigation were included in the analysis, the risk of re-report was lower for children with drug-abusing parents.[45] When analysis was limited to only those children remaining in-home, as we have done here, substance abuse was no longer a significant factor in re-reports. One explanation for that finding is that a higher proportion of children with substance-abusing parents are placed in out-of-home care, thereby virtually eliminating the risk of a re-report of abuse by the parents.[46]

The outcome of the re-report(s) shows that more than half (52.5 percent) of families never received services following a re-report. However, as the number of re-reports grew, families were much less likely to have their case closed to services. In fact, nearly all (97 percent) of those families with at least four re-reports received either in-home or out-of-home services. With more re-reports, placement in out-of-home care was more likely, as was receipt of in-home services. It appears that some families must be involved with child welfare agencies multiple times before services are deemed necessary to protect their children. Several encounters with a family may also be needed before child welfare workers understand the dynamics of the family well enough to take the steps necessary to serve the family.

Statistical Note

The proportion of children who had one or more re-reports, the proportion of children who had substantiated re-reports, and the likelihood that in-home or out-of-home services were provided following a re-report were determined by using contingency table analyses with chi-square tests. A multivariate model of re-report was estimated using logistic regression analysis.

Because NSCAW is a nationally representative sample with a complex sample design, we employed the SUDAAN software package in the data analysis. SUDAAN allows the analyst to account for clustering and other complex sampling effects and to use appropriate sample weights in statistical inferences. The sample sizes varied somewhat due to missing responses on some variables.

Relationships were considered to be statistically significant if the *p* value was less than 0.05. In some instances, trends also were discussed (*p* < 0.10).

Notes

1. Adoption and Safe Families Act, 42 U.S.C.A. §§ 672 et seq., P.L. 105-89.

2. For example, see Vincent J. Palusci, Elliot G. Smith, and Nigel Paneth, "Predicting and Responding to Physical Abuse in Young Children Using NCANDS," *Children and Youth Services Review* 27 (June 2005): 667–82.

3. Susan J. Wells and Michelle A. Johnson, "Selecting Outcome Measures for Child Welfare Settings: Lessons for Use in Performance Management," *Children and Youth Services Review* 23 (February 2001): 169–99.

4. Lodi L. Lipien and Melinda S. Forthofer, "An Event History Analysis of Recurrent Maltreatment Reports in Florida," *Child Abuse & Neglect* 28 (September 2004): 947–66.

5. David B. Marshall and Diana J. English, "Survival Analysis of Risk Factors for Recidivism in Child Abuse and Neglect," *Child Maltreatment* 4 (November 1999): 287–96.

6. Susan J. Wells, "Decision Making in Child Protective Services Intake and Investigation," *Protecting Children* (Fall 1985): 3–8.

7. A substantiated maltreatment report is an allegation of maltreatment that is supported by state law or state policy, while indication is a case determination used by some states when there is reason to suspect maltreatment but it cannot be substantiated under state law. See John D. Fluke, Ying-Ying T. Yuan, and Myles M. Edwards, "Recurrence of Maltreatment: An Application of the National Child Abuse and Neglect Data System (NCANDS)," *Child Abuse & Neglect* 23 (July 1999): 633–50.

8. U.S. Department of Health and Human Services, Administration for Children and Families, *Child Maltreatment 2003* (Washington: U.S. Government Printing Office, 2005).

9. Patricia L. Kohl, C. Gibbons, and the NSCAW Research Group, "Safety from Recurrent Maltreatment and Victimization," paper presented at the 9th Annual Conference of the Society for Social Work and Research, Miami (January 2005).

10. U.S. Department of Health and Human Services, *Child Maltreatment 2003.*

11. For differences between males and females in report rates, see George E. Fryer and Thomas J. Miyoshi, "A Survival Analysis of the Revictimization of Children: The Case of Colorado," *Child Abuse & Neglect* 18 (December 1994): 1063–71. For no differences in rates, see Howard H. Levy and others, "Reabuse Rates in a Sample of Children Followed for Five Years after Discharge from a Child Abuse Inpatient Assessment Program," *Child Abuse & Neglect* 19 (November 1995): 1363–377; Lodi L. Lipien and Melinda S. Forthofer, "An Event History Analysis," pp. 947–66.

12. For significant difference in race and ethnicity, see John D. Fluke, Ying-Ying T. Yuan, and Myles M. Edwards, "Recurrence of Maltreatment"; Lipien and Forthofer, "An Event History Analysis"; Isabel Wolock and others, "Child Abuse and Neglect Referral Patterns: A Longitudinal Study," *Children and Youth Services Review* 23 (January 2001): 21–47. For no association, see Howard H. Levy and others, "Reabuse Rates."

13. Lipien and Forthofer, "An Event History Analysis"; Department of Health and Human Services, *Child Maltreatment 2003.*

14. For the Colorado study, see George E. Fryer and Thomas J. Miyoshi, "A Survival Analysis of the Revictimization of Children." For the Washington study, see Diana English and others, "Characteristics of Repeated Referrals to Child Protective Services in Washington State," *Child Maltreatment* 4 (November 1999): 297–307.

15. Vincent J. Palusci, Elliot G. Smith, and Nigel Paneth, "Predicting and Responding to Physical Abuse."

16. Jill Duerr Berrick and others, *The Tender Years: Toward Developmentally Sensitive Child Welfare Services* (New York: Oxford, 1998).

17. For any prior CPS involvement and placement followed by reunification, see Diana English and others, "Characteristics of Repeated Referrals"; for unspecified post-investigation services, see Fluke, Yuan, and Edwards, "Recurrence of Maltreatment," pp. 633–50.

18. David B. Marshall and Diana English, "Survival Analysis of Risk Factors."

19. For substantiation as not a significant predictor of re-report, see Susan J. Wells, "Decision Making in Child Protective Services"; Isabel Wolock and others, "Child Abuse and Neglect Referral Patterns." For substantiation as a significant predictor, see Marshall and English, "Survival Analysis of Risk Factors"; Lipien and Forthofer, "An Event History Analysis."

20. For a review of recurrent maltreatment research, see Diane DePanfilis and Susan J. Zuravin, "Rates, Patterns, and Frequency of Child Maltreatment Recurrences among Families Known to CPS," *Child Maltreatment* 3 (February 1998): 27–42. Five of the eight reviewed studies reported the highest recurrence rates when neglect was identified as the index maltreatment type. For more recent studies demonstrating that neglect is significantly associated with maltreatment recurrence, see Lipien and Forthofer, "An Event History Analysis"; and English and others, "Characteristics of Repeated Referrals."

21. For domestic violence, see English and others, "Characteristics of Repeated Referrals"; Diane DePanfilis and Susan J. Zuravin, "The Effect of Services on the Recurrence of Child Maltreatment," *Child Abuse & Neglect* 26 (February 2002): 187–205; Palusci, Smith, and Paneth, "Predicting and Responding to Physical Abuse." For caregiver substance abuse, see English and others, "Characteristics of Repeated Referrals," pp. 297–307; Wolock and others, "Child Abuse and Neglect Referral Patterns," pp. 21–47. For caregiver's own childhood history of abuse and neglect, see English and others, "Characteristics of Repeated Referrals," pp. 297–307. For caregiver's emotional problems, see Palusci, Smith, and Paneth, "Predicting and Responding to Physical Abuse."

22. Wolock and others, "Child Abuse and Neglect Referral Patterns."

23. Ineke Way and others, "Maltreatment Perpetrators: A Fifty-Four-Month Analysis of Recidivism," *Child Abuse & Neglect* 25 (August 2001): 1093–108.

24. Moira Inkelas and Neal Halfon, "Recidivism in Child Protective Services," *Children and Youth Services Review* 19 (1997): 139–61.

25. U.S. Department of Health and Human Services, Administration on Children, Youth and Families, *National Survey of Child and Adolescent Well-Being: Children Involved with the Child Welfare Services* (Baseline Report) (Washington: GPO, 2005).

26. Roy C. Herrenkohl and others, "The Repetition of Child Abuse: How Frequently Does It Occur?" *Child Abuse & Neglect* 3, no. 1 (1979): 67–72; Fluke, Yuan, and Edwards, "Recurrence of Maltreatment"; Lipien and Forthofer, "An Event History Analysis."

27. Diane DePanfilis and Susan J. Zuravin, "The Effect of Services."

28. Terence P. Thornberry, Timothy O. Ireland, and Carolyn A. Smith, "The Importance of Timing: The Varying Impact of Childhood and Adolescent Maltreatment on Multiple Problem Outcomes," *Development and Psychopathology* 13 (December 2001): 957–79.

29. Christine A. Ateah and Joan E. Durrant, "Maternal Use of Physical Punishment in Response to Child Misbehavior: Implications for Child Abuse Prevention," *Child Abuse & Neglect* 29 (February 2005): 169–85.

30. Murry Straus, *Handbook for the Conflict Tactics Scale* (University of New Hampshire Family Research Laboratory, 1991). As recommended by the developer, midpoint scoring was used to assess the frequency of each violent act, with one time scaled to 1, two times scaled to 2, three to five times scaled to 4, six to ten times scaled to 8, eleven to twenty times scaled to 15, and more than twenty times scaled to 25.

31. Thomas M. Achenbach, *Manual for the Child Behavior Checklist/4–18 and 1991 Profile* (University of Vermont, Department of Psychiatry, 1991); *Manual for Child Behavior Checklist/2–3 and 1992 Profile* (Burlington: University of Vermont, Department of Psychiatry, 1992).

32. Joseph Dalaker, U.S. Census Bureau, Current Population Reports, Series P60-214, "Poverty in the United States: 2000" (Washington: GPO, 2001).

33. Independent variables included in the logistic regression model were in-home service setting at baseline, child age, child gender, child race and ethnicity, Child Behavior Checklist score, prior reports of maltreatment, prior child welfare services, most serious maltreatment type of index report, substantiation of index report, domestic violence, caregiver mental health problem, caregiver substance abuse problem, caregiver history of child abuse and neglect, financial difficulties, poverty, urbanicity, and receipt of parenting support services.

34. Marshall and English used a study period of two years. See Marshall and English, "Survival Analysis of Risk Factors." Wells used a study period of four years. See Wells, "Decision Making in Child Protection Services."

35. Diane DePanfilis and Susan J. Zuravin, "Epidemiology of Child Maltreatment Recurrences," *Social Service Review* 73 (June 1999): 218–39.

36. Diana J. English and others, "Defining Maltreatment Chronicity: Are There Differences in Child Outcomes?" *Child Abuse & Neglect* 29 (May 2005): 575–95.

37. U.S. Department of Health and Human Services, *National Survey of Child and Adolescent Well-Being*.

38. Bruce D. Perry, "Traumatized Children: How Childhood Trauma Influences Brain Development," *Journal of the California Alliance for the Mentally Ill* 11, no. 1 (2000): 48–51; Edward F. Zigler, Matia Finn-Stevenson, and Nancy Hall, *The First Three Years and Beyond: Brain Development and Social Policy* (Yale University Press, 2002).

39. Department of Health and Human Services, *Child Maltreatment 2003*.

40. Fluke, Yuan, and Edwards, "Recurrence of Maltreatment"; Lipien and Forthofer, "An Event History Analysis."

41. See, for example, Susan Schechter and Jeffrey L. Edleson, *Effective Intervention in Domestic Violence and Child Maltreatment Cases: Guidelines for Policy and Practice* (Reno, Nev.: National Council of Juvenile and Family Court Judges, 1999); Patricia L. Kohl and others, "Child Welfare as a Gateway to Domestic Violence Services," *Child and Youth Services Review* 27 (November 2005): 1203–221.

42. Kohl and others, "Child Welfare as a Gateway"; Randy H. Magen and others, "Identifying Domestic Violence in Child Abuse and Neglect Investigations," *Journal of Interpersonal Violence* 16 (June 2001): 580–601; Melanie Shepard and Michael Raschick, "How Child Welfare Workers Assess and Intervene around Issues of Domestic Violence," *Child Maltreatment* 4 (May 1999): 148–56.

43. Diana J. English, Jeffrey L. Edleson, and Mary E. Herrick, "Domestic Violence in One State's Child Protective Caseload: A Study of Differential Case Dispositions and Outcomes," *Children and Youth Services Review* 27 (November 2005): 1183–201; Patricia L. Kohl and others, "Domestic Violence and Pathways into Child Welfare Services: Findings from the National Survey of Child and Adolescent Well-Being," *Children and Youth Services Review* 27 (November 2005): 1167–182.

44. English and others, "Characteristics of Repeated Referrals"; Wolock and others, "Child Abuse and Neglect Referral Patterns."

45. Patricia L. Kohl, Gibbons, and the NSCAW Research Group, "Safety from Recurrent Maltreatment."

46. Department of Health and Human Services, *National Survey of Child and Adolescent Well-Being*.

13

Physical Abuse and Adolescent Development

JOHN ECKENRODE, CHARLES IZZO,
AND ELLIOTT G. SMITH

The National Survey of Child and Adolescent Well-Being (NSCAW) is a unique resource for exploring a number of important questions regarding children who come in contact with the child welfare system because of abuse or neglect. In this chapter we address two major issues related to the physical abuse of adolescent children. First, we present a method for classifying youth as physically abused that uses multiple sources of data in the NSCAW study. Second, we relate the occurrence of physical abuse to several outcomes, including decreases in socioemotional well-being and academic achievement and an increase in behavior problems. Previous research has supported some links between physical abuse and such outcomes, but typically the results have relied on a single source of information about the abuse, such as agency or court records. In addition, much more information is needed regarding how the effects of physical abuse vary by characteristics of the child, such as gender and age.

Identification of Maltreated Children and Youth

National data available to researchers and policymakers on the nature and scope of maltreatment have come from three main sources: annual reports from the

Support for this research was provided by the Administration for Children and Families, U.S. Department of Health and Human Services, through RTI International. Additional support was provided by the Children's Bureau (Grant 90CA1750).

National Child Abuse and Neglect Data System (NCANDS); the series of National Incidence Studies (NIS); and national surveys such as the National Family Violence Surveys by Straus and colleagues or the 1995 Gallup Poll on child abuse.[1] NCANDS represents administrative data that come from official reports to state child protective agencies. Since only a portion of maltreated children ever become known to child protective services (CPS), NCANDS is generally viewed as yielding conservative or lower-bound estimates of the true number of maltreated children. For example, in 1993, NCANDS showed that 4 children per 1,000 were physically abused.[2] In contrast, NIS studies, which do not rely on CPS reports but survey professionals who interact with families with children, yield a higher rate of maltreatment. The 1993 NIS estimate of physical abuse, for example, was 9.1 children per 1,000, more than twice the NCANDS rate.[3] Surveys that question parents directly about their parenting behaviors (or adult recollections of their own maltreatment experiences) yield a still higher rate of maltreatment. The 1985 National Family Violence Resurvey, using the Conflict Tactics Scale (CTS), reports a yearly rate of severe violence to children of 110 per 1,000 and a rate of very severe violence of 23 per 1,000.[4] A more recent study by Theodore and colleagues used the CTS in a telephone survey of mothers in North and South Carolina. The harsh physical discipline measure used in the study consisted of parents' self-reported behaviors of shaking a child two years of age or younger; beating, burning, or kicking a child; or hitting a child with an object somewhere other than on the buttocks in the year before the interview. The study reports a rate of harsh physical discipline of 43 per 1,000 children, similar to the rate found in the Gallup survey (49 per 1,000), which used a similar measure.[5]

The field of child maltreatment research has been hampered by a lack of clear definitions of child abuse and neglect, which are crucial to estimating the size and nature of the maltreatment problem.[6] In part that is because the origins and purposes of research definitions (for example, of harsh parenting practices) may differ from those of the legal definitions codified in state child welfare laws. Also, the field is evolving, and there is a lack of consensus about what types of parenting behaviors may be dangerous or may compromise development, especially in the long term (witness the controversy about the developmental consequences of spanking).[7] Finally, the social context of parenting and modes of contact with children change over time. For example, the emergence of the Internet has opened up new ways to victimize children (see recent results of the National Juvenile Online Victimization Study).[8]

Even with common definitions, different informants (caseworker, parent, child, and so forth) may have access to different types or amounts of information about maltreatment. Thus, one recommendation for improving research in the field is to use multiple informants when possible. Cathy S. Widom and

R. L. Shepard were able to compare official reports of physical abuse with adult recollections of physical abuse for the same time period, yielding important information about the relative strengths and weaknesses of each source.[9] In a longitudinal study of 100 physically abused school-age children, Stockhammer and colleagues found that abuse information from CPS records differed somewhat from information from parent interviews (parents underreported physical abuse incidents).[10] In addition, there were differences in the patterns of predictions of child outcomes depending on whether the abuse data came from CPS records or parent reports. In general, given the weaknesses of any one source of information on victimization, it seems wise to include several sources when possible. CPS data have the benefit of resulting from in-depth examinations of alleged abuse incidents. Investigations often are flawed, however, because investigators lack firsthand knowledge about the incident and critical facts about a case often come from unreliable sources. Also, the decision to substantiate often relies on factors other than whether the maltreatment incident in fact occurred.[11] Parent and youth reports have their own sources of bias and inaccuracy, stemming from cognitive factors (for example, comprehension and recall) and situational factors (for example, desire for attention, fear of reprisal, or interviewing conditions). Each of these factors may be linked to over- or underreporting.[12]

The NSCAW study, which includes data drawn from a nationally representative sample of children entering the child welfare system, provides an opportunity to make significant contributions to the understanding of these issues. Estimates of maltreatment derived from caseworker data can be compared with estimates from state administrative data supplied through NCANDS. While NCANDS represents a complete census of official CPS reports, it contains scant information about the children or families besides their demographic characteristics; in contrast, NSCAW contains detailed child and family data. In addition, NSCAW used multiple informants to uncover victimization, especially in the case of physical abuse, which was reported by caseworkers, parents, and youths eleven years of age and older.

In this chapter we describe an approach to defining cases of physical abuse that makes maximum use of all sources of information within the NSCAW data. In doing so, we highlight the benefits of using multiple sources of information. We chose physical abuse as the starting point because there are child and parent self-report data for this domain (youths were not asked about neglect or sexual abuse) that allow us to examine consistency across sources of information. In the future we will extend our analysis to other forms of maltreatment.

Physical Abuse and Developmental Outcomes

Physical abuse has been linked to a number of short- and long-term outcomes related to physical health, social functioning, mental health, academic achievement, substance use, and antisocial behavior.[13] Some of the best-documented consequences of physical abuse are related to aggression and other externalizing behaviors, such as stealing. Physically abused children display increased rates of aggression and an associated inability to interpret others' behavior accurately; they are likely, therefore, to attribute aggression and hostility to others.[14] These developmental changes and their social consequences have long-term effects, as shown by Widom, who reported that a history of physical abuse is associated with a significantly increased risk of juvenile or adult arrest for violent crime.[15]

The nature and consequences of physical abuse in adolescence may differ somewhat from physical abuse in infancy or childhood (for example, fatalities are more frequent among infants), but there also are some coherent effects across development. For example, there is evidence that physical abuse that occurs in adolescence may increase the likelihood of externalizing behaviors more than does the persistent influence of maltreatment in childhood.[16] Adolescence is an important life stage for study because young people may display the cumulative impact of a history of maltreatment as well as the short-term effects of recent maltreatment. They also create a bridge to violence in the next generation as they reach young adulthood and have children themselves.

In this chapter we explore several developmental outcomes of physical abuse for adolescents in the NSCAW sample in the domains of problem behavior, psychosocial functioning, and academic achievement. We also examine the associations between abuse and those outcomes to evaluate the relative advantages of using different sources of information to classify youths as physically abused. Specifically, the validity of a given source of information about abuse is reflected in part in the number of outcomes to which the information derived from this source is significantly related. If abuse as reported by children was related to several outcomes whereas abuse reported by parents was related to fewer outcomes, we would take this result as an indication that child reports of abuse were more valid than reports by parents.

Methods

Our study used data from the CPS sample of the NSCAW, the details of which are described elsewhere in this volume. We focused on the subset of youths ages eleven and older at wave 1 ($N = 1,179$) because those are the ages at which NSCAW assessed many of the key variables of interest. Youths were 42.1 percent male, and their ages ranged from eleven through sixteen, with a mean age of 12.7 years (although the NSCAW targeted children aged fourteen and younger, 99 children aged fifteen or sixteen were included in the sample). The sample was racially diverse: 30.6 percent Black, 44.8 percent White, 15.5 percent Hispanic, and 9.1 percent other races. The sample was predominantly low income, with 47.8 percent of caregivers reporting a total household income of less than $20,000 a year and 74.3 percent reporting less than $35,000 a year. Caregivers in the sample reported an average of 4.5 people living in the home, and 100 percent indicated that at least one household member received some type of financial support from the government. Finally, in 36.2 percent of the sample families, the investigative caseworker indicated that the target child was the subject of a prior substantiated report of maltreatment.

Measurement of Physical Abuse

We examined physical abuse by using three independent sources of information, all collected at the time of entrance of the parents and children into the NSCAW study, as well as a measure that combined all three sources of information.

Self-reports from caregivers and youths. Only caregivers who were living at home at the time of data collection were interviewed. Caregivers responded to the physical abuse subscales of the CTS, indicating how often they engaged in several behaviors toward the target child in the twelve months preceding the interview.[17] We selected a subset of items from the Severe and Extreme Physical Abuse subscales that were most easily interpreted as causing serious harm to the child and that were serious enough to substantiate a physical abuse report if verified in a CPS investigation. The following behaviors were included in the abuse measure: respondent hit child with fist or kicked child hard, hit child somewhere other than on the buttocks with a hard object, threw or knocked child down, grabbed or choked child, beat child as hard as he or she was able, burned child on purpose, and threatened child with a knife or gun. We computed a dichotomous prevalence score indicating whether the caregiver engaged in any of these behaviors at least once in the previous twelve months.

Youths responded to the same items, indicating how often they had been subjected to those behaviors by any adult who lived with them in the previous twelve months. We computed a dichotomous prevalence score for youths using the same items and method as were used for the caregivers.

Report from investigative caseworker. In most instances, caseworkers indicated what types of maltreatment were alleged in the case report (that is, the report that triggered each participant's entry into the study) and whether that allegation was substantiated, indicated (that is, the agency had reason to suspect maltreatment but could not substantiate it), or unfounded. When there was more than one allegation, caseworkers reported which allegation they believed to be the most serious and whether that allegation was substantiated, indicated, or unfounded. In those cases, we coded the case report as positive for physical abuse if the allegation (or the most serious allegation when there was more than one) involved physical abuse and was either substantiated or indicated.[18]

Combination of caseworker, parent, and youth reports of physical abuse. In combining each source of information into an aggregate physical abuse measure, we coded a child as positive for physical abuse if the caseworker, parent, or youth

Table 13-1. *Summary of the Physical Abuse Coding Scheme Combining Caseworker, Parent, and Youth Reports of Physical Abuse*

Code	Rule	Number of children
Positive	At least one source indicates presence of abuse	484
Negative	No source indicates abuse, and at least two sources report absence of abuse	643
Unknown	All other combinations	52
		1,179

Source: Authors' calculations.

report indicated the occurrence of abuse, regardless of what was reported by the other two sources. This method maximizes the chance of detecting abuse by drawing from three sources rather than one. A child was coded as not physically abused if no source indicated the occurrence of physical abuse and if at least two sources indicated the absence of physical abuse. When there was only one source of information and that source reported no physical abuse, the physical abuse variable was coded as missing. The coding scheme is summarized in table 13-1.

In addition to information on physical abuse, we obtained other information about each case in the sample, including the child's gender, age, and race (coded as Black, Hispanic, White, or other); previous maltreatment (caseworker report of whether the child had a substantiated CPS report before entering the study); and family income (measured as the caregiver's report of the total combined family income from all sources). We also computed three indicators of whether youths had experienced a form of maltreatment other than physical abuse, to be used as covariates in the regression models. One variable indicated whether the case report was substantiated for a reason other than physical abuse. A second variable indicated whether the parent reported engaging in neglectful behaviors (based on a set of neglect items on the CTS) or whether the child experienced sexual abuse (based on the two sexual abuse items on the CTS) at least once in the previous twelve months. A third variable indicated whether other, nonphysical abuse occurred, as reported by either a caseworker or parent.

We examined eighteen outcome variables in three domains of adolescent functioning. In the behavior problems domain, caregivers reported children's problem behaviors at waves 1, 3, and 4 using the Child Behavior Checklist (CBCL), which yielded two composite scores reflecting internalizing and externalizing behavior problems. At wave 2, they completed the Behavior Problem Index, which yielded a total problem score.[19] Youths reported their own problem behaviors using the Youth Self-Report, which also yielded internalizing and externalizing behavior problem scores.[20] The Self-Report of Delinquency was used to obtain youths' reports of delinquent behaviors (for example, skipping school, carrying a weapon, and stealing).[21] We assessed youths' tobacco, alcohol, and drug use with a set of items derived from the Drug-Free Schools Outcome Study.[22] For frequency of tobacco use, we used two questions on the number of days that youths smoked or chewed tobacco in the previous thirty days. We coded frequency as the highest score on either the smoking or chewing tobacco items. The frequency of drug or alcohol use was assessed by using several questions about the number of days that youths used alcohol or any one of several illicit drugs in the previous thirty days. Frequency was coded as the highest score on any single drinking or drug use item. We also assessed sexual activity, using a single question asking whether the youths had ever had sexual intercourse. That item was part of the larger instrument assessing sexual activity.[23]

In the domain of psychosocial functioning, we included youths' reports of their depressive symptoms during the previous two weeks using the Children's Depression Inventory.[24] Youths reported on their expectations about their future by using three items from the Future Expectations scale derived from the Adolescent Health Survey and about their trauma-related symptoms using a measure adapted from the Trauma Symptom Checklist for Children.[25] Caregivers rated youths' social skills using the Social Skills Rating System. [26]

In the domain of school functioning, youths were administered the Mini-Battery of Achievement, a standardized test of reading and math achievement.[27] Finally, youths completed a scale measuring school engagement, which was derived from the Drug-Free Schools Outcome Study.[28]

Results

The following discussion describes three sets of findings that reflect the value of using a measure of physical abuse that combines information from the caseworker, parent, and youth reports. We first describe how the use of multiple sources allows for the classification of youths as abused or not abused even when the caseworker data were missing. Then we discuss the correspondence between the three sources of information about abuse. Finally, we relate our combined measure of abuse to several developmental outcomes.

The Effects of Reclassifying Cases According to Our Coding Method

One criterion for judging the value of a combined measure is how well it increased our ability to detect physical abuse among youths in the NSCAW sample. We found that in many cases in which young people were classified as not abused on the basis of one source of information, the presence of abuse was reported by at least one of the other two sources. For example, 127 of youths who were classified as not physically abused by using case reports alone were reclassified as physically abused after either a parent or a youth report of abuse. In addition, many cases that were retained in the analytic sample would have

Table 13-2. *Estimates of the Prevalence of Physical Abuse
Based on Individual and Combined Reports*[a]

	Type of report (percent)			
	Caseworker	Parent	Youth	Combined (parent, youth, and caseworker)
Prevalence estimate	(*N* = 1,072)	(*N* = 818)	(*N* = 1,104)	(*N* = 1,127)
Weighted	9.2	15.8	27.1	40.7
Unweighted	16.2	16.0	27.4	43.0

Source: Authors' calculations.

CPS = child protective services.

a. The design of the CPS sample targets some subpopulations (for example, children younger than one-year-old, those receiving services, and victims of sexual abuse) for sampling at a higher proportion to ensure a sufficient number of completed cases for precision in statistical analysis. Given the complex design and oversampling, sample weights must be applied to the observations to obtain unbiased estimates of the population parameters.

been lost because of missing data had we relied on a single source of information. For example, among the cases for which there was no case report substantiating abuse, 189 of 217 cases were reclassified either from the estimation procedure or from parent or youth reports. In those 189 cases, 77 youths were reclassified as physically abused and 112 were reclassified as not physically abused.

Correspondence between Victim Definitions Based on Case Report and the CTS

A second criterion for judging the value of the combined measure is whether different sources tend to agree about whether physical abuse occurred. If there was high agreement, it would matter less which source of information was used because predicted outcomes would not differ greatly across each abuse measure. Our estimate of the prevalence of physical abuse varied considerably among each of the three sources that we used. As shown in table 13-2, the prevalence rates ranged from 9 percent to 27 percent across the three single-source measures. The highest estimate for the prevalence of physical abuse came from the youth reports; in our weighted estimates, it was nearly two times higher than the estimate from parent reports and nearly three times higher than the estimate from case reports. The combined measure yielded the highest estimate, which was about 50 percent higher than the highest estimate from any single source.

Overall, agreement among sources about the absence of abuse was moderately high, ranging from 62.9 percent to 70.7 percent. There was less agreement among sources about whether abuse occurred, and the rate of agreement differed depending on the sources being compared. Only 32.9 percent of youths with a positive case report indicated that they had experienced abuse, and only

16.0 percent of their caregivers reported engaging in abusive behaviors. For the youths who reported experiencing abuse, only 21.4 percent of caregivers reported engaging in abusive behaviors. It is worth noting that the correspondence was low partly because youths reported abuse by any adult living in the household, whereas caregivers reported only their own abusive behaviors. In 40.5 percent of cases, only one adult lived in the household; in 43 percent of cases, there were two adults; and in 14.3 percent of cases, there were three or more adults.

Relationship between Maltreatment and Outcomes

A third criterion for evaluating the combined measure is whether it is a better predictor than the single measures of outcomes that have been linked to physical abuse in the child maltreatment literature. To address this issue, we examined the relationship between each indicator of physical abuse at wave 1 and several outcome variables, measured at waves 1, 2, 3, and 4.

Data analysis strategy. We conducted regression analyses to examine the relationship between physical abuse and each outcome variable. Each regression model controlled for youths' gender, race, and age at wave 1; total family income; previous maltreatment; and the presence of forms of maltreatment besides physical abuse. We conducted two sets of analyses to examine whether the relationship between physical abuse and each outcome variable differed according to gender or age at wave 1.

There was considerable variability across physical abuse measures in the number and type of wave 1 youth outcomes for which significant effects were found (table 13-3). Both the combined and youth report measures showed a significant relationship between abuse and at least one outcome in all three domains. In the problem behavior domain, the results indicated that physical abuse predicted more externalizing behaviors (parent and youth reported) and internalizing disorders (youth reported only) and greater delinquency, tobacco use, alcohol and drug use, and sexual activity as reported by the youths.

In the psychosocial domain, results from both measures showed that abuse was related to more trauma and depressive symptoms and poorer expectations about the future. For the combined measure, there was a trend suggesting that abuse was related to poorer social skills, but there was no such association for the youth report measure. In the academic domain, both the youth and combined measures showed a significant negative relationship between abuse and school engagement. Results from the youth reports indicate that abuse was related to poorer reading achievement and a trend toward poorer math achievement. The combined measure showed no relationship between abuse and academic achievement.

The effects for both case reports and parent reports were more sporadic on all the outcome measures. Parent-reported abuse was significantly related to more

Table 13-3. *Association of Each Physical Abuse Variable with Wave 1 Child Outcomes*[a]

	Type of report			
Outcome measure	Caseworker	Parent	Youth	Combined
Problem behavior				
Externalizing (parent)	4.41**	6.65***	4.51***	8.28***
Externalizing (youth)	0.77	0.14	5.21***	4.35***
Internalizing (parent)	1.10	3.76***	0.77	1.34
Internalizing (youth)	−0.11	−0.46	5.46***	3.78**
Delinquency	0.01	−0.05	1.63***	1.62***
Frequency of tobacco use	0.69	0.67**	0.84***	0.83***
Frequency of drug or alcohol use	0.39	1.07**	1.19***	1.17**
Sexual intercourse	−1.06*	0.88	1.63***	2.08***
Psychosocial				
Trauma symptoms	0.09	0.71	3.63***	3.77***
Depression	−1.26*	1.98	5.70***	5.12***
Future expectations	0.18*	−0.15	−0.36**	−0.28**
Social skills	−0.85	−0.72*	−0.06	−0.82*
Academic functioning				
Reading achievement	6.82*	−0.16	−7.34**	−1.77
Math achievement	8.57**	−0.07	−5.87*	−4.27
School engagement	−0.01	−0.09	−0.20**	−0.27***

Source: Authors' calculations.

***$p < 0.01$, **$p < 0.05$, *$p < 0.10$.

CPS = child protection services.

a. All analyses were conducted on weighted data. Unweighted Ns range from 566 to 874. Regression coefficients for the effect of physical abuse on the outcome variables are shown. Each model contained the following covariates: child's age; race and gender; family income; the child being a victim in a substantiated CPS report prior to the case report; and a dichotomous indicator of the presence of maltreatment other than physical abuse, assessed at wave 1. For "social skills," we used the square root to adjust for skewed distribution.

externalizing (parent-reported) and internalizing (parent-reported) behaviors, greater tobacco use, and a trend toward poorer social skills. Abuse based on case reports was significantly related to more externalizing behavior (parent reported). However, several other findings involving the case report measure ran counter to our expectations. Those results showed that abuse was significantly related to greater math achievement and marginally related to greater reading achievement, less sexual activity, less depression, and higher future expectations.

The moderating effects of age and gender. Using the combined measure of physical abuse, we found that for several outcomes the effects of abuse were concentrated among children who were older at baseline (table 13-4). For children aged fourteen at wave 1, abuse was significantly related to youth-reported internalizing behaviors at wave 1, delinquency at wave 3, and poorer social skills at

Table 13-4. *Significant Age and Gender Differences in the Effects of Maltreatment*[a]

Outcome measure	Abuse by age interaction	Simple effect test by age			
		11	12	13	14
Externalizing, parent (wave 1)	6.95***	0.22	10.69***	9.36***	12.64***
Externalizing, parent (wave 4)	3.44**	0.85	5.56**	3.94	11.57***
Internalizing, youth (wave 1)	2.25*	3.34	2.35	0.88	8.13***
Depression (wave 1)	3.57**	4.04**	2.84	2.28	10.32***
Delinquency (wave 3)	2.41*	−0.34	0.14	0.58	0.97***
Social skills (wave 4)	3.03**	0.06	−0.10	0.09	−2.04**

Outcome measure	Abuse by gender interaction	Simple effect test by gender	
		Boys	Girls
Internalizing, parent (wave 3)	4.69**	1.40	5.22***
Sexual activity (wave 3)	4.13**	4.44***	1.59
Substance use (wave 4)	3.20*	−0.22	0.89*

Source: Authors' calculations.

***$p < 0.01$, **$p < 0.05$, *$p < 0.10$.

CPS = child protection services.

a. All analyses were conducted on weighted data. Unweighted Ns range from 621 to 867. Interaction and simple effect regression coefficients are shown. Only tests with significant abuse by age or abuse by gender interactions are presented. Each model contained the following covariates: child's age; race and gender; family income; the child being a victim in a substantiated CPS report prior to the case report; and a dichotomous indicator of the presence of maltreatment other than physical abuse, assessed at wave 1. For "social skills," we used the square root to adjust for skewed distribution.

wave 4. The effect of abuse on those outcomes was nonsignificant for children ages eleven through thirteen. The effect of abuse on wave 1 depression was limited to the eleven- and fourteen-year age groups. In addition, at wave 1, the effect of abuse on parent-rated externalizing problems was limited to the twelve-, thirteen-, and fourteen-year-old age groups, and at wave 4, it was limited to the twelve- and fourteen-year-old age groups.

Results also indicated that for girls, the effect of abuse was significant for wave 3 parent-reported internalizing problems and approached significance for wave 4 substance use. Abuse was unrelated to those variables among boys. Conversely, the effect of abuse on wave 3 sexual behavior was significant for boys but not for girls.

Stability of effects over time. Finally, as shown in table 13-5, although the combined measure predicted the majority of outcomes at wave 1, most of the associations became attenuated over time. The effect for tobacco use disappeared by wave 3, as did the effects for trauma symptoms, future expectations, and social skills. The effects for delinquency, alcohol and drug use, depression, and school engagement disappeared by wave 4. In contrast, associations remained significant

Table 13-5. *Associations with Physical Abuse Using the Combined Measure with Child Outcomes at Waves 1 through 4*[a]

	Wave			
Outcome measure	*1*	*2*	*3*	*4*
Problem behavior				
Externalizing (parent)	8.28***	3.97***	7.08***	5.71***
Externalizing (youth)	4.35***	. . .	2.87*	2.26*
Internalizing (parent)	1.34	1.08***	3.75***	2.39**
Internalizing (youth)	3.78**	. . .	2.71**	2.58**
Delinquency	1.62***	. . .	0.79**	0.45
Frequency of tobacco use	0.83***	. . .	0.47	0.42
Frequency of drug or alcohol use	1.17**	. . .	1.00***	0.54
Sexual intercourse	2.08***	. . .	1.20**	2.15***
Psychosocial				
Trauma symptoms	3.77***	. . .	1.19	1.20
Depression	5.12***	. . .	3.29***	0.70
Future expectations	−0.28**	. . .	−0.15	−0.06
Social skills	−0.82*	. . .	−0.70	−0.56
Academic functioning				
Reading achievement	−1.77	. . .	−1.07	−1.17
Math achievement	−4.27	. . .	2.45	−7.06
School engagement	−0.27***	. . .	−0.22***	−0.07

Source: Authors' calculations.

***$p < 0.01$, **$p < 0.05$, *$p < 0.10$.

. . . Not applicable.

a. All analyses were conducted on weighted data. Unweighted Ns range from 566 to 868. Table entries are regression coefficients for the effect of physical abuse on the outcome variables. Each model contained the following covariates: child's age; race and gender; family income; the child being a victim in a substantiated CPS report prior to the case report; and a dichotomous indicator of the presence of maltreatment other than physical abuse, assessed at wave 1. For "social skills," we used the square root to adjust for skewed distribution.

or nearly significant in all later waves for internalizing and externalizing behaviors and sexual activity. It is also notable that the effect for parent-rated internalizing behaviors, which was nonsignificant at wave 1, became significant in later waves. Overall, it appears that the effects on variables in the problem behavior domain last somewhat longer than the effects on those in the psychosocial or academic domains.

Discussion

In this chapter we examine physical abuse within the adolescent sample of the NSCAW data (ages eleven through sixteen). We show that the use of case reports along with parent reports and youth self-reports yielded a larger number of physical abuse cases than would have appeared if only one source were used.

There was only a moderate degree of correspondence between sources; therefore, in many instances youths were classified as abused by one source and as non-abused by another. In addition, in many cases the occurrence of abuse was detected in cases that would have been classified as missing if only one source were used. The youth self-reports yielded the highest percentage of abuse cases, followed by parent reports and then case reports. Overall, about 40 percent of youths were classified as experiencing physical abuse when all sources of information were used.

Several patterns were detected when we related each physical abuse variable to developmental outcomes. First, youth reports of abuse were related to a larger number of outcomes than either parent or case reports. Youth reports of abuse were significantly associated with almost every outcome that we examined, including behavior problems, psychosocial outcomes, and academic outcomes. In contrast, parent reports of abuse were related to parent and youth reports of externalizing problems, parent reports of internalizing behaviors, youth-reported tobacco use, and parent-reported social skills. Abuse based on caseworker reports was also related to more externalizing behaviors. Surprisingly, caseworker reports of abuse were related to less sexual activity and depression and better reading and math scores. The combined measure yielded data most consistent with the pattern of findings for the youth reports, with a few exceptions noted below. Overall, the data from the combined measure are consistent with the research literature regarding the consequences of physical abuse for youth.

The second pattern was that for some outcomes there was consistency in effects regardless of the abuse variable used, as was the case involving parent reports of externalizing behaviors where measures of abuse reported by each of the three sources as well as the combined measure predicted this outcome. The consistency of these effects adds credence to similar findings reported by other researchers.[29] In other instances, only one or two abuse measures were related to an outcome (for example, parent reports of internalizing behaviors). In cases in which the only effect noted was based on data that came from a common source (for example, parent abuse reports related to parent reports of internalizing behavior), a concern could be raised about common rater bias. Results that held across more than one source should be seen as more credible.

Third, for some outcomes, effects (for example, on reading and math scores) differed among sources, so the combined score showed a nonsignificant effect. While we argue that in most cases the combined abuse measure is preferable to any individual source, our data also suggest that associations involving individual sources of abuse should be checked to be sure that significant but opposing effects at the individual source level are not masked at the level of the combined abuse variable. We have not yet begun to determine why case reports of abuse would be related to better math and reading scores. Recall that these effects control for the presence of neglect or sexual abuse. Also, diagnostic analyses revealed no artifactual explanations, such as a few influential cases with high analysis weights. One possible explanation is that substantiated reports may have triggered the provision of services to children that gave them greater support and supervision and improved their school attendance and performance.

Finally, we examine the effects of the combined measure across all waves of data collection. There were more effects at wave 1, as might be expected given the proximity of the outcomes to the assessment of abuse. There also were some consistent effects across time, such as externalizing behaviors (parent and youth reports), internalizing behaviors (youth reports), and youth-reported delinquency. This finding provides evidence for the robustness and stability of the effects that we present. For some outcomes, effects observed at wave 1 were no longer significant at wave 4, such as delinquency and tobacco use. In part, that may reflect the fact that some youths abused at wave 1 were no longer being abused three years later at wave 4. For an outcome like tobacco use, normative increases in tobacco use from mid to late adolescence may also serve to mask the effects of abuse, which may emerge later in the form of persistent substance abuse in young adulthood. One limitation of the current analyses is that each time point was examined separately; future analyses of the data will use more dynamic longitudinal methods.

We also found that the effects of physical abuse were not uniform across children of all ages or for boys and girls. For example, the relationship between physical abuse and behavior problems, delinquency, and poor social skills was concentrated among older children and in several instances was significant only among children who were fourteen years old at baseline. That finding may be related to the fact that age fourteen coincides with the transition into high school, a period considered to be highly sensitive for adolescents' social and emotional development.[30] Therefore, viewed from the perspective of developmental psychopathology, our results may reflect a process whereby the vulnerabilities resulting from abuse manifest themselves most strongly as children encounter new developmental challenges.[31] Also, many behaviors comprised by the delinquency and CBCL scales tend not to emerge until later in development.[32]

The effects of abuse also varied according to gender, with abused boys showing more sexual activity and girls showing more internalizing problems and substance abuse. Both the age- and gender-specific results parallel findings from other studies of the impact of child maltreatment on adult pathology. For example, Widom's prospective study of abused and neglected children reported that boys were more likely than girls to display antisocial behaviors and that girls were more likely than boys to abuse alcohol.[33] Taken together, our results might be viewed as an earlier glimpse into some of the longer-term patterns identified in previous studies. It is important to keep in mind that we restricted our analyses to youths who were age eleven and older at the start of the study, so we cannot be certain that the findings that we report here would be the same for younger children.

Overall, our findings are relevant for child welfare practitioners because they illustrate how the sensitivity of an abuse investigation might be improved by obtaining accounts from both youths and adults. It is possible that the more structured format of the CTS may make it easier for some informants to disclose abuse. Although it is common practice to gather abuse-related information through in-person interviews, investigators may improve the accuracy of their judgments about physical abuse by providing both youths and adults the opportunity to disclose abuse through a questionnaire, such as the CTS. Our data also have implications for researchers who seek to characterize the victim status of children and youth in the NSCAW study. Choosing one source over another can affect conclusions about the prevalence of maltreatment and the impact of maltreatment on health and developmental outcomes. Ultimately, having better data on maltreatment incidence and prevalence is crucial to gauging the impact of service provision, prevention programs, and social policies.

Notes

1. Murray A. Straus and R. J. Gelles, "How Violent Are American Families? Estimates from the National Family Violence Resurvey and Other Studies," in *Family Abuse and Its Consequences: New Directions in Research,* edited by Gerald. Hotaling and others (Newbury Park, Calif.: Sage, 1988); Gallup Organization, "Gallup Poll: Child Abuse Study 1995," available from the National Data Archive on Child Abuse and Neglect (www.ndacan.cornell.edu).

2. U.S. Department of Health and Human Services, Administration on Children, Youth and Families, *Child Maltreatment 1994* (Washington: Government Printing Office, 1994).

3. Andrea J. Sedlak, I. Hantman, and D. Schultz, *Third National Incidence Study of Child Abuse and Neglect (NIS-3) Public Use Files Manual* (DHHS, 1997).

4. Murray A. Straus and R. J. Gelles, "How Violent Are American Families?"

5. Adrea D. Theodore and others, "Epidemiologic Features of the Physical and Sexual Maltreatment of Children in the Carolinas," *Pediatrics* 115, no. 2 (2005): 331–37; Gallup Organization, "Child Abuse Study 1995."

6. Dante Cicchetti and D. Barnett, "Toward the Development of a Scientific Nosology of Child Maltreatment," in *Thinking Clearly about Psychology: Essays in Honor of Paul E. Meehl,* edited by Dante Cicchetti and William M. Grove (University of Minnesota Press, 1991), pp. 346–77; National Research Council, *Understanding Child Abuse and Neglect* (Washington: National Academy Press, 1993).

7. Corina Benjet and A. E. Kazdin, "Spanking Children: The Controversies, Findings, and New Directions," *Clinical Psychology Review* 23, no. 2 (2003): 197–224.

8. Kimberly Mitchell, D. Finkelhor, and J. Wolak, "Victimization of Youth on the Internet," *Journal of Aggression, Maltreatment, and Trauma* 8, nos. 1-2 (2004): 1–39.

9. Cathy S. Widom and R. L. Shepard, "Accuracy of Adult Recollections of Childhood Victimization: Part 1. Childhood Physical Abuse," *Psychological Assessment* 8, no.4 (1996): 412–21.

10. Tanya F. Stockhammer and others, "Assessment of the Effect of Physical Child Abuse within an Ecological Framework: Measurement Issues," *Journal of Community Psychology* 29, no. 3 (2001): 319–44.

11. Gail L. Zellman, "The Impact of Case Characteristics on Child-Abuse Reporting Decisions," *Child Abuse & Neglect* 16, no. 6 (1992): 57–74.

12. Nancy D. Brener, J. O. G. Billy, and W. R. Grady, "Assessment of Factors Affecting the Validity of Self-Reported Health-Risk Behavior among Adolescents: Evidence from the Scientific Literature," *Journal of Adolescent Health* 33, no. 6 (2003): 436–57.

13. Robin Malinosky-Rummell and D. J. Hansen, "Long-Term Consequences of Child Physical Abuse," *Psychological Bulletin* 114, no. 1 (1993): 68–79; David J. Kolko, "Child Physical Abuse," in *The APSAC Handbook on Child Maltreatment,* edited by John E. B. Myers (Thousand Oaks, Calif.: Sage Publications, 2002), pp. 21–54.

14. Kenneth A. Dodge and G. S. Pettit, "Mechanisms in the Cycle of Violence," *Science* 250, no. 4988 (1990): 1678–683.

15. Cathy S. Widom, "Does Violence Beget Violence? A Critical Examination of the Literature," *Psychological Bulletin* 106, no. 1 (1989): 3–28.

16. Carolyn Smith and T. P. Thornberry, "The Relationship between Child Maltreatment and Adolescent Involvement in Delinquency," *Criminology* 33, no. 4 (1995): 451–77; Jeffrey M. Williamson, C. M. Borduin, and B. A. Howe, "The Ecology of Adolescent Maltreatment: A Multilevel Examination of Adolescent Physical Abuse, Sexual Abuse, and Neglect," *Journal of Consulting and Clinical Psychology* 59, no. 3 (1991): 449–57.

17. Murray Straus and others, "Identification of Child Maltreatment with the Parent-Child Conflict Tactics Scales (CTSPC): Development and Psychometric Data for a National Sample of American Parents," *Child Abuse & Neglect* 22, no. 4 (1998): 249–70.

18. There were 109 cases of children aged eleven or older missing caseworker data related to the type of alleged maltreatment. We developed a statistical method to code those cases as being substantiated or not based on three other pieces of information: whether the child was placed into foster care after the case report, the caseworker's rating of the amount of evidence available to substantiate the allegations in the report, and the caseworker's rating of the level of harm suffered by the child.

19. Thomas M. Achenbach, *Manual for the Child Behavior Checklist/4–18 and 1991 Profile* (Burlington: University of Vermont, Department of Psychiatry, 1991).

20. Thomas M. Achenbach, *Manual for the Youth Self Report and 1991 Profile* (Burlington: University of Vermont, Department of Psychiatry, 1991).

21. Delbert S. Elliott, D. Huizinga, and S. S. Ageton, *Explaining Delinquency and Drug Use* (Beverly Hills, Calif.: Sage Publications, 1985).

22. E. Suyapa Silvia and J. M. Thorne, "School-Based Drug Prevention Programs: A Longitudinal Study in Selected School Districts," Technical Report (Research Triangle Park, N.C.: Research Triangle Institute, 1997).

23. Desmond K. Runyan and others, "LONGSCAN: A Consortium for Longitudinal Studies of Maltreatment and the Life Course of Children," *Aggression and Violent Behavior: A Review Journal* 3, no. 3 (1998): 275–85.

24. Maria Kovacs, *The Children's Depression Inventory (CDI) Manual* (Toronto: Multi-Health Systems, 1992).

25. Peter S. Bearman, J. Jones, and R. J. Udry, *The National Longitudinal Study of Adolescent Health: Research Design* (Chapel Hill, N.C.: University of North Carolina, Carolina Population Center, 1997); John Briere, *Trauma Symptom Checklist for Children: Professional Manual* (Lutz, Fla.: Psychological Assessment Resources, 1996).

26. Frank M. Gresham and S. N. Elliot, *Social Skills Rating System* (Circle Pines, Minn.: American Guidance Service, 1990).

27. Richard W. Woodcock, K. S. McGrew, and J. K. Werder, *Mini-Battery of Achievement* (Riverside, Calif.: Riverside Publishing, 1994).

28. E. Suyapa Silvia and J. M. Thorne, "School-Based Drug Prevention Programs."

29. Tanya F. Stockhammer and others, "Assessment of the Effect of Physical Child Abuse within an Ecological Framework."

30. Kristin Isakson and P. Jarvis, "The Adjustment of Adolescents during the Transition to High School: A Short-Term Longitudinal Study," *Journal of Youth and Adolescence* 28, no. 1 (1999): 1–26; Terri E. Moffitt, "Adolescence-Limited and Life-Course-Persistent Antisocial Behavior: A Developmental Taxonomy," *Psychological Review* 100 (1993): 674–701.

31. Dante Cicchetti and S. L. Toth, "A Developmental Psychopathology Perspective on Child Abuse and Neglect," *Journal of the American Academy of Child and Adolescent Psychiatry* 34, no. 5 (1995): 541–65.

32. Rolf Loeber and D. Hay, "Key Issues in the Development of Aggression and Violence from Childhood to Early Adulthood," *Annual Review of Psychology* 48 (1997): 371–410.

33. Cathy S. Widom, "Childhood Victimization: Early Adversity, Later Psychopathology," *National Institute of Justice Journal* (January 2000): 2–9.

14

Addressing the Educational Needs of Children in Child Welfare Services

MARY BRUCE WEBB, PAMELA FROME,
BRENDA JONES HARDEN, RODNEY BAXTER,
KATHERINE DOWD, AND SUNNY HYUCKUN SHIN

Children in the child welfare system have a variety of special needs with respect to their cognitive and academic functioning as well as their physical and mental health. Research documents adverse developmental outcomes for many children in the child welfare system resulting from perinatal problems, maltreatment, changes of residence, and a host of other risk factors.[1] One of the most important outcomes, and one that is well documented by research, is the poor educational attainment of these children.[2] Many of the factors that compromise a child's achievement may exist before the child welfare system becomes involved; even so, evidence of educational deficits has spurred the policy and practice communities to examine the school experiences of these children, especially with regard to whether and how they receive supportive or individualized education services.

Although federal mandates require local child welfare agencies to attend to the safety, permanence, and well-being of children in their systems, often well-being, in terms of children's functioning, adjustment, and optimal development, is de-emphasized in the face of legislative, administrative, fiscal, and public pressure to ensure the children's safety and secure permanent homes for them.[3] For children with diagnosed special needs, having access to special education services

"The information and opinions expressed herein reflect solely the positions of the authors. Nothing herein should be construed to indicate the support or endorsement of its content by ACF/DHHS.

243

represents a critical step toward achieving well-being. To date, no large-scale, nationally representative study has addressed the child welfare system's response to the special education needs of the children in its care, and evidence is ambiguous regarding whether these children receive the special education services to which they are entitled. This chapter uses data from the National Survey of Child and Adolescent Well-Being (NSCAW) to estimate the prevalence of the need for special education services among children of elementary school age who are in the care of the child welfare system and to document the extent to which the system recognizes and addresses their needs.

Academic Needs and Experiences of Children in Child Welfare

Maltreated and foster children have been found to perform below grade level on academic subjects and standardized tests.[4] In addition, they are more likely than other children to repeat a grade and to attend special education classes, and they are less likely to graduate from high school.[5] They also are more likely to experience disciplinary action, suspension, and expulsion.[6]

Multiple factors explain a child's involvement in both the child welfare and special education system. One factor is maltreatment, which a variety of small- and large-scale studies have linked to poor academic achievement.[7] Maltreated children have a higher likelihood of receiving poor grades and low achievement test scores and of repeating a grade.[8] Some studies have documented significant declines over time in grades, attendance, and behavior as well as an increase in placement in special education classes, repeating of grades, referrals for disciplinary action, and suspensions.[9] Another explanation is that maltreated children may have cognitive deficits (that is, low IQs) that explain their relatively poor academic functioning.[10] Maltreated children also have been found to lack other skills that are related to academic competence, such as school engagement.[11]

Further, many maltreated children have social and emotional difficulties that result in their being placed in special education classes. For example, increased aggression, difficulties with peers, depression, and emotional dysregulation have been documented in maltreated children.[12] Some research has suggested that such children are more likely to be placed in special education classrooms reserved for children with social-emotional disabilities.[13] Taken together, studies on the cognitive and social-emotional consequences of child maltreatment provide a solid explanation for the elevated rates of placement in special education classes found among maltreated children.

Being placed in foster care is another factor that may contribute to a child's poor academic performance. An independent link between placement in foster care and academic outcome is difficult to establish because by the time that foster children enter care, they have had a series of life experiences that affect their educational success. Moreover, some scholars argue that foster care acts as a protective factor. For example, Horwitz and colleagues concluded that foster care actually has the potential to improve academic outcomes;[14] in contrast, Evans concluded that foster care has no effect on academic achievement.[15] Other scholars have focused specifically on the substantial educational risks that foster children face at the time of placement and then argued that the instability associated with foster care leads to high rates of absenteeism and school changes during the academic year, which negatively affect children's academic outcomes.[16]

Many studies have documented that school outcomes in the cognitive and social-emotional domains for foster children are poorer than those of children not in foster care.[17] More specifically, the studies show that more foster children perform below grade and age expectations on cognitive, language, and achievement tests;[18] that they are more likely to repeat a grade; and that they have lower graduation rates.[19]

Research also suggests that foster children are more likely to have mental health problems than children not in foster care.[20] They tend to have poorer social and adaptive skills, to exhibit aggressive and impulsive behavior more often, and to suffer more from depression—all conditions that may precipitate school failure and result in their being placed in special education.[21] In addition, temporary adjustment difficulties arising from the trauma of transitions between foster care placements may increase the likelihood that foster children are referred for special education because of behavioral problems.[22]

Overall, the research strongly suggests that foster children have increased rates of cognitive, social-emotional, and academic difficulties, which lead to a higher proportion being referred for special education.[23] However, the findings are complex and thus must be interpreted with caution. Findings may emerge from studies that have methodological flaws that prevent the drawing of definitive conclusions; for example, a study may use convenience samples or have no control for previous maltreatment or other adverse experiences. Further, it may be the characteristics of a child's foster care experience—specifically, the type of setting (for example, kinship home), the stability of placement, and the quality of the environment—that reduce or increase academic difficulties rather than foster care placement per se.[24]

The Special Education System and the Child Welfare Population

The Individuals with Disabilities Education Act (IDEA) defines federal policy regarding the education of children with special needs.[25] Although subject to local interpretation, the act sets out the process by which children are identified as needing special education and through which they receive the required services. Eligibility for special education placement is determined through a comprehensive assessment of the child's abilities, which also forms the basis for determining the type and level of service a child receives. Children may be diagnosed as having health, cognitive, or emotional problems that must be addressed within the educational setting.

It is well established that children who come from a high-risk background (characterized, for example, by low income, low maternal education, and physical health risks arising from trauma and neglect), as do most of the children in the child welfare system, are at a markedly increased risk for school failure.[26] Therefore, it is not surprising that children in the system have high rates of referral to special education classes. One study of youths aging out of foster care found that nearly 50 percent of the children had been placed in special education at least once.[27]

Despite the established link between the child welfare and special education systems, there is a paucity of evidence regarding the link between children's needs and receipt of appropriate special education services.[28] For example, in the wake of the establishment of loosely articulated yet mandated standards to ensure the well-being of children in the welfare service sector, it is not yet known whether caseworkers are more likely to attend to the academic needs of children in their caseloads. Extant data also do not address more refined questions, such as whether children who have a documented need for special education at the time of child welfare entry subsequently receive it or whether the special education that they receive effectively addresses the issues that contributed to their compromised school achievement, particularly cognitive and social-emotional difficulties. The educational needs of younger children also have received less attention than those of adolescents, whose high rates of school dropout and transition into adulthood with poor job skills have been well-documented. Finally, existing research has focused primarily on children in foster care; little attention has been paid to children who receive child welfare services while living in their original home. Reports from the first round of Child and Family Service Reviews, required by federal legislation enacted in 1997, suggest that states are struggling to identify and provide services to children who have special needs of any kind, particularly those who are receiving in-home services.[29] Nor is much known about the role of caseworkers in ensuring that children in the child protection system receive appropriate education services.

This chapter addresses special education services for elementary school-aged children in the Child Protective Services (CPS) sample of NSCAW. The analysis includes children who were receiving child welfare services, whether they remained at home or were placed in foster care. Although children of all ages in the child welfare system are likely to be at high risk for poor educational outcomes, children in their early school years were chosen for this analysis because early difficulties in school are likely to persist if left unaddressed.[30] Intervention for children in this age group therefore may be especially important. The chapter has three aims: to examine the cognitive and social-emotional functioning of elementary school-aged children as assessed at baseline, to determine the proportion of children who are likely to be eligible for special education services, and to explore the link between documented cognitive and social-emotional needs and the receipt of special education, with special attention to the actions of child welfare workers in identifying and referring children who are likely to have special educational needs.

Methods

This analysis uses data from the NSCAW baseline interviews and the eighteen-month follow-up. On average the baseline interviews with children and care-givers were conducted four months after the close of a maltreatment investigation or assessment, and the follow-up was conducted nineteen months after the close of the investigation or assessment. Only children of elementary school age (six through eleven years) whose cases were opened to services after a maltreatment investigation were included in this analysis (N = 1,760). A small number of children being home schooled were excluded because their access to special education services is markedly different from that of children in the school system.

Measures of behavior and functioning included the Parent Report Form (PRF) from the Achenbach Child Behavior Checklist (CBCL)[31] and the Vineland Adaptive Behavior Scale (VABS) Screener.[32] Children were considered to be at serious risk for behavioral problems and in need of special education services if they scored two or more standard deviations above the mean on the CBCL or if they scored two or more standard deviations below the mean on the VABS.

The Kaufman Brief Intelligence Test (K-BIT) and the reading and math sections of the Woodcock-Werder-McGrew Mini-Battery of Achievement (MBA) were used to estimate cognitive needs.[33] Children were considered to be at serious risk for cognitive delay and in need of early intervention services if their overall scores on the K-BIT or their score on the MBA reading or math tests were two or more standard deviations below the mean.

Children were separated into four categories: those who showed need of special education services because of cognitive problems (identified by their scores on the K-BIT or MBA), those who showed need because of behavioral problems (identified by their scores on the PRF or VABS), those who showed need because of both types of problems, and those who showed neither problem.

In addition to the assessments, a second measure of need for and use of special education services was obtained by asking the current caregiver—including biological, adoptive, or foster parents or relatives who had primary responsibility for the child's care and who had resided with the child for at least thirty days—about diagnoses made by professionals and about the child's need for and receipt of specific types of school-based special education services.

Caseworker interviews collected at baseline and at the eighteen-month follow-up were the basis for determining the actions taken by the child welfare system to refer children for special education services. Approximately one year after the close of an investigation or assessment, caseworkers were identified and

Table 14-1. *Percentage of Children Defined as Needing Special Education Services at Wave 1, by Need*[a]

Need	Number	Percentage of all children
Cognitive	137	7.3
Behavioral problems	331	16.4
Cognitive and behavioral problems	143	6.6
Total	611	30.3

Source: Authors' calculations.

a. All *N*s are unweighted, while all percentages are weighted estimates. This table is based on the cross-tabulation of children showing need for services based on low scores on cognitive and behavioral assessments. About 8 percent of children who were identified as needing special education are not included in this table, because while data on the behavioral assessment were available for them, data on the cognitive assessment were missing.

interviewed regarding children who were in the "services received" (services provided or paid for by CPS) category of the NSCAW sampling domains or for children whose caregiver reported receipt of CPS services since the baseline interview.[34]

Data on the type of maltreatment were collected from the investigative caseworker as part of baseline data collection. The measure of urbanicity derives from the county in which the baseline investigation for maltreatment took place.

Results

Overall, 30.3 percent of all children ages six through eleven in the child protection system showed some type of need for special education services based on low scores from cognitive assessments, behavioral assessments, or both (table 14-1).[35] The majority of the children needed special education because of behavioral problems (23.0 percent, including children with both types of need). Fewer children showed need because of cognitive problems (13.9 percent, including children with both types of needs).

Table 14-2 presents information regarding child gender, race and ethnicity, first language, urbanicity, and maltreatment type classified by type of need. Overall, well over half of the children identified as having need for special education services were male (59.9 percent). Most of the children showing need were White (49.9 percent); 29.6 percent were Black. Very few children spoke English as a second language (7.7 percent), and the majority lived in an urban environment (69.5 percent). The most significant types of maltreatment for most of the children were physical abuse (30.8 percent) and neglect or failure to supervise (24.7 percent). There were no significant differences in the demographic variables based on type of need.

Table 14-2. *Child Sociodemographic Characteristics and Maltreatment Type, by Type of Need*[a]

	Type of Need			
Characteristic and maltreatment type	Cognitive (n = 137)	Behavioral (n = 331)	Cognitive and behavioral (n = 143)	Total (N = 611)
Gender				
Male	52.3	66.2	52.6	59.9
Race and ethnicity				
Non-Hispanic Black	37.4	29.0	22.6	29.6
Non-Hispanic White	39.4	54.2	47.5	49.9
Hispanic	9.6	9.5	26.2	13.2
Other	13.6	7.2	3.7	8.0
English as second language	5.8	5.7	15.0	7.7
Urbanicity	72.2	69.0	67.8	69.5
Maltreatment type				
Physical	21.3	37.2	25.5	30.8
Sexual	3.7	7.5	24.8	10.0
Failure to provide	34.5	15.5	25.8	22.4
Failure to supervise	28.9	26.8	14.0	24.7
Other	11.6	13.1	9.9	12.1
Percentage of U.S. children represented in sample (number)	24.2 (62,661)	54.1 (140,184)	21.7 (56,351)	100 (259,196)

Source: Authors' calculations

a. All *N*s are unweighted, while all percentages are weighted estimates. Data entries are percentages. There were no significant differences between the types of need on any measure of sociodemographic characteristic or maltreatment type.

As another measure of the need for special education services, caregivers were asked whether a professional had told them that their child had learning problems, special needs, or developmental disabilities. According to that measure, 31.3 percent of children had a need for special education services. We next looked at the overlap of identification by assessment and identification by caregiver of children having need. Both sources identified about one-third of children as having need (assessment, 30.3 percent; caregiver, 31.3 percent). However, there was some disagreement on which children needed services ($\chi^2 = 56.3$, $p < 0.001$). Only 17.3 percent of children were identified as having need by both sources. The assessments identified 11.3 percent of children not identified by caregivers, and caregivers identified 14.0 percent of children not identified by assessment.

There were some differences by age for the children who showed a need for special education services according to both the assessments and the caregivers.

For both sources, children ages nine to eleven (34.2 percent by assessment; 36.2 percent by caregiver) were significantly more likely to be identified as having need than children ages six to eight (23.6 percent by assessment; χ^2 = 7.3; p < 0.01 and 27.0 percent by caregiver; χ^2 = 5.7; p < 0.05).

Children identified by assessment as needing services were significantly more likely to have repeated a grade (23.6 percent) than children without need (14.7 percent; χ^2 = 5.4; p < 0.05). For children identified as having need of services, there were differences in rates of repeating a grade based on the type of need. Children identified only on the basis of behavioral need were the least likely to have repeated a grade (14.9 percent), while those identified on the basis of cognitive need or both were more likely to have repeated a grade (37.0 percent and 32.2 percent, respectively; χ^2 = 12.9; p < 0.01).

Need, Referral, and Receipt of Services

Table 14-3 shows the percentage of children referred to and receiving special education services, as reported by caseworkers, caregivers, or both.[36] Only 16.1 percent of children identified by assessment as needing special education services were referred by the caseworker within twelve to eighteen months after the close of an investigation. An additional 27.4 percent of children identified as needing special education services were not referred because they already were receiving services at the time of an investigation. According to caseworker reports, a total of 42.3 percent of identified children were already receiving services or began receiving services following a referral after the close of an investigation. However, that means that 57.7 percent of children who were identified as needing services did not receive them after the close of an investigation. Ninety-three percent of children referred to services received them, so the discrepancy between need and receipt of services appears to be based on children not being referred to services.

According to caregiver reports, 54.4 percent of children identified by assessment as needing special education services were receiving them within twelve to eighteen months after the close of an investigation. Thus, of the children in need of services based on assessment, 45.6 percent were not receiving them. Combining all available information about receipt of services from caregivers and caseworkers, 57.8 percent of children identified by assessment as needing services were receiving them within twelve to eighteen months after the close of an investigation. Overall, that means that 42.2 percent of children who were identified as showing need were not receiving them. Since most children who were referred to services by their caseworkers received them, it is likely that the discrepancy between need and receipt of services was caused the lack of a referral.

The only significant difference in receipt of services based on type of need was that caregiver reports indicate that children having both cognitive and

Table 14-3. *Percentage of Identified Children Referred to and Receiving Special Education Services within Twelve to Eighteen Months of Baseline, by Person Reporting and by Category of Need*

	Need			
	Cognitive			
			Cognitive	
	Cognitive	Behavioral	and	
Referred for or received special education	only	only	behavioral	Total
Caseworker report[a]				
Referred to special education by caseworker	12.1	13.8	26.9	16.1
Receipt of special education as reported by caseworker 1	12	13.3	22.4	14.9
Receipt of special education as reported by caseworker 2	35.3	40.9	54	42.3
Caregiver report[b]				
Receipt of special education*	59.1	45.6	71.3	54.4
Caseworker or caregiver report[c]				
Receipt of special education	60.5	50.9	72.4	57.8

Source: Authors' calculations.

*$p < 0.05$.

a. Ns for cognitive need, behavioral need, cognitive and behavioral need, and total across all need categoires are 92, 248, 106, and 446, respectively.

b. Ns for cognitive need, behavioral need, cognitive and behavioral need, and total across all need categoires are 119, 311, 137, and 547, respectively.

c. Ns for cognitive need, behavioral need, cognitive and behavioral need, and total across all need categoires are 132, 326, 138, and 596, respectively.

behavioral problems were more likely to receive special education services (71.3 percent) than were children with cognitive problems only (59.1 percent), who in turn were more likely to receive services than were children with behavioral problems only (45.6 percent; $\chi^2 = 6.85$; $p < 0.05$). However, there were no differences in caseworker reports of rates of receipt of services based on type of need.

Table 14-4 shows the percentages of need and receipt of services broken down by gender, race and ethnicity, language, urbanicity, and maltreatment type. Males were more likely to need services (33.3 percent) than females (23.3 percent; $\chi^2 = 9.81$; $p < 0.01$). Of students identified as needing services, males were more than twice as likely to be referred to services (19.8 percent) as females (9.0 percent; $\chi^2 = 4.03$; $p < 0.05$), and they also were more likely to receive services (64.8 percent, including students reported by caseworker or caregiver as newly or already receiving services at the time of interview) than females (48.9 percent; $\chi^2 = 4.373$; $p < 0.05$). Nonurban students were more likely to show need of services (37.3 percent) than were urban students (25.9 percent; $\chi^2 = 5.71$; $p < 0.05$). Children for whom neglect or failure to provide was the

Table 14-4. *Percentages of Children Needing, Being Referred to, and Receiving Services, by Sociodemographic Characteristics*

Sociodemographic characteristic	Show need of services at baseline	Identified cases referred to services within twelve to eighteen months after baseline[a]	Identified cases referred to services within twelve to eighteen months after baseline and newly receiving services at waves 2 or 3[b]	Identified cases receiving services within twelve to eighteen months after baseline as reported by caseworker or caregiver[b]
Gender				
Male	33.3**	19.8*	18.5	64.8*
Female	23.3	9.0	8.4	48.9
Race and ethnicity				
Non-Hispanic Black	28.6	12.4	12.3	56.4
Non-Hispanic White	31.7	18.2	16.0	60.4
Hispanic	20.0	29.3	28.5	41.6
Other	29.7	7.4	7.4	79.1
Language				
English as first language	29.7	15.6	14.4	59.0
English as second language[c]	19.7	25.0	24.6	53.1
Urbanicity				
Urban	25.9*	16.3	14.9	60.0
Nonurban	37.3	15.9	15.9	55.1
Maltreatment type[d]				
Physical	28.8	12.0	9.2	51.4
No physical	28.1	18.8	18.1	60.6
Sexual	28.6	34.4	32.7	63.5
No sexual	28.3	15.0	13.8	57.1
Failure to provide	37.6*	7.9*	7.8	62.6
No failure to provide	26.3	20.0	18.4	56.3
Failure to supervise	26.3	28.6	27.7	50.5
No failure to supervise	29.0	13.4	12.2	60.0
Other abuse	20.2	11.3	11.1	73.6
No other abuse	29.9	17.9	16.5	55.7

Source: Authors' calculations.

Chi-square values: *$p < 0.05$, **$p < 0.01$.

a. Based on caseworker report; students who did not receive a referral because they already were receiving services are not represented in this column but are represented in the "receiving services" column.

b. Based on caseworker report. Includes both children who already were receiving services and kids who newly began receiving services within twelve to eighteen months of the close of the investigation.

c. Caregiver reports that another language besides English is spoken in the home.

d. Each type of maltreatment is analyzed as an individual variable.

most significant type of maltreatment were more likely to show need (37.6 percent) than were children for whom it was not (26.3 percent; $\chi^2 = 4.09$; $p < 0.05$). Of children identified as needing special education services, those for whom failure to provide was the most significant type of maltreatment were less likely to be referred to special education services (7.9 percent) than children for whom it was not (20.0 percent; $\chi^2 = 4.08$; $p < 0.05$). There were no differences in likelihood of needing, being referred to, or receiving services based on race and ethnicity or on English being a child's second language.

Discussion

This chapter examines the educational needs of elementary school–age children who are in the care of the child welfare system, whether living in their own home or out-of-home. About 30 percent of the maltreated children in this age group, representing almost 260,000 children in the United States, may need special educational assistance, whether a caregiver's report or direct assessment is used as the indicator of need. That rate of need is substantially higher than would be expected in the general population of children, where placement rates under the Individuals with Disabilities Education Act are around 9 percent.[37] Older elementary school children in the system are at somewhat higher risk than those in the earliest grades, but NSCAW assessments did not find differences based on race or home language. Children whose primary maltreatment classification was failure to provide were more likely to demonstrate need for services (based on assessment), but they were less likely than those in other maltreatment categories to be identified by caseworkers as having educational needs. Males were more likely to be referred than females with a similar level of need.

NSCAW represents a unique data source since direct assessments and ratings of children provide firsthand data about their special education needs. Direct assessments show that 13.9 percent of children who are involved with child welfare services have cognitive deficits, while 23 percent are identified through caregiver ratings as exhibiting maladaptive behavior. A conservative standard (in a general population of children, less than 2 percent would be expected to score below the cut-points chosen) was used for measures in both domains, so that the measures identify children for whom success in an average school environment, without additional support, would be highly unlikely. While not all children identified by these measures would necessarily be eligible for special education services, the presence of a risk of this magnitude should, at a minimum, be a trigger for referral for a complete educational evaluation. Unfortunately, such problems often go unaddressed by child welfare workers. Only 16.1 percent of the children exhibiting these high levels of risk were referred by workers for special education services, while an additional 27.4 percent were reported as already receiving services. That leaves 54.4 percent whose potentially serious educational needs go unrecognized by the child welfare system. Caregivers report that more children are receiving special education services than child welfare workers report, but substantial numbers still are not receiving services to meet their needs.

What should be the child welfare system's responsibility for children's educational placement and adjustment? Child welfare systems are understandably reluctant to assume responsibility for outcomes that clearly are under the control of another child service system, in this case, the educational system. Moreover, there may be reluctance to add to the time demands on child welfare workers, who already have large caseloads and who deal with families with multiple problems. Nonetheless, standards employed in the federally mandated Child and Family Services Reviews require that workers attend to children's educational needs. Moreover, the child welfare system is coming to recognize that safety, permanence, and well-being are not independent of one another. Children with disabilities and behavior problems are at higher risk for continued maltreatment,[38] and behavioral and school difficulties have been documented as contributing to instability in foster care placements.[39] A well-functioning child welfare system, then, would do best to make educational assessment a routine part of the intake process and to adopt standardized protocols for making and following through on educational referrals. Training of workers to increase their awareness of special education regulations as well as to deepen their understanding of school system procedures and policies should be ongoing. Finally, training and information resources for parents and foster parents regarding school services and procedures may help caregivers advocate effectively for the educational needs of children in their care.

The educational system, of course, bears the primary responsibility for meeting these children's needs. The Individuals with Disabilities Education Act, as well as section 504 of the Rehabilitation Act of 1973, guarantees the right of children with special needs to receive a free and appropriate public education. Further, there are provisions in IDEA that require school systems to actively seek out and identify children who may have learning or behavioral issues that interfere with their educational progress. It is critical that school personnel become more aware of the likely risks faced by children involved with the child welfare system and that they develop strategies for dealing with their needs. Training for teachers and other school personnel should address the types of risks faced by children who are served in child welfare and should provide information to facilitate outreach and service coordination.

Attention to structural aspects of the school environment is needed to reduce barriers to identifying and providing services to children in need as well as to facilitate cooperation across agencies. For example, implementation of policies that allow foster children to remain in the same school even if their place of residence changes would enhance the continuity of their schooling and allow them to maintain potentially important relationships with peers and teachers. When children cannot stay in their original school, procedures should be established for the efficient transfer of records, particularly special education records, to ensure that assessments are not duplicated and that valuable time is not lost because school personnel are unaware of plans that already have been developed. In some school systems, attention should be paid to eliminating administrative barriers so that classroom teachers and child welfare personnel can more effectively coordinate services.

Some child welfare and education systems in the nation have adopted best practices designed to ensure that children's educational needs are addressed. Other jurisdictions should consider adopting these or similar practices:

—A number of states have passed legislation aimed at allowing foster children to remain in the same schools when they are placed out-of-home or moved to new placements.[40]

—California's Foster Youth Services Program, based in the educational system, resulted from a legislative mandate that each local education agency employ a liaison to work with child welfare to identify children who are in foster care and ensure that their educational needs are addressed.[41]

—The California legislation also encouraged interagency agreements governing the sharing of records.[42]

—Grants for coordinated Systems of Care demonstrations, funded by the federal Center for Mental Health Services or the Children's Bureau within the U.S. Department of Health and Human Services, allow agencies to employ multiagency teams to develop individual case plans for children across service sectors and also feature liaisons or case managers who are expected to work across systems to make sure the needs of children and families are addressed in the most efficient manner.

In addition to model practices in the United States, the United Kingdom has a statutory requirement for the development of personal education plans for all children in foster care. These plans require initial assessment of educational needs, employ school system liaisons, involve caregivers and children as well as child welfare and school personnel in plan development, and provide guidelines for regular monitoring to ensure that plans are implemented.[43]

The acceptance of child well-being as part of the mission of the child welfare system has resulted in growing attention to the educational and other special needs of the children within its care. To date, however, most of the attention has been directed toward children who are in foster care, with less emphasis on children who are served within their own homes by child welfare personnel. Previous NSCAW reports have pointed out that children who come to the attention of child welfare authorities, regardless of whether their cases are substantiated or opened to services, are at similar risk for poor developmental outcomes.[44] The child welfare system could serve as an important gateway to educational and other services for this high-risk group of children. The more complex question of the effectiveness of those services requires more focused attention.

Notes

1. U.S. Department of Health and Human Services, Administration for Children and Families, *National Survey of Child and Adolescent Well-Being: Characteristics of Children and Families at Intake into Child Welfare Services* (Washington: DHHS, 2005); DHHS, Administration for Children and Families, *National Survey of Child and Adolescent Well-Being: One Year in Foster Care Report* (Washington: DHHS, 2003).

2. Mark Courtney and others, "The Educational Status of Foster Children," Issue Brief 102 (Chicago: Chapin Hall Center for Children, 2003); Kathleen Konenkamp and Jennifer Ehrle, *The Well-Being of Children Involved with the Child Welfare System: A National Overview* (Washington: Urban Institute, 2002); Marijcke Veltman and Kevin Browne, "Three Decades of Child Maltreatment Research: Implications for the School Years," *Trauma, Violence, and Abuse* 2, no. 3 (2001): 215–39.

3. Fred Wulczyn and others, *Beyond Common Sense: Child Welfare, Child Well-Being, and the Evidence for Policy Reform* (Piscataway, N.J.: Aldine Transaction, 2005).

4. Joseph C. Crozier and Richard P. Barth, "Cognitive and Academic Functioning in Maltreated Children," *Children & Schools* 27, no. 4 (2005): 197–206; Konenkamp and Ehrle, *The Well-Being of Children.*

5. Kathleen Konenkamp and Jennifer Ehrle, *The Well-Being of Children;* C. Smithgall and others, *Educational Experiences of Children in Out-of-Home Care* (Chicago: Chapin Hall Center for Children, 2004); Melissa Jonson-Reid and others, "A Prospective Analysis of the Relationship between Reported Child Maltreatment and Special Education Eligibility among Poor Children," *Child Maltreatment* 9, no. 4 (2004): 382–94.

6. Kathleen Kendall-Tackett and John Eckenrode, "The Effects of Neglect on Academic Achievement and Disciplinary Problems: A Developmental Perspective," *Child Abuse & Neglect* 20, no. 3 (1996): 161–69; Mark Courtney, Sherri Terao, and Noel Bost, *Midwest Evaluation of the Adult Functioning of Former Foster Youth: Conditions of Youth Preparing to Leave State Care* (Chicago: Chapin Hall Center for Children, 2004).

7. For example, Joseph C. Crozier and Richard P. Barth, "Cognitive and Academic Functioning in Maltreated Children"; DHHs, *National Survey of Child and Adolescent Well-Being: Characteristics of Children and Families at Intake;* DHHS, *National Survey of Child and Adolescent Well-Being: One Year in Foster Care.*

8. Kathleen Kendall-Tackett and John Eckenrode, "The Effects of Neglect"; John Eckenrode, Molly Laird, and John Doris, "School Performance and Disciplinary Problems among Abused and Neglected Children," *Developmental Psychology* 29, no. 1 (1993): 53–62.

9. Kendall-Tackett and Eckenrode, "The Effects of Neglect"; Jeffrey Leiter and Matthew Johnsen, "Child Maltreatment and School Performance Declines: An Event History Analysis," *American Educational Research Journal* 34, no. 3 (1997): 563–89; Elizabeth Rowe and John Eckenrode, "The Timing of Academic Difficulties among Maltreated and Non-Maltreated Children," *Child Abuse & Neglect* 23 (1999): 813–32.

10. DHHS, *National Survey of Child and Adolescent Well-Being: Characteristics of Children and Families at Intake;* Marijcke Veltman and Kevin Browne, "Three Decades of Child Maltreatment Research."

11. School engagement refers to the student's active involvement in the learning environment and includes constructs such as school attachment and commitment to achievement.

With regard to maltreated children, see, for example, Susan Shonk and Dante Cicchetti, "Maltreatment, Competency Deficits, and Risk for Academic and Behavioral Maladjustment," *Developmental Psychology* 37, no. 1 (2001): 3–17.

12. Kenneth Dodge, Gregory Pettit, and John Bates, "Effects of Physical Maltreatment on the Development of Peer Relations," *Development and Psychopathology* 6, no. 1 (1994): 43–55; Jennifer Lansford and others, "Long-Term Effects of Early Child Physical Maltreatment on Psychological, Behavioral, and Academic Problems in Adolescence," *Archives of Pediatrics and Adolescent Medicine* 15, no. 8 (2002): 824–30; Eric Trupin and others, "Children on Child Protective Service Caseloads: Prevalence and Nature of Severe Emotional Disturbance," *Child Abuse & Neglect* 17, no. 3 (1993): 345–55.

13. Richard Mattison and others, "Psychiatric Background and Diagnoses of Children Evaluated for Special Class Placement," *Journal of the American Academy of Child Psychiatry* 25, no. 4 (1986): 514–20.

14. Sarah Horwitz, Kathleen Balestrucci, and Mark Simms, "Foster Care Placement Improves Children's Functioning," *Archives of Pediatric and Adolescent Medicine* 155, no. 11 (2001): 1255–260.

15. Larry Evans, "Academic Achievement of Students in Foster Care: Impeded or Improved?" *Psychology in the Schools* 41, no. 5 (2004): 527–35.

16. Courtney and others, "The Educational Status of Foster Children."

17. Ibid.

18. Crozier and Barth, "Cognitive and Academic Functioning in Maltreated Children"; DHHS, *National Survey of Child and Adolescent Well-Being: Characteristics of Children and Families at Intake;* DHHS, *National Survey of Child and Adolescent Well-Being: One Year in Foster Care.*

19. Mason Burley and Mina Halpern, *Educational Attainment of Foster Youth: Achievement and Graduation Outcomes for Children in State Care* (Olympia: Washington State Institute for Public Policy, 2001); Konenkamp and Ehrle, *The Well-Being of Children.*

20. E. Stein and others, "The Mental Health of Children in Foster Care: A Comparison with Community and Clinical Samples," *Canadian Journal of Psychiatry* 41, no. 6 (1996): 385–91.

21. June Clausen and others, "Mental Health Problems of Children in Foster Care," *Journal of Child and Family Studies* 7, no. 3 (1998): 283–96.

22. Courtney and others, "The Educational Status of Foster Children."

23. Ibid.; Sunny H. Shin, "Building Evidence to Promote Educational Competence of Youth in Foster Care," *Child Welfare* 82, no. 5 (2003): 615–32.

24. Mason Burley and Mina Halpern, "Educational Attainment of Foster Youth," *Future of Children* 14, no. 1 (2004): 31–47; Rebecca Sawyer and Howard Dubowitz, "School Performance of Children in Kinship Care," *Child Abuse & Neglect* 18, no. 7 (1994): 587–97.

25. Individuals with Disabilities Education Act of 1990, P.L. 101-476, 20 U.S.C. §§ 1400–1485.

26. M. Suzanne Donovan and Christopher T. Cross, eds., *Minority Students in Special and Gifted Education* (Washington: National Academies Press, 2002).

27. Mark Courtney, Sherri Terao, and Noel Bost, *Midwest Evaluation of the Adult Functioning of Former Foster Youth.*

28. Cynthia Godsoe, "Caught between Two Systems: How Exceptional Children in Out-of-Home Care Are Denied Equality in Education," *Yale Law and Policy Review* 19, no. 1 (2000): 81–164.

29. Department of Health and Human Services, Administration for Children and Families, "General Findings from the Federal Child and Family Services Review," (Washington:

DHHS, 2004) (www.acf.hhs.gov/programs/cb/cwmonitoring/results/genfindings04/gen findings04.pdf [February 23, 2007]).

30. See, for example, National Research Council, *Preventing Reading Difficulties in Young Children* (Washington: National Academies Press, 1998); Terry Moffitt and others, "Childhood-Onset vs. Adolescent-Onset Antisocial Conduct Problems in Males: Natural History from Ages 3 to 18 Years," *Development and Psychopathology* 8, no. 2 (1996): 399–424.

31. Thomas Achenbach, *Integrative Guide for the 1991 CBCL 4-18, YSR, and TRF Profiles* (Burlington: University of Vermont, Department of Psychiatry, 1991).

32. Sara Sparrow, Alice Carter, and Dominick Cicchetti, *Vineland Screener: Overview, Reliability, Validity, Administration, and Scoring* (Yale University, Yale Child Study Center, 1993).

33. Alan Kaufman and Nadine Kaufman, *Kaufman Brief Intelligence Test Manual* (Circle Pines, Minn.: American Guidance Service, 1990); Richard Woodcock, Kevin McGrew, and Judy Werder, *Mini-Battery of Achievement* (Itasca, Ill.: Riverside Publishing, 1994).

34. Note that these trigger mechanisms for child welfare worker interviews were undoubtedly imperfect and likely resulted in some missed caseworker interviews for children who actually were receiving child welfare services.

35. The assessments used to determine a child's need for special education services were conducted about four months, on average, after the child's case was closed.

36. Wave 2 data were used to determine referral and receipt of services; however, if a child did not have wave 2 data, wave 3 data were used. The 37.9 percent of children who were identified in wave 1 as needing special education services but who did not have caseworker data for wave 2 or wave 3 were not included in counts and percentages of rates of referral and receipt throughout the chapter (except for certain cases in which caregiver data were also used to determine receipt of services). Caseworker interviews were conducted at wave 2 and wave 3 only if a service that the child was receiving was provided or paid for by CPS; that happened only in very rare situations. Therefore there will be selection bias differences between the group of children who received a caseworker interview in waves 2 or 3 and were included in our reports of referral and receipt and the group of children who did not receive a caseworker interview in waves 2 or 3 and thus were not included. For example, children likely received a caseworker interview in waves 2 or 3 for issues other than the need for special education, which means that they were dealing with more than one issue or perhaps more severe issues.

37. *Twenty-fifth Annual Report to Congress on the Implementation of the Individuals with Disabilities Education Act, 2003* (Washington: U.S. Department of Education, Office of Special Education and Rehabilitative Services, 2003).

38. Patricia Sullivan and John Knutson, "Maltreatment and Disabilities: A Population-Based Epidemiological Study," *Child Abuse & Neglect* 24, no. 10 (2000): 1257–273.

39. For example, see Sonya Leathers, "Foster Children's Behavioral Disturbance and Detachment from Caregivers and Community Institutions," *Children and Youth Services Review* 24, no. 4 (2002): 239–68.

40. For example, see National Conference of State Legislatures, *State Child Welfare Legislation 2005,* July 2006 (www.ncsl.org/print/cyf/cwlegislation05.pdf [February 23, 2007]).

41. Steve Christian, "Educating Children in Foster Care" (Washington: National Conference of State Legislatures, December 2003).

42. Ibid.

43. Carol Hayden, "More Than a Piece of Paper? Personal Education Plans and 'Looked After' Children in England," *Child and Family Social Work* 10, no. 4 (2005): 343–52.

44. DHHS, *National Survey of Child and Adolescent Well-Being: Characteristics of Children and Families at Intake.*

Contributors

RICHARD P. BARTH
University of Maryland, School of Social Work

RODNEY BAXTER
Research Triangle Institute, Durham, North
    Carolina

BARBARA J. BURNS
Duke University, School of Medicine

CYNTHIA D. CONNELLY
Child and Adolescent Services Research
    Center, Rady Children's Hospital and
    Health Center, San Diego; University of
    San Diego, Hahn School of Nursing and
    Health Science

KATHERINE DOWD
Research Triangle Institute, Center for Survey
    Research, Durham, North Carolina

JOHN ECKENRODE
Cornell University, Family Life
    Development Center

PAMELA FROME
Research Triangle Institute, Durham,
    North Carolina

REBECCA L. GREEN
University of North Carolina at Chapel Hill,
    School of Social Work

SHENYANG GUO
University of North Carolina at Chapel Hill,
    School of Social Work

LAUREN HAFNER
Safe Place: Center for Child Protection,
    Children's Hospital of Philadelphia

BRENDA JONES HARDEN
University of Maryland, Department
    of Human Development

ANDREA L. HAZEN
Child and Adolescent Services Research
    Center, Rady Children's Hospital and
    Health Center, San Diego; San Diego
    State University, Department of
    Psychology

RON HASKINS
Brookings Institution, Center on Children
    and Families

MICHAEL S. HURLBURT
Rady Children's Hospital, San Diego

CHARLES IZZO
Cornell University, Family Life
    Development Center

KELLY J. KELLEHER
Office of Clinical Sciences, Columbus
    Children's Research Institute, Ohio

PATRICIA L. KOHL
Washington University, George
    Warren Brown School of Social Work,
    St. Louis

JOHN A. LANDSVERK
Child and Adolescent Services Research
    Center, Rady Children's Hospital and
    Health Center, San Diego; San Diego
    State University, School of Social Work

ARLEEN LEIBOWITZ
University of California–Los Angeles,
    School of Public Affairs

LAUREL K. LESLIE
Child and Adolescent Services Research
    Center, Rady Children's Hospital and
    Health Center, San Diego; Institute for
    Clinical Research and Health Policy
    Studies, Tufts-New England Medical
    Center, Boston

ARNOLD LEVINSON
University of Colorado at Denver, Department
    of Preventive Medicine and Biometrics
    and Health Sciences Center

ANNE M. LIBBY
University of Colorado at Denver, School of
    Medicine and Health Sciences Center

A. RUSSELL LOCALIO
University of Pennsylvania, School of
    Medicine and Department of
    Biostatistics, Center for Clinical
    Epidemiology and Biostatistics,
    Philadelphia

XIANQUN LUAN
Division of Biostatistics, Children's
    Hospital of Philadelphia

JULIE S. MCCRAE
University of North Carolina at Chapel Hill,
    School of Social Work

AMANDA L. R. O'REILLY
Safe Place: Center for Child Protection,
    Children's Hospital of Philadelphia

HEATHER D. ORTON
University of Colorado at Denver, School
    of Medicine and Health Sciences Center

RAMESH RAGHAVAN
Washington University, George Warren
    Brown School of Social Work and
    Department of Psychiatry, St. Louis

STEVEN A. ROSENBERG
University of Colorado at Denver,
    Department of Psychiatry and
    Health Sciences Center

DAVID M. RUBIN
University of Pennsylvania, School of
    Medicine, Department of Pediatrics;
    Safe Place: Center for Child Protection,
    Children's Hospital of Philadelphia

SUNNY HYUCKUN SHIN
Boston University

ARON SHLONSKY
University of Toronto, Faculty of Social
    Work; Bell Canada Child Welfare
    Research Center, Toronto

ELLIOTT G. SMITH
Cornell University, Family Life
    Development Center

MARY BRUCE WEBB
Office of Planning, Research and Evaluation,
    Administration for Children and Families,
    Washington

JUDITH WILDFIRE
University of North Carolina at Chapel Hill

FRED WULCZYN
University of Chicago, Chapin Hall Center
    for Children

Index